Bowling For The Mob

Bob Perry

with Stefan Bechtel

I want to dedicate this book to all the people on the street who didn't make it, and to all the people in the rooms who couldn't find their way home.

-Bob

CONTENTS

ACKNOWLEDGMENTS

Bob, Stefan, and the rest of the team behind Bowling For The Mob would like to thank our supporters, especially those who backed our Kickstarter campaign in the fall of 2013 to make production of the book possible.

Pat Spadafora
Lilly Bechtel
Debra Pick
Teresa Cooper
Andrea & Steve Holmberg
L. Jay Bourgeois
mike calbi (lodi lanes)
Nicholas R. Duke Sr.
Bob Hadley
J. Dean A.
Ian Wren
Jon Emm
Stuart England
Sari Bennett
steve chevy chiarella
Roni Del Rio
Jay Flanagan
Matthew J. Kessler, DVM
Lawrence Bechtel
The Madara Family
Kimi Wren
Pat
Joseph Ardolino
Taylor Barnett
Chris & Cynthia Buck
Tracy A. Campbell
Monica Chieco
joseph conigliaro
Jeff Corwin

Jim "Crazy Horse" Crawford
Caryolyn Friedman
lewis c johnson jr (aka jr Johnson)
Paul Levesque
philip maturo
William Mullin
Viktoria Parvin
ANN PURZYCKI
Sarah E. Ray
Susan & Kent Rychcik
Jamie Sacco
James Salisbury
Eric and Nancy Schmitz
Joseph Schwartz
Bob Sieski
Mary Jane Strickland
James Burnett
Tim Michel
Francesco Ruffa
Matthew Strickland
Ring Fever Productions
Howard & Elizabeth Barnett
Len Nicholson
Bill Spigner
Storm Bowling Products
Corbett Austin
Nick Duke
Gardy Bloemers

1 THE BEGINNING OF THE END

I was twenty-three years old the summer of 1975 and I looked like John Travolta in that movie *Saturday Night Fever*. No, wait: It was the other way around. John Travolta looked like *me*, 'cuz that movie didn't come out until a few years later and I'd been rocking out at the discos for ages by then – since even before "The Hustle" got big.

My best buddy Cadillac Nicky and I used to go down to this place in Paterson, New Jersey called Mr. Stag's and we'd buy more clothes in a month than some people bought in a year. There was this Jewish guy, Irv, who'd actually let us buy stuff on credit because we were such righteous customers. Other times, we'd go into the city to a place in the Village, on Sixth, where Doc Severenson from the Johnny Carson Show used to buy his shit.

We were stylin', man!

I'd wear these real nice pants, with creases like a knife. I'd wear these Italian knit shirts, like the gangsters wore. I had a couple of eight, nine-hundred-dollar leather jackets that I'd wear, and another one, with a belt, that came down almost to my ankles, that musta cost a thousand bucks. I had this one velour jacket with flowers all over it, that might seem kind of faggoty today but in them days everybody in the clubs loved it. I'd wear two, three-inch platform shoes. I didn't go for them five-inch ones, mainly because it was hard to dance in them.

Yeah: It was a time when white guys dressed up like black guys. I'd do my hair with one of them hot combs. Gold chains weren't popular in them days, but I used to wear a couple of gold "300" rings, that the Professional Bowlers Association gave out when you bowled a perfect game. And about two in the morning when I went out to the after-hours clubs in Manhattan, or this place called Mr. Ds in Saddlebrook, with all the lights and people and music, I looked like a million fuckin' bucks.

Nicky had this totally pimped-out white 1968 Cadillac El Dorado. He would scrub and shine that thing until it looked like a white spaceship, like the goddam thing just touched down from Mars. And when we showed up at Mr. Ds on a Friday or Saturday night, he'd park that bitch right on the sidewalk in front of the club. These two brothers that owned the place let us do it, because we were the deal, man — we walked into the place and it was like one of them movies where, just for a second, everything stopped. We were like Starsky and Hutch.

Back in them days, though, all I really wanted was to float on top of the music and dance all night with all those hot women, all that heat, all that noise. I was a really good dancer — I kind of took lessons from this Hispanic girl, who would go out to the clubs with me and show me the moves. And since most guys didn't dance, I could dance with anybody's girlfriend and it was cool. It was like walking into a pinball arcade and playing every single machine for free.

The music in them days was Teddy Pendergrass and The Tramps, Marvin Gaye, Barry White, Soul Train, Double Exposure, The Jackson Five, The Bee Gees, Frankie Valli and the Four Seasons. They got their name from a bowling alley in Jersey called The Four Seasons. Joe Pesci used to work there, before he got famous. That's where I met him. All those songs, with that pounding beat! "Stayin' Alive," "I Will Survive," "Ten Percent," "Shake Your Booty," "Black Skinned Blue Eyed Boys," "I'll Always Love My Momma." All that shit.

Everybody drank in the clubs, of course. And everybody did coke, too, but usually not too much, because it was so expensive. But it wasn't like all that shit was no big problem. It was just, you know, party time. Coke was the club drug.

So where did a couple of twenty-three-year-old kids have all that money to throw around? Well, first of all, me and Cadillac Nicky both worked full-time at my dad's appliance store in Paterson, PK Appliance, basically schlepping refrigerators and dishwashers all the fuck over New Jersey. That's the job we were trying to escape when we'd get decked out to go to the clubs.

A much more entertaining source of income, of course, was Uncle Raymond, "the fat man," the smartest man I ever knew, who taught me and Cadillac Nicky and a few scary-looking older guys how to use our brains to consistently win money at the racetrack. When it was rainy, Uncle Raymond would wear a black fedora and a long black trenchcoat, and just park himself at the rail watching the ponies come pounding down the straightaway. That man had so much brainpower underneath that black hat that it was almost like a giant magnet in there, sucking up the right answers like them iron filings in some science experiment. Unfortunately, all Uncle Raymond's brains couldn't save him, or me, or anybody else, when the

2

shitstorm finally came down.

And there were also times when I could make five or six thousand dollars in a night from "action bowling" – the after-hours betting game that drew all the gamblers and hoodlums and derelicts from all over the Tri-State area. I might have been a hot-shit dancer in the disco clubs. I might have been studdly-ass dresser. But as a bowler, I was phenomenal. And I was the best action bowler walking.

Howard Barnett (childhood friend from Paterson, now a financial advisor in Virginia): *"I remember the first time I met Bob Perry, at the Bowl-O-Mat in Paterson. Of course I'd heard of him by then – everybody had heard of Bob Perry. He was very nice to me, even though I was only 13 or 14. He went behind the counter of the snack bar and made me a sandwich, actually. He seemed to live at the bowling alley. But when I actually watched him bowl – that was something else. You don't have to be an expert in baseball to see that when Mickey Mantle swings, it's just different than everybody else. That's the way it was with Bob – it was just different than everybody else. It was amazing. It was a beautiful thing to watch."*

"Fat Joey" Ardolino (bowler from New Jersey, now selling mattresses in Florida): *"One time I ran into Earl Anthony [one of the most famous bowlers on the East coast] in Paramus Lanes. I was a teenager at that time. Anthony bowled anchor for D'amato Paperstock, and Bobby Perry introduced me to him. Bobby walked away and Earl said to me, "You know, he's the best bowler in the world," nodding his head, pointing to Bobby. Bobby was the best, unequivocally, without a doubt. Anyone who truly knows bowling knows that on a given night even a blind squirrel could find a nut. But a lion will always eat. Bobby Perry was a lion on the lanes. You didn't have to like Bobby, but when it came to bowling you had to respect him. Anyone who didn't, became the next victim."*

Joe Tolvay: *"Bobby's future at the age of 16 was as bright as it could be in the sport of bowling. Everybody was jealous. When he picked up a bowling ball, he was the man. His bowling ability got him a lot of free passes, whether it was league bowling or action bowling. People would sponsor him for anything. People used him to make money, they tried to take advantage of his abilities."*

Here's what I'd do: During the day, for work at the appliance store, I'd wear my schmuck clothes, that practically had "Bobby" printed over the pocket. Then after work, I'd go out to dinner or whatever and then, at eleven or midnight, I'd change into my pimped-out disco clothes that I had nicely arranged on hangers in the back of my car and me and Cadillac Nicky would make our big entrance at Mr. Ds. After that, maybe around one or two in the morning, we'd change clothes again and go out to whatever bowling alley had some action. And I'd be a superstar again, but this time

3

in a different way. Sometimes I wouldn't get home until four in the morning. Sometimes Cadillac Nicky wouldn't come home for two or three days. When did we sleep in them days? I dunno. I just know there was more than one time when me and him were so tired we dropped a goddam Frigidaire.

Well, that's how it all started out, anyhow – with late nights, hot-combed hair, stacked-heel shoes and a white Cadillac El Dorado. But before it was all over, people couldn't believe I was even still alive. I'm sixty now, and my health is pretty much shot from everything that happened – I got prostate cancer, diabetes, I got chemo burns in my throat and whatnot – and all those fabulous clothes are long gone. They're so long gone they're a joke. But here I am anyhow: A man who was destroyed, almost lost, found by an angel, and brought back to life.

I'm a friggin' miracle, really.

I grew up in a kind of ordinary house, with four sisters, on East 26th Street, in Paterson, New Jersey. It was in a neighborhood that was ethnically mixed-up, lots of Polacks, lots of Italians, lots of hard-drinking Irish. It was an OK neighborhood I guess, but it was only, like, a block away from the projects and six blocks away from murderville, down on Governor Street where there were bars on all the windows and the brothers hung out on the streetcorners selling heroin. It was a big heroin area down there. Man, you let one of them brothers stick his head in your car window, and you got a gold chain on, he'll grab that chain and yell, "five-oh!" which means the cops are coming, so you'll boogie out of that place so as not to get caught copping and the brother will just run away with the gold.

In the old days, supposedly, up until the First World War or whatever, Paterson was the "silk city of the world," because of all the textile mills that were there. But when I was growing up, all that was long gone. Most of them mills were boarded up, and that whole end of town was just a nasty spooky ghetto.

Paterson wasn't a great place to be a small, shrimpy kid who got pushed around and bullied a lot. But that's what I was. Big kids would corner me on the way to school and steal my lunch money. I always felt tense, like there was danger lurking around every corner. Plus, I was blind in one eye from a childhood accident. And there was another terrible thing that was happening to me then that I'll tell you about later, if I can. Nowadays people talk about dysfunctional families, but Paterson in them days was a dysfunctional town – it was a very mean, tough place for a skinny little kid like me.

There was more drunks living on my street than you can imagine – guys coming home shit-faced and yelling and screaming at their kids and their wives and whatnot. I think the only person on my street who didn't drink was my dad. And there was this other thing that would go on in my

$1.00 OFF

103305

ONE COVERGIRL® Product (excludes accessories and trial/travel size)

| MANUFACTURER COUPON | EXPIRES 05/30/15 |

CONSUMER: LIMIT ONE COUPON PER PURCHASE of products and quantities stated. **LIMIT OF 4 IDENTICAL COUPONS PER HOUSEHOLD PER DAY.** Any other use constitutes fraud. Coupons not authorized if purchasing products for resale. VOID if transferred, sold, auctioned, reproduced or altered from original. You may pay sales tax. Do not send to Procter & Gamble.

DEALER: Sending to Procter & Gamble, 2150 Sunnybrook Drive, Cincinnati, OH 45237 signifies compliance with policy; includes 8¢ handling fee. Copy available at above address. No cash or credit in excess of shelf price may be returned to consumer or applied to transaction. Cash Value 1/100 of 1¢.

NOT VALID IN PUERTO RICO.

Procter & Gamble 150503
©2015 P&G

0022700-109305

neighborhood, which was that some guy, like the Italian guy next door, would just kind of disappear. And I'd ask some older person where so-and-so went and they'd say, "He went to college." That was the terminology. It was only later that I realized, in my world, nobody went to college, especially thugs and tough guys. They weren't going to college. They were going to prison. So I guess you could say that, later in life, I had some real bad examples to look back on from when I was a kid.

In them days, in Paterson, there was really only one place that felt clean and safe, a place full of light and people laughing. A place families could go. Really, it was a place sort of like the places in them impossible TV shows — *Lassie, Leave It To Beaver, Ozzie and Harriet, My Three Sons* — where people had little problems that always got solved in half an hour, and there were mothers and fathers and dogs and nice lawns and whatnot. Not like the rundown part of Paterson where I grew up, where things felt raggedy and edgy and I was never quite safe.

That place was the bowling alley. It was bright and cheerful and noisy, with the sound of jukebox music and tenpins clattering off the pindeck. I felt at home there. I felt safe. In Paterson, the place everybody went was a place called Bowl-O-Mat lanes. I started going there with my mom and dad and sometimes a couple of my sisters when I was just a punk kid, maybe six or seven. My dad was a good bowler, who bowled in a league. Later on, just for use in bowling, he started going by the last name "Perry" instead of "Purzycki," which is my birth name, a Polack name. When I got a little older I changed my name to Perry, too.

My dad could tell at a pretty young age that I just had a gift for the game. I just understood naturally that you didn't want to hit the tenpins head-on; you wanted to hook the ball so it would come in, hard, in the "pocket" just behind the head pin. I had a knack for doing that, and I loved the sound of those pins clattering across the hard-maple lane when I threw a strike. My dad and mom screamed and yelled when that happened. I joined one of the New Jersey leagues and by the time I was 12 I was averaging over 200 a game.

Plus, you gotta understand: Bowling scores nowadays are way higher than they used to be in the old days, because of the introduction of synthetic lanes and high-performance balls (which we used to call "cheater balls" when they first came out). It's the same way new-fangled baseballs and bats have made it much easier to hit a home run than it was in Babe Ruth's day. So for a 12-year-old to be averaging over 200 — that made people sit up and take notice of this skinny little kid from Paterson.

Chuck Pezzano (prominent bowling writer and inductee into the Professional Bowling Hall of Fame): *"Even when Bobby was 15 years old, you could see that he had a spectacular talent. It had to have been a natural ability, because he was too young to have much training at that age. He had a lot of guts, he wasn't afraid of anybody, and I thought right from the beginning that he could be great."*

Mike Stella (bowler from North Arlington): *"I remember once Earl Anthony said to me, 'There's only one bowler I fear on the PBA Tour [Professional Bowlers Association] and that's Bob Perry.' And Earl Anthony, of course, was one of the greatest bowlers ever."*

This was a time when top professional bowlers could make real money. Not as much as professional golfers, but still, a lot. And, in them days, it seemed like bowling was a sport that was taken more seriously than it is now. Nowadays you only see bowling in cartoony movies like The Big Lebowski, but when I was growing up there were all these bowling shows on TV, like Bowling For Dollars and Make That Spare. And then, of course, there was all the TV coverage of the big professional tournaments, with big-money purses. That was before the Super Bowl High Roller tournament was started in Vegas, which became the biggest-money bowling competition in the country, with a total purse of over a million bucks. That didn't come around until 1981. Even so, I started to realize it might just be possible for me to have a golden career as a professional bowler – maybe even take my place among the Great Ones. People like Dick Webber, or later Earl Anthony and Mark Roth.

In 1964, when I was 13, my dad found out about this national youth bowling competition, that was going to be held at the World's Fair in Flushing, New York. This would be my first chance to get up on the national stage and show the world what I could do.

Two days before I was supposed to go to Flushing to this tournament, my dad gave me a croquet set for my birthday. He told me not to use it until after the tournament. I don't know, maybe he got a little worried about them long-handled wooden mallets around a 13-year-old kid. (So what did he give them to me for then?) Well, so me and this neighbor kid named Ricky unpacked the croquet set anyway and we're playing with it in my back yard when Ricky somehow loses control of one of them wooden mallets, it goes flying through the air and smashes me in the left side of my face. It felt like a bomb going off in my head. It crushes my left eyeball and a bunch of the bones around it, too.

Patsy Purzycki (Bob's sister): *"I was across the street at my girlfriend's house and I just remember hearing this screaming, and Bobby came out from behind the house holding his face and there was blood everywhere. Somebody called my dad at work at the appliance store and it seemed like he was there in two minutes. I remember Bobby lying there on the sidewalk, all covered in blood, holding my hand, saying 'Please don't leave me! Please don't leave me!' He seemed so alone."*

When I got back from the hospital I had to lay on the bed in a dark room for weeks. Needless to say, the youth bowling tournament at the World's Fair was totally off. The doc thought maybe I'd be able to see a little out of that left eye, but when he took the patches off it turned out that eye was almost completely blinded. To this day, I can only see a little bit of blurry light out of that eye.

The great, golden bowling career I had imagined in my head, the chance to be somebody, to touch my dreams – all that seemed to fall away, like dust. I felt crushed, defeated. Just pounded down. But, I don't know what it was, somehow I just reached down inside myself and found a lion down there, ready to fight. I was pissed off at this fucking kid Ricky, of course. But mainly I was focused on getting up out of that bed and coming back to life. I didn't care if I only had one eye. I didn't care if I never heard of a one-eyed bowler. I wanted to get back to bowling, and become the best athlete I could become – maybe even the best ever. So I started practicing like a maniac, bowling and bowling and bowling, trying to train myself to see down the lane with one eye and no depth perception at all. I trained myself to hit a mark on the lane over and over and over again, just exactly the same way, like a machine.

Patsy: *"I remember Bobby was always getting yelled at because he spent all his money at the bowling alley. One time he spent his haircut money at the bowling alley and he came home all scared and said, 'Patsy, you gotta cut my hair! I spent all my money bowling!' My girlfriend and I cut his hair, but it looked sort of like a bad Mohawk."*

Over the next few years I started coming back, big time. I learned to use that same inner lion, that ferocious drive, that had helped me overcome my blindness, to become a phenomenal bowler. I was still in my teens or early twenties when I won four regional titles. In one of them, I beat the legendary bowler Ralph Engan. I won the Regional Championship Classic tournament, in New York. I competed in the Firestone Tournament of Champions. Someday, I realized, I might even win a national tournament like the High Roller.

I had a way of throwing the ball that just hooked harder than anybody else, and when that solid-rubber ball hit those rock-solid maple tenpins, they just exploded off the pindeck with an incredibly loud clatter. I loved that sound. It was so loud, so confident, so dominating, that it scared other bowlers; I could tell. One of the pin chasers where I used to bowl told me he could always tell when I was in the house because my strikes were louder and scarier than anybody else's. Bowling is a beautiful game, involving skill and strategy, and some of it has to do with psyching out the other guy. Intimidation. I was great at all that shit, and scattering them pins as if you were blowing up the dude was part of it.

Now, other bowlers not only admired me, they had started to fear me. Now, when I walked into the Bowl-O-Mat in Paterson or any of the other bowling alleys in Passaic or Nutley or Clifton or Hoboken or any of them other places, Lodi Lanes or Wallington, with my hot-combed hair and my fancy pants, everybody looked at me. Everybody knew who I was. I was like a movie star. Because when I got up to bowl and addressed that line, I was fearless. I was practically unbeatable. When people went up against me, they couldn't win. They could not win. I'd beat their brains out. I'd wipe the floor with them. I was the best. And I was still just a kid. Who knew how far I could go? I had no idea how blind I really was, or how far down the wrong road I was getting ready to go.

2 SOUL TRAIN

I dunno, it's possible this is a story about a guy that got everything too easy. A guy that was cursed by God or the Devil saying, "Go on, help yourself. Have another! Everything is free."

All I knew was that I just kept winning. The trophy shelf at my parents' house started getting more and more crowded. In 1973 and then again in 1974 (when I was in my early 20s) I won Regional Bowler of the Year, which meant that I was the best bowler on the East coast, where most of the good bowlers in the whole country lived.

In them early days, I was totally focused on the sport of bowling. I was like a top athlete in training – no drinking or drugs or staying out late or horsing around. I was bowling, almost every day. Monday nights, I'd bowl for the action. Tuesday nights, I'd bowl in the Bronx. Wednesday, I'd bowl in the doubles leagues against the best bowlers in the East. Thursday nights, I'd be back in New York or Long Island, Friday was Lyon's Lanes, and Saturday was the big money, in the tournaments. I was not only learning how to play the lanes, I was also learning how to psych out my opponents – how to dominate them, mislead them, how to play them like a fiddle. I had a real good teacher, Al Fuscarino, and he taught me a lot about the game, how to play the outside or the inside, how to work the angles. He also helped me develop a swing that nobody else had – this tremendously high back swing, which creates a great knee bend and a powerful hook that just demolishes the pins.

By the time I was 17, Al told me I was destined to be the best.

In them days, in the bowling alleys, everybody bragged about how good they were. But everybody was not as good as they said they were. All except me.

I start winning all kinds of "legitimate" trophies and tournaments – the official stuff. At the same time, though, there was this whole 'nother world that was going down – late at night, off the books, when the bowling alley was closed to the public. Like I say, it was known as "action bowling." It was where the hotshot young bowlers, like the gunslingers in the Wild West, got to compete for money. The bowling alley would fill up with shadowy older men, gamblers and gangsters, who would bet big money on the superstars like me.

It didn't take me long to figure out that you could make a whole lot more money as a late-night action bowler than you could as a dufus in the local league wearing a stripey shirt playing pot games. The whole impossible dream of someday competing in a national tournament like the High Roller started to pale in comparison to the money I was already making. Who needs clean money for hard work when you can get dirty money a whole lot easier? And I was quickly developing a reputation as one of the best money bowlers anywhere.

Plus, action bowling was a whole lot more fun. I was great at winning money because I loved the game: It was exciting and complex, it involved not just skill but cunning, intimidation, bluffing, strategy and human psychology. I instinctively knew how to scare the shit out of my opponents, rattle their cage, mess with their minds.

Stepping out onto the approach at the top of the lane, it's almost like you're walking onto a stage. For a few seconds, you're the center of attention. And if you were someone like me – the guy who was probably going to win a lot of money – you never knew who was watching. Especially when I started one of those runs where I'd be throwing strike after strike after strike.

One night, before the action started, a guy walks up to me out of the shadows while I was sitting in the settee area, getting ready to bowl. He was this huge man, not very tall, but he probably weighed 240. He was "fat" like an oak tree is fat. He had dirty blonde hair and he was wearing glasses, sort of like Clark Kent. He was maybe 18 or 20 years older than me, not old enough to be my dad but old enough to be my older brother or uncle.

"How ya doin'?" the guy says.

"Okay."

"Wanna bowl? Five or ten bucks a game?"

I just laughed.

"Fuggedaboutit," I says. "No way, man. I'll CRUSH you."

I was an arrogant sonofabitch in them days.

"No, seriously – I'll bowl you," the guys says.

"Look, mister, you can't win. You cannot win. Piss off, man."

"Well, let's bowl anyway. I can afford to lose a few bucks."

So after awhile, just to humor the old guy, I threw a few games with him. I destroyed him, just like I said I would.

But this guy, who turned out to be Raymond – he was pretty smart. Actually, very smart. He'd been watching me and all the other action bowlers from the shadows for a long time before he came up to talk to me. He knew all about me. He'd been making money off me for months. He also knew a lot about the horses, too, and at least according to him he'd been making a lot of money at the track. He told me he was in the trucking business, bringing shrimp and seafood up from the Gulf, and moving ingots and other stuff from one foundry to another all across the East coast, from Pennsylvania down to the Deep South.

We kind of hit it off, I guess, and after that Raymond started coming around the bowling alley quite a lot. He'd sit there at the bar drinking Manhattans made with VO – that shit is like rat poison, and it makes people mean – watching me bowl. Sometimes he'd come with this real old guy, a plumber name Nicky, who would fall asleep at the bar half the time.

One day Raymond asked me to give him a ride someplace. So I took the wheel of Raymond's car and drove him and Nicky the Plumber over someplace near North Arlington, where he lived, I guess to meet some guys. He told me to wait in the car while him and Nicky the Plumber went upstairs, so I did, because now I knew Raymond would pay me for my trouble. Whenever I got through driving him, he'd hand me a little wad of cash.

So that's the way it started to go. I started driving Raymond and his friends around in his car – these guys were always drinking, and I guess they needed a "designated driver," even though nobody used that term in them days. They were always going to see people. I'd drive them someplace and these guys – big guys, nicely dressed, always smoking – they'd get out of the car and go into a house or an apartment. I'd always wait in the car. I think they liked me because I was always reliable and they knew I wouldn't blab about where I'd taken them. I would just shut up and drive, and at the end of the night Uncle Raymond would give me cash. Then I'd go to the after-hours clubs in New York and party.

I don't know when it was, exactly, but at some point I started calling Raymond "Uncle Raymond," and he'd tell people I was his nephew, Bobby. There was one other kid, Bobby Schumacher, that Raymond also called nephew, so sometimes us two Bobbys would wind up driving Uncle Raymond around from place to place, like we really were his nephews for real.

And, OK, look: I ain't stupid. I grew up in a bad part of Jersey. There were a lot of towns that were known to be places that were "mobbed up." There were a lot of diners known for having a lot of Mob sit-downs. But the thing is, you just didn't talk about it. You didn't go sticking your nose into it. Except for people like Bobby Schumacher, who wanted to be in the Mob in the worst way and eventually wound up serving some serious time for it.

Uncle Raymond? I didn't know what he did in his private time. I didn't know what he really did for a living. I actually didn't believe he was in the Mob, even though he definitely knew people who were. I came to think he was probably "in the rackets," as they say in Jersey, meaning he might have had a legitimate business but part of the time he stepped over onto the shady side of the street. Maybe most of the time. Anyway, I just knew he was very nice to me, like a real uncle, that he was the smartest man I ever knew, and that over time I came to admire him more than any other person I ever met.

Patsy Purzycki (Bob's sister): *"Uncle Raymond was a heavy man who drove a Lincoln Continental and smoked constantly. He was always at the bowling alley. More and more, Uncle Raymond became a fixture in Bobby's life. It worried a lot of us. Supposedly Raymond was in the Mafia — that's what people said. And considering where he was from, North Arlington, I wouldn't doubt it for a minute. But all I really I knew was that when you were around him, you felt his power. You felt protected. You felt safe."*

Joe Tolvay (Bob's bowling teammate): *"Bobby talked about Uncle Raymond a lot — 'I gotta go do such-and-such for Uncle Raymond' or 'Uncle Raymond will take care of this or that for me' — but I never actually met him. I sometimes wondered if he was fictional. I just know that Uncle Raymond was Bobby's savior. He gave him a lot of power."*

About this same time, the best thing that ever happened to me, happened. Her name was Debbie LaRusso.

I'd met Debbie at the Paramus Bowl, in Paramus, New Jersey, a couple of years earlier, and God, she was beautiful! She looked like Barbara Streisand. She was everything a man could want. Blonde, about five-foot-five, with a fantastic body — a wonderful body. She had one of those bodies that was so curvaceous you could see her naked through her clothes — her breasts, her hips, her thighs, her ass.

You kept trying not to look at her, but you couldn't. She was a good bowler herself, and as we got to know each other I'd come to watch her bowl, and she'd come watch me bowl in tournaments. I know she loved it that I was a big star in the bowling world. Plus, we couldn't keep our hands off each other.

I guess it was a little unusual for that time, but we were so crazy about each other that we moved in together, first in Garfield, New Jersey, and then into a one-bedroom apartment with garage on East 16th Street in Paterson, because it was cheaper. It was a nice little apartment, and pretty cheap (our rent was $237 a month). We had a dog named Jackson that somebody gave us – he was half beagle and half German Shepherd – and we were both very attached to that dog. We lived there in that little apartment, just the three of us – me, Debbie and Jackson, like a little family.

Debbie had a real good job with this insurance agency, so she made a good income. Unfortunately, her mother hated me and the people I had started to hang out with. She was really angry and worried whenever she saw me leaving the bowling alley with Uncle Raymond and these other older guys wearing long coats and hats. She kept warning Debbie against getting involved with me and those scary-looking men.

One day I got Debbie a little ring and asked her to marry me. But when her mom found out, she exploded. She told Debbie, "If you marry Bobby, I'll disown you." I couldn't let that happen, of course. So we just lived together without getting married. Debbie would have married me if she could, and I would have married her, too. But we couldn't. My sisters, especially Patsy and Jeannie – they just loved Debbie. She was part of the family.

But it wasn't just that Debbie's mother didn't like me. Looking back on them days now, forty years later, I can see that my whole life was starting to run off the rails, but I had no fucking idea what was starting to happen to me. I had no idea where I was getting ready to go.

Partly, it was all that easy money – being able to go down to the bowling alley pretty much day or night and walk away with a fistful of cash. Alcohol was all over the place, but so was coke. And now I could afford enough of it to get myself into trouble. So I started drinking and doing blow all the time, whenever and wherever I could get it. And I couldn't get enough of that stuff. My nose had started to close up; I think I already had a deviated septum already, but I just kept going. Without my really knowing it, my life story was gradually getting taken over by booze and dope and all the lying it takes to keep that going.

In July of 1981, just after my dad died, I went out to Vegas for my first High Roller tournament. It was the kind of huge national tournament I'd dreamed of ever since I was a little punk kid, and this was the big kahuna, the biggest of the big, with total prizes over two million. It cost you $1100 to enter, but if you won your first two matches, you broke even. So I go out to Vegas, all full of my own shit and swagger, but also (I figured out later) heartbroken 'cuz my dad died. I won my first five matches, though, and then I got knocked out. Well, at least I had a few grand in my pocket, so I started drinking, started snorting blow, and then I got totally out of control, just drunk and obnoxious as hell. We was throwing dice and I got mad and threw the dice everywhere. I was impossible, but I didn't know it. I did not realize how far down I'd already gone.

After that Debbie and I started arguing, mainly about my staying out half the night and drinking. I'd go out to have a couple of drinks, then wind up going out to the after-hours clubs and not get home, really toasted – forget about it! – until five in the morning or something. I'd be lying all the time. I'd tell her, oh, I had to help Uncle Raymond with something, or I had to go into the city to make some money, or I had to go meet somebody about a job, or this or that. But it was all a pack of lies, and I think she knew it. My whole life was turning into a pack of lies.

In them days, the PBA (Professional Bowlers Association) would give you a gold ring if you threw a 300 game, a perfect game. By that time I was getting so good that I had at least 15 or 20 of these rings (although I'd already sold some of them for dope.) Well, one night Debbie takes a hammer and just starts smashing the shit out of them. That made me mad, of course, and we had another big fight over that. All her friends were telling her to get away from me, to get away from the gamblers and hoodlums I'd started hanging out with. I didn't want her to leave, but I couldn't stop drinking and doing drugs real bad, pretty much around the clock, really, and lying to cover it all up. It was tearing me apart. I was on the wrong side of the street, I can tell you that.

Patsy: *"My bedroom was right next to Bobby's at home, and one time I went into my jewelry box and found forty thousand dollars, cash. You gotta understand: We were a nice middle-class family, and we didn't have money like that. It was like drug money. It was scary. And then the very next day, it would be gone and Bobby would be broke again. I didn't know what was going on, but I started to get very frightened for him. I didn't know what was going to happen next, but I just knew it was going to be bad."*

3 RUBY RED

Back in them days there was a guy named Arthur Prysock, a black jazz singer who had this big soulful baritone voice. He had some big disco hits, but the main thing people remember him for is a beer commercial he did in the '70s where he sang, "Tonight, tonight let it be Lowenbrau." Helluva thing to be remembered for, huh? Well, anyway, Arthur Prysock and his wife were big supporters of bowling for kids in Harlem. Lots of these youth bowling events they did were in a place called Lenox Lanes, on Lenox Avenue right in Harlem. Every once in awhile, I'd go down to Lenox Lanes with other local bowling professionals to do some kids' event in Harlem.

Well, so one night after I finished bowling for Arthur I had a few vodkas and smoked some pot and I was just hanging out at one of the tables in the bar at Lenox Lanes, watching the action, and this guy comes up to me.

He knew who I was – everybody knew who I was.

And I knew who he was – everybody knew who he was.

He was known as "Ruby Red," and he was a pretty unforgettable guy. A black guy, six feet tall, who was an outrageous dresser even though he was kind of a quiet guy. He'd wear a full-length red fur coat and a red fur hat, with red pants. Sometimes the fur was white or gray or green or black, but there was always fur all over the place. He'd wear these real expensive shoes – everything he wore was expensive. He was loaded with gold, gold chains, gold on his fingers, all kinds of bling. He always drew a crowd wherever he went, and I knew that he was feared. I knew he had to be a tough guy to be feared like that.

Everybody said that Ruby Red and his brothers were loaded with money. Supposedly they were some of the biggest heroin dealers on the East coast, working out of Harlem.

(I am not 100 percent sure of this, but I'm convinced that "Ruby Red" was actually Frank Lucas, the subject of the movie "American Gangster," starring Denzel Washington. He was originally from a little town in North Carolina, but later he and his brothers established a huge heroin ring based in Harlem in the late 60s and 70s. They brought in incredibly dangerous and powerful heroin, called "Blue Magic," from Thailand, shipped over in the body bags of dead soldiers returning from Vietnam. Lucas was famous for being a flamboyant dresser, especially his fur coats and fur hats. He was still active in the mid-1970s, before he went to prison.)

I had heard that Ruby Red was at the action in New Jersey on Friday nights because that was the predominant place where people went to bet for a lot of money. After midnight, on Friday nights, in Jersey, is where it was all happening.

"Hey, Money Bowler – what you doing here?" Ruby Red says to me. "Money Bowler": That's what he called me. (Later he sometimes just called me "Money.")

"I was here for Arthur's thing," I says. "The youth bowling thing."

"Are you bowling?" he says, meaning, was I bowling for the action.

"No."

"Why not?"

"There's no money here, man."

"Well, I heard if we beat you, we can make a lotta money."

"That's true, but you gotta have a lotta money to win a lotta money. You don't get nothin' for nothin.'"

Like I say, I was an arrogant sonofabitch in them days.

"How much is a lot?" Ruby Red says, and then he reaches in his pocket and pulls out this big fat wad of hundreds, folded over and wrapped with an elastic band, and throws it on the table. There was probably, I don't know, maybe five thousand dollars in there.

"Is this enough money?" he says.

"No, that's not enough," I say.

I mean, just arrogant as hell.

He throws down another wad on the table.

"Is this enough?"

"No, sorry," I say.

He throws down another wad.

"Is this enough?"

"No."

Then Ruby Red calls over another black guy, maybe one of his brothers, and the two of them start throwing wads of money down on the table, until the entire table – it was one of them bar tables, not too big – was completely covered with money.

The truth is, I was kind of just kidding. I had never seen so much goddam cash money in one place in my life. I mean, it might have been fifty thousand dollars, cash, or more, on that table. That's a lot of money, for a 23-year-old kid, especially in them days.

"Okay," I says. "Sure – I'll bowl your guy. Where do you want to do it? We can't bowl here, that's for sure."

Look: I knew that if this match really happened, it would attract all the degenerate gamblers and mobsters and hoodlums in New Jersey to the action. And the white mobsters weren't going to come to Harlem. They just wouldn't do it. In them days everybody pretty much stayed in their own neighborhoods – blacks with the blacks, Italians with the Italians, Polacks with the Polacks, whites with the whites.

Plus you had a situation where, if they did come, you'd have guys with tens of thousands of dollars in cash leaving the bowling alley late at night, and if somebody tried to rob them, it could turn into a real ugly situation. The guns would come out, and there'd be black gangsters shooting at white gangsters and the whole nine yards. If a stickup happened the Italians would be the worst. Uncle Raymond always said he hated the Italians because they were the only people who would kill for money.

"Boys play, men kill," he'd say, speaking about them.

"Let's just bowl in Jersey," Ruby Red says.

"OK," I says. "You pick the house."

So Ruby Red and a couple of his guys wrote some names on pieces of paper, and put them in a hat. Then Ruby Red picked one: Olympic Bowl, in Bellevue. I found out later that all the pieces of paper had Olympic Bowl written on them – he was already trying to rig the match. Olympic Bowl was next to Newark and Nutley, and it sounded OK to me, even though I'd actually never bowled there before. At that point, twenty-three years old and totally full of myself – invincible, unbeatable, a lion on the lanes – I figured I could crush Ruby Red's guy anytime and anyplace. It didn't really matter who the guy was, or where we bowled. The guy was dead. I was already counting my money.

"OK," Ruby Red says, "You pick the time."

"Next Sunday night, ten o'clock."

"OK, see you then. Just be sure your guys bring a lot of money."

By this time, it was obvious to me and everybody else in my life that I "belonged" to Uncle Raymond. I was part of his crew, part of his outfit. Uncle Raymond was like one of them great big fish in the ocean, that's got a whole lot of littler fish swimming alongside.

A "crew" was sort of like a Mafia-type setup, even though Uncle Raymond wasn't in the Mob. If I went somewhere and told people off, those people couldn't do nothing to me until they went to Uncle Raymond and got his permission. If somebody slapped me, they'd have to answer to Uncle Raymond. When I went out on one these swag jobs in the middle of the night, I knew that Uncle Raymond would protect me if we got into trouble. That's the way it worked.

One of the crew was me, of course. Nicky the Plumber, who was an old guy maybe seventy – he was always around. I figured out later that Nicky the Plumber was an old, old friend and also kind of a first lieutenant to another of Uncle Raymond's friends, Bobby Cabert. Cabert really was in the Mafia. Cabert and I just kind of hit it off from the beginning – maybe because I was always making him money, maybe because I just liked his style. He looked and acted and sounded like a gangster. But whatever Cabert's personal life was, who else he hung out with? It was none of my fuckin' business. Years later, when Cabert died in federal prison, The New York Times pointed out that Joe Pesci's character in the Mob movie Goodfellas was based on Cabert. That's the guy who is kind of a psychotic killer, who shoots this kid in the foot who is waiting on their table, and then kills him. Which doesn't surprise me, because I knew them guys knew each other. And Cabert sort of was like that gangster in the movie – kind of dangerous and unstable.

Then there was this new guy who'd started hanging around a lot. Some people called him "Johnny Boy," but Uncle Raymond just called him "the other guy" or "your friend." Like he'd say, "what happened to the other guy?" Or, "are you gonna give your friend a ride, or what?" It was like Uncle Raymond was afraid the Feds were listening in, even if we were just standing there at the bowling alley or sitting in a bar.

People said the other guy was a hoodlum, a gangster, from Ozone Park, in Queens. He'd spent two or three years in federal prison. He was only about ten years older than me, but he had this silvery hair all done up nice, and most of the time he had a nice tan. The old ladies said he looked like a movie star. He had a pretty deep scar on his right upper lip, that made him look like he was sneering a lot of the time. He also walked a little funny. I found out later that it was because when he was fourteen years old, he was trying to boost a portable cement mixer from a construction site and the thing tipped over and crushed his foot. I picked up a few other tidbits about the guy, just from people talking, even though this was the kind of a guy you had to be extra careful knowing anything about. Like that he came from a family of thirteen and grew up real poor. That when he was my age he used to run with a bunch of thugs and knucklebreakers called the Fulton-Rockaway Boys. And that he loved to bet – on the horses, cards, dice and sports events like action bowling.

There was another thing I learned pretty quick about "Johnny Boy": If you were a winner, if you made him money, he loved you. And I was a superstar out there – the best action bowler walking. Another good part of it was that "Johnny Boy" told me, if I ever got into trouble, just to call him. He was a thug, I guess, an enforcer. But he was also a guy who genuinely

18

liked people in general, and me in particular. Knowing "Johnny Boy" was like knowing Uncle Raymond, twice.

I'd picked Sunday night for the match with Ruby Red because Sunday night, after all the league play was over and all the mothers and fathers and kids were gone, when the bowling alley was closed to the public, was a perfect time for action bowling. That's when everybody who was there was a gambler, or a gangster, or both. On Sunday nights there was nothing else to bet on – the racetracks were closed, football was over for the weekend. All that was left was bowling, and there were bowling alleys all over the place. That's why bowling turned into such a huge betting sport, an action sport, a money sport. There was a whole lot more money won – and lost – in these late-night action games than any of the professional bowlers were making on the pro tour.

I knew that.

And so did Ruby Red.

"Who's your guy?" I asked Ruby Red, wanting to find out who I'd be bowling against, although it really didn't matter all that much.

"Guy Fisher," he says. Guy Fisher, a black guy, was a good bowler but absolutely no contest against me. It was a total mismatch. I was going to humiliate and destroy this guy.

I got back to the apartment late that night. Debbie was already asleep, so there was no big argument, but first thing the next morning the phone rings. It's Uncle Raymond.

"Why were you in Harlem last night?" he says, kind of accusing me.

"How did you know I was there?"

"Somebody told me."

"Who told you?"

"None of your business."

I had no idea how he did it, but Uncle Raymond always seemed to know where I was at. He had people watching me. He could protect me and love me and sometimes I could do no wrong. At the beginning, I wasn't afraid of him at all – why should I be? But later, when I did bad things and started to get him mad at me – really, I broke his heart – then he started to get scary.

"Look," I says, "I was up there for one of Arthur Prysock's things for the kids," I says to Uncle Raymond. "I met up with that black guy Ruby Red, the guy with the fur coats. He wants to bowl for a lot of money."

"How much money?"

"The most cash money I ever seen in my life."

"How much is that?"

"I don't know – fifty, sixty, seventy-five thousand maybe. But if the word gets out I think people will show up with hundreds of thousands."

"Yeah, that nigger got a lot of money," Uncle Raymond says. (I don't mean no disrespect – but that's what he said.) "Where does he want to bowl?"

"Olympic Bowl, over in Bellevue."

"When?"

"Next Sunday night, ten o'clock."

"Why so late?"

"Because it's the best time. This guy and his brothers and them guys – they're loaded. They've got piles of cash. He says we gotta show up with a lotta money, so you gotta call your friend to make the match." Meaning: I was asking Uncle Raymond to call "Johnny Boy" and all his mobster friends to come to the match and bring plenty of cash to bet.

"OK," Uncle Raymond says, "so I gotta go away for a few days but I'll be back by the end of the week. What you doing this week?"

"I probably gotta work for my dad at the appliance store, and I'll go practice at the Bowl-O-Mat."

"Well, don't you be stayin' out all night drinkin' like you do. You make sure to watch your ass and don't screw around. Practice. And don't drink so goddam much."

"OK," I said.

But, in reality, I kind of didn't give a shit. I guess I didn't actually believe that this match would really happen. Guys were always trying to set up action games for big money, and it usually didn't happen. Shit like that just never happened. But I just knew, if it did happen, I would beat the living shit out of whoever stood up to me.

Howard Barnett: *"I've seen Bob bowl 36 consecutive strikes – that's three perfect games in a row, or what's known as a '900 series'. This is really an incredible athletic achievement. The first guy to ever do it in officially sanctioned league play was a guy named Glenn Allison, back in 1982 (this feat was later disallowed because of lane conditions). Since then, according to the American Bowling Congress, only 19 other bowlers have done it. The ABC keeps a list of these people, what they call the '900 Club.' But Bob has thrown 900 series in practice and in informal games so often he doesn't even mention it anymore. I mean, the guy is phenomenal."*

Mark Brady (Bob's bowling teammate): *"One time we brought Bobby Perry on with Mark Roth [considered one of the greatest bowlers ever] and Bobby was the better bowler, the smarter bowler. He had better instincts. If Bobby could have kept his head, he had the potential to be the best of anybody. His potential was unlimited."*

So anyhow, I was at Lyons Lanes on Monday or Tuesday night and I happened to run into Ruby Red, all decked out in his fur coat and fur hat and whatever.

"We still on for the match at Olympic Bowl on Sunday night?" I asked him.

"Yeah, and you better bring a lot of money," he says.

By then, everybody seemed to have heard about the match. People were getting their cash together. People were getting excited about this.

The commotion was in the air because all kinds of people were coming. And because there'd be so much betting going on, anybody could get in on the action, even with a hundred bucks. There'd be the big, main bet, and all kinds of side bets also. Lots and lots of action, just like the gamblers loved.

Even so — don't ask me why — I still didn't really take Ruby Red seriously.

So on Monday night I bowled in the big league in Paramus, with some of the best bowlers in the country. I told a lot of people about The Match and that there was going to be a lot of money there. They said they'd already heard about it. The next night I went out for a couple of drinks and then to the disco and I wound up staying out half the night. Then I went out and drank all night Wednesday. As usual, Debbie got really pissed at me when I got home so late. Afterwards she just got up and went to work without speaking to me. But that was not so unusual. I was used to it by now. Thursday was always a good disco night, so I went out that night too. On the way back home I just wanted to stop somewhere and have a drink, but the next thing you know I was drinking all night long. Again.

The truth was that I didn't really practice at all. I didn't really care. I didn't really give a rat's ass, for some reason. The truth — the truth that I had never really looked square in the eye — was that I was lazy, I was egotistical, I was unbelievably arrogant, I was completely blind, and most of all, I had turned into a round-the-clock alcoholic and a dope addict.

I was, actually, getting into very serious trouble in my life.

My boat had already gone over Niagara Falls and I was going down.

But, at the time, I just thought I was the greatest boater in the world.

BOB PERRY WITH STEFAN BECHTEL

4 PISSING OFF JOHNNY BOY

So Saturday morning rolls around, and Uncle Raymond calls.

"Where you been?" he says.

"Do you mean have I been practicing, minding my own business? Yeah, sure. I been doing that."

"That's not what I heard."

"Well, maybe you didn't hear right."

"Where are you now?"

"I'm home, at my apartment. With Debbie."

"Come over to my house."

"I can't. I might have to work for my dad today, in the store."

"I just got home, and nobody knew where you been. Where you been all week?

"I was working."

"Did you practice?"

"Yeah, sure."

"I want you to come over to my house."

"Why?"

"Cuz I got some things for you to do."

Then he switches to his growly voice, very threatening:

"Perry! Come over here!"

I didn't really want to. Sometimes he was a real headache to be around because he was always bitching at me, and I couldn't drink when I was over there, he was always keeping an eye on me, and he'd make me do these bullshit jobs around his house. But I went over there anyway. It was the middle of the day but he could tell that I had already been drinking. He didn't say nothing about this, though. He made me mow the grass, clean up the garage, this kind of shit.

"You gotta bowl tomorrow," he told me in that way he had that was

23

really threatening at the same time it sounded friendly. "Either you show up here first thing tomorrow morning – and no fuckin' drinking! – or you just stay over here tonight."

I didn't stay over at Uncle Raymond's that night. But Sunday morning he called me at 8:30 in the morning.

"Come over here," he says.

"I can't – I gotta go bowl at Palladium Lanes."

This was in Orange, New Jersey. I used to go over there to bowl on Sunday mornings a lot. Uncle Raymond didn't give me no grief about it, because at least I'd be practicing, but by one o'clock I'd had a few drinks at the bowling alley and I was started to get a little toasted. Afterwards, I went over to Uncle Raymond's house, and all we did was drive around and run errands, and then we picked up the "friend" in Queens, around Ozone Park. Then, sometime after nine that night, we drove over to Olympic Bowl in Bellevue, which was around five miles outside the city, maybe 45 minutes from Queens.

And when we walked into that bowling alley, I'd never seen anything like it. The place was packed. There must have been two hundred people there that night – every lowlife gambler in New Jersey was there, black people, white people, Hispanics, hoodlums, mobsters, heroin dealers – anybody who had money to bet was there, and they were ready for the action. Nobody knew where anybody else got their money from, and nobody was gonna ask. In them days – well, maybe today, too – it was also unusual for black people to be carrying a lot of heavy cash, but Ruby Red's guys seemed to be loaded with it.

I wasn't scared. I felt good. I felt like a winner, like I always felt. I was the guy who couldn't lose, and I was ready to go against this joker. I even had a guy carrying my bowling balls. I walked in with my hot-combed hair and my fancy leather jacket, surrounded by the Who's Who, Uncle Raymond, my friend Bobby Cabert, the gangster, Nicky the Plumber, the gangster's apprentice, and some other big scary-looking guys. This was not a bunch of "fugazis" – phony gangsters, a bunch of fake Italians. This was for real.

Because – oh, yeah, maybe I forgot to tell you – the guy people called "Johnny Boy" or "the other guy" was actually the silver-haired mobster John Gotti, who eventually became the head of the Gambino crime family and wound up dying in the federal supermax prison at Marion after being given a life sentence for all kinds of crimes. I know he put out the hit on Paul Castellano and all that. But all I got to say is, he was never anything but nice to me. (Well, except for this one particular night we're talking about here.) I just knew him as a guy who loved to gamble, a guy who loved action bowling, a guy who loved people. And he loved me, especially, at least he loved me when I won.

It's funny, though: I never actually called him by his name.
I didn't actually call him anything.
"How ya doin'?" he'd say to me.
"Okay."
"That's good. Did you come to bowl?"
"Yeah."
"Let me know who you're gonna bowl."
"Okay."
And that was it. That was how we'd said "hello."

Other times, I'd just identify the guy by the places I seen him. Like when somebody asked who the guy was, I'd say I seen him at Hollywood Lanes, downstairs, on Queens Boulevard. Or I'd see him at Garden City, Long Island. And later, I'd say I seen him at the action in Deer Park, but by then I was on the long, slippery slide and I don't remember too much.

Anyhow, on this particular night, I was John Gotti's golden boy. I was going to make this tough guy and his pals a shitload of money that night.

Like I say, I had never bowled at Olympic Bowl before, but I knew it was a Brunswick house, and I knew I did good in Brunswick houses, plus it was in New Jersey, my home turf, so how hard could it be? That just shows you how arrogant I was: Here was this huge money match, and I hadn't even taken the trouble to bowl there.

Olympic Bowl was a 36-lane house, 18 lanes on a side. So since Ruby Red had picked the house, I got to pick the lanes. I picked the end pair of lanes, 17 and 18, right on the outside, because I had been told by older bowlers that those are the toughest lanes in the house, no matter where you go. Nobody ever bowls good on end pairs. I wanted to make it as tough as possible on the other guy, because I knew I would do great no matter which lane we used.

You gotta understand: At that level of play, every little thing makes a difference, including the way the lanes are oiled. When the lane is dry, the ball behaves differently than if it's oiled. People who own bowling alleys, and people who like to bet in them, have also figured out that there are ways to rig the game by oiling, or not oiling the lanes, depending on who is bowling. A lot of bowlers are terrific in the lane conditions they're used to, but they can't adapt to different lane conditions. Being able to adapt is what makes the difference between somebody who is good and somebody who is great. I was convinced I could bowl great on any lane, in any condition, anywhere, against anybody. So who needed to practice?

Once we got there, I got out of my fancy clothes, just put on dungarees and a T-shirt, and then I went up to the bar. All I needed was a vodka-and-orange-juice to grease my wheels. But the fucking bar was closed. I asked the bartender for a drink anyhow, but he said it was against the law to serve me.

I walked back to the lane, just a little bit panicked, picked up a ball and addressed the line to throw a few practice balls, just to get the feel of the lanes. And the first ball I threw hooked sharply to the left and thunked into the gutter. I just threw a gutterball! Holy shit. I couldn't believe it. I hadn't thrown a gutterball since I was a little punk kid. I threw again, and again, and again, but I couldn't get lined up. My timing was way off. I was amazed. I was just off. I already felt tired, and the match hadn't even begun. The truth was, I was hungover, but I wasn't prepared to admit that. I just thought I couldn't seem to throw the ball hard enough to hit the pocket.

I glanced over at the other bowler, Guy Fisher, and I noticed he wasn't doing much better. But he was still doing a lot better than me.

"You ready?" he said, after a few more practice throws.

"Yeah, sure," I said, even though I knew I wasn't. I could tell everybody was getting impatient. Some people had gotten there at, like, 6 pm and they'd been waiting all that time.

I figured the first game would start off with a bet of two, three thousand, but the first bet was $6,800. That was the main bet, but with all those gamblers, and all that cash, there were lots of other smaller bets going down. Gamblers will bet on anything. I looked around this crowd and there a whole bunch of guys who were big and strong that I had never seen before, who had lots of money and who had been told I was the best money bowler that ever lived. And they'd just seen me throw a gutterball. I had no idea what they were thinking now.

Well, the first game I got killed. I couldn't believe it. Guy Fisher threw a 210, which normally I could have easily beaten, but I only bowled 160. It was nothing but splits, and the lanes were hooking real bad. I had only seen the ball make that kind of extreme hook once before in my life. I was a great curve bowler sometimes, but tonight I seemed to be fighting everything – fighting to get in line, fighting the lanes, fighting the hook, and fighting those two guys behind me who had all this money on the line and were putting all this pressure on me.

After the first game, Gotti walks up to me.

"What's the matter?" he says. He was looking at me funny, like he was surprised and a little suspicious.

And you don't want to make John Gotti suspicious.

"The lanes are hooking real bad," I says. "I can't throw the ball hard enough to hit the pocket. I'm just not lined in yet – don't worry. I'll get it."

Actually, though, I was worried. Still, Guy Fisher was throwing the best he could and he was only hitting 210. I just needed to get back to my usual game, and I could demolish this guy.

The next game, the main bet went from $6,800 to $13,000. Ruby Red's brothers parlayed their bets – whatever they won in the first match, they bet again. They had confidence in their guy, and the second game went in his favor, too. In fact, it was no contest whatsoever. I was totally off. Terrible. The other guy was getting looser, and I was getting worse.

After the second game, it was Uncle Raymond's turn to come up and grill me.

"Is this on the up-and-up?" he says, and I heard that same pissed-off suspicion in his voice.

He was suspicious that somebody was paying me to take a fall, to deliberately lose, because I could probably actually make a lot more money that way than by winning.

"Of course this is on the up-and-up," I says, starting to get angry myself. "Why would you ask me that?"

"Because you look terrible!"

"The goddam lanes are hooking."

"Then throw the fucking thing harder!"

But the lanes were so dry that every time I threw the ball it would curve to the left. I couldn't get no timing together. It was like a pitcher in baseball, hitting the dirt instead of the strike zone. Actually, I knew what I needed to make me right: A goddam drink. A goddam vodka-and-orange-juice.

In the third frame of the third game, it was Gotti's turn to come up and rattle my cage.

"How come we ain't making any money?" he says. "Are you tankin'?"

You could tell he was getting really, really mad. He was not one of these guys who yelled when he got mad; he was quieter. But you got the point. This was a guy who'd gotten where he got by intimidating people, and he was pretty goddam intimidating right now.

"You tell me the truth: Are you fuckin' tanking?"

"No, of course not!"

"Well, that's what it fuckin' looks like!"

"I got some problems."

"Well, get rid of your problems, and start bowling! We're losing a lot of money here!"

The third bet was for $26,668. I remember this number, because it was the most money I ever bowled for in a single game. People were getting all excited by now, you could hear arguments over money in the back, all these complicated bets going down.

"What the fuck's going on?" he kind of half-yells at me. "I want to know!"

"I need a goddam drink. I've spent this whole week trying not to drink, and I need a goddam drink!"

"What kind of a drink?"

"A mixed drink – I need some fuckin' vodka and orange juice."

27

"Well, why didn't you say so?"

"I asked the guy up at the bar earlier and he said the bar's closed. It's against the law."

"Well it's open now."

Gotti shoved his way up to the bar and confronted the bartender, who was standing there watching the action like everybody else.

"My guy needs a drink."

"Bar's closed."

"My guy needs a drink, you hear me? Open the bar and gimme a bottle of vodka!"

"The bar's – " then I guess the guy got a real clear shot of John Gotti, the pissed-off mobster, and figured he'd better open the bar. Fuck the law. Gotti came over to where I was with a bottle of vodka, some orange juice and a glass. I filled the glass about three-quarters full of vodka and orange juice, knocked it back, and poured another. Right away I stopped being tired, stopped being exhausted. I got an oomph, I started getting lined in. I relaxed, my concentration came in and I stopped worrying about everything and everybody. This is what was supposed to happen in the first game, not the third, and it would have if I'd had a drink before the match started.

By the fourth frame of that third game, before I had a drink, I was down by 42 fucking pins. But then I started to throw. I took another drink and threw two strikes. Then he threw two strikes.

Then, as I'm walking past the guy up to the line, I kind of growl at him, "Throw bad, you fuckin' rat!"

By now, the vodka was kicking in and my old, arrogant, sonofabitch, fuck-you self was coming back. My asshole self.

Then I threw two strikes. He threw two strikes. By the last frame, the guy was standing at 254. He was doing pretty good. Real good, actually. All I needed was two strikes in the tenth to win.

"Lock the doors!" I yelled out. "This guy is dead!"

Then I threw the ball. I thought I threw it perfect. But it went sailing down the lane, off-center, and only knocked down nine pins. Guy Fisher won, 254 to 247 – three in a row.

By now the place is going nuts. Ruby Red and his guys are winning all kinds of money, and other guys are losing all kinds of money, and the guy who supposedly cannot lose, is losing.

But then I look over at Guy Fisher and I see he's sitting down, taking off his bowling shoes. He'd won the first three games, but I was coming back, big time, and he could see it. The kid knew he could not win against me.

I walk over to him.

"What are you doing?" I say.

"I'm quitting," he says.

"Why are you quitting?"

"Because you're drinking. I've seen you before, and when you're drinking you can't be beat. There's no way I can beat you."

Ruby Red and his guys might have gave Guy Fisher ten thousand bucks for bowling three games, so that was a good night for him. But this is also what is known as "bad action" – when somebody is winning and they quit while they're ahead. The guys who are losing don't get a chance to win their money back, and they tend to be seriously jerked around about this.

"You can't do that," I says.

"Who's gonna stop me?"

"They are."

"Who are they?"

"Them guys," I says, hooking my finger over at Uncle Raymond and Bobby Cabert and the other guy.

Then Ruby Red walks over.

"What's going on?" he says.

"Your man's quitting," I says.

"So? He's allowed to quit," Ruby Red says.

"No, he's not."

"Who's gonna stop me?" Guy Fisher says.

"Nobody stops Ruby Red," Ruby Red says. "He does what he wants."

So then Uncle Raymond and the other guy walk over. You know, you really don't want to get these two aggravated.

"What's the matter?" they say.

So then I jump in.

"Well, we got two problems," I say. "Number one is, this guy is quitting" (and here I'm pointing at Guy Fischer, who has stopped taking off his shoes). "And number two, this other guy says that's OK" (and here I'm pointing at Ruby Red).

So then Gotti jumps in. He gets right up in Ruby Red's face.

"You told us to bring a lot of money, and we brought a lot of money," Gotti yells at him, probably busting the guy's eardrum. "There could be three, four hundred large out in this crowd. So here's what's gonna happen. Lock the doors, nobody's going home! We're staying here until I win all your money, or you win all our money, or somebody gets killed! I will kill you or shoot you where you stand."

This was no longer the John Gotti I knew, the guy who loved people, the guy who loved me and loved to bet on bowling. This was the John Gotti who scared the shit out of people.

Ruby Red just stood there for a second, with his full-length fur coat and his fancy shoes and all his bling.

"Let's bowl," he said.

I guess he figured the other guy was serious.

Well, by then I was getting seriously toasted on vodka and I bowled fantastic. I just crushed the poor bastard, nine out of the next ten games. I fuckin' cleaned his clock. It wound up one of the ways Gotti said it would: With Ruby Red and his guys losing all their money.

So Gotti goes up to Ruby Red and hands him a big wad of cash – maybe ten or twenty thousand.

"Here," he says, "here's some pocket change to get you home."

"I don't need your money."

"Go on, take it anyway – no hard feelings. I don't want any repercussions over this. Maybe we can do business together in the future sometime."

This was the way things were done in them days. It was a standard gambler's thing. You never let a guy go home broke. For one thing, you wanted to be able to gamble against the guy some other time in the future. And also, it was just a matter of etiquette, kind of "honor among thieves." So Ruby Red took the money.

I put my bowling balls in my bag and me and Uncle Raymond and the other guy walked out to my car in the parking lot. We got in the car in our usual way – Raymond in the front passenger seat, me in the driver's seat and Gotti in the back seat, directly behind me.

"So we did good, huh?" I says. I'm happy. I'm rubbing my hands together. I knew I did great them last ten games.

"How did you like how I bowled?" I says to them.

"You were terrific for those last ten games," Uncle Raymond says.

"So you think we did good, huh?"

"Yeah, I think I did good. We won a lot of money. How much do I get?" I says, as I started turning the key in the ignition.

And that's when Gotti reached around from behind me, grabbed my whole head in his hands like a melon, and slams it into the driver's side window so hard it cracks the glass. Then he slams it into the glass again and again, as hard as he can, and the glass starts to shatter in my face. The side of my face splits open and blood gushes everywhere.

"You think you did good, huh? You think you did good? Don't you ever, EVER do that to me again!" Uncle Raymond yells at me, right up in my face.

Then he grabs my head and takes his turn, slamming it into the glass a few more times until the glass is busted all over the place and there's blood splattered all over my clothes, all over the seat.

"You put us in a real bad spot – we put big money on the line and you showed up with your head up your ass! You could have lost us a lot of money!"

I have to say, thinking back on it now, I was not totally surprised when this happened. I really did put them in a big-time bad situation because first they thought I was tanking and second, for the first time in my life, I really wasn't ready to bowl. I showed up hung over and out of practice and way off, mentally. I had had no desire to practice or anything.

On the other hand, they weren't looking to kill me or anything, they didn't throw me out of the car onto the ground. They didn't want the cops coming around. This was just a family argument. They just wanted to smack me around, teach me a lesson.

Still, I was busted up so bad, and bleeding all over the place, that Uncle Raymond had to take the wheel. He and Gotti both felt bad about what they'd done, I think. Uncle Raymond drives over to his doctor's house, someplace in North Arlington — by now it's, like, one o'clock in the morning — and he gets the doc up out of bed to stitch me up. It took forty stitches to put me back together, the doc said. I got $4,000 and forty stitches out of that night.

When I finally got home, I told Debbie I fell down the stairs.

I don't know if she bought it.

But at least she didn't throw me out of the house.

And the way our relationship was going, I considered that a good night.

.

5 THE EMPTY ROOM

Look, you gotta understand: Debbie LaRusso was the love of my life. She was fantastic – beautiful, caring, sexy, funny, somebody who cared about the stuff I cared about, somebody who fit into my family as if she was born there. She was so kind to my mom and dad and my sisters. She was the woman most guys are never lucky enough to meet in their lives.

But yet I was lucky enough to meet her, fall in love with her, and most amazing of all she fell in love with me, too. If there ever was a person for me forever, it was her.

If everything had worked out like I thought it was gonna, we would have gotten married and spent the rest of our lives together. We'd have had grandkids by now. I'd be grandpa Bobby.

Who wouldn't love a woman like that? But it didn't go down that way. Not at all.

And it was all because of me – because, by the time I was 25, I was turning into a lying scumbag and an addict. And I lost the love of my life.

How do you live with regret like that?

All these years later, I still don't know exactly how.

The night of the Ruby Red match, Debbie wasn't there. She didn't want no part of that shit. Plus, it was kind of a total guy thing – I don't think there was a single woman in the crowd that night.

But she wasn't there also 'cuz I was leading two lives now. One was the life where I loved Debbie, and kind of divided my time between staying with her at her apartment, or at my parents' house in Paterson. That was a life full of love and hot meals and going to the bowling alley with this great, funny, beautiful lady. And the other life was the late-night life, full of jacked-up, coked-up energy and booze, action bowling, the excitement of big bets hanging on a single moment, getting drawn deeper and deeper into a world full of people like John Gotti and Bobby Cabert and other shadowy, dangerous characters. I started to act and think and lie like these guys.

I don't remember how I first met them, but I started hanging out with some guys in the Bergen County mob – real low-lifes they called Crooked-Eye Phil and Little Al and Malinky and them guys. And one day I gave these Bergen County mobsters a major league gambler, this guy Chuck, who was involved with the "coupon king," the guy that invented grocery store coupons or whatever. This guy Chuck had too much money for his own good –he'd bet four or five thousand a match, fifty thousand in a night.

When you bet five thousand on a game, of course, you had to lay down an additional five hundred as the vig, the juice, the percentage. That money went to the mob or whoever "owned" the game. So if you got a guy betting fifty thousand a night, the vig is big enough to get the mob interested.

So this guy Chuck goes out and bets a lot of money and wins a lot of money until one day he don't. He gets crushed. And he winds up owing the Bergen County mob like, twenty or thirty thousand dollars in vig. And right after that, Chuck pulls a Houdini act and disappears. He don't come around no more.

This is a really, really bad idea.

But since the Bergen County boys can't find Chuck, they send Little Al over to see me. Little Al is little, but he's tough.

"You need to pay up," he says.

"I'm not paying nothing. I don't owe you a thing. You need to go find Chuck yourself."

"Where is he? Where's the guy live?"

"I don't know where he lives. That's your problem."

Then Little Al starts getting real nasty with me, all up in my face with that weird spooky glint in his eye.

"If we can't collect the vig, I'm coming after you, you little prick. I'm holding you responsible."

Meanwhile, while I'm slipping into these sorts of situations with all kinds of degenerate characters, I'm also slipping deeper and deeper into the grips of that beautiful white powder called cocaine. What had started out as a little club drug now and then had turned into a whole driving obsession, almost like a reason for living. I couldn't stop. Whatever started out as so-so use turned to extensive use turned to totally abusive use. Every dollar I made action bowling went straight up my nose, or down my throat.

And gradually, something else had started to happen: Addiction may start out as this big social party scene, this club scene, but it starts to turn into something completely unsocial. You start to get more and more focused on your own little self, and your next high: How am I gonna get the money to get high, how am I going score, how am I gonna get loaded, how am I gonna get the money to do it again. I wasn't Debbie's boyfriend no more. I was the boyfriend of booze and little razor-sharp lines of white powder.

Debbie wasn't stupid. More and more, she was getting suspicious and mistrusting of me. And I gotta say, she had good reason. I'd tell her I was going to be home at eight or ten or whatever and then I wouldn't show up until midnight or two even around daylight the next day. And, look: I wasn't no womanizer. I wasn't carrying on with some other lady at the clubs. I was carrying on with two other ladies: Alcohol and cocaine.

By Christmas, 1978, when I was 26 years old, I'd been deeply involved with Debbie for a couple of years. And, like I told you earlier, we would have been married if Debbie's mom hadn't threatened to disown her if she done that. So most of the time we was "living in sin."

Then, on December 18th, 1978, a Monday just before Christmas, something happened that I will never forget, something that showed what sort of magical stuff Debbie was made of.

The whole thing kind of began a couple of days earlier, on Friday. That day, my sister Patsy calls me up and asks me if I want to go to a party in Totowa, New Jersey, with her best friend. I told her I was bowling but I'd come pick her up after that. So I go pick her up and we go to this hoity-toity house and when we get there and knock on the door, this tiny little peephole opens up, like where the boogie man would look out, and then somebody opens the door and lets us in. This is the sort of place I don't belong. And when we go inside, it's this big spaghetti-bender party. I say "spaghetti-bender" to mean Italian, not mobbed-up.

And I'm sort of wandering around the party awkwardly, kind of stumbling into the potted palms or whatever, 'cuz these ain't my people and I don't belong here, and neither does Patsy. And then I look into the next room and I see this huge guy starting to fuck with my sister, and I can tell she's a little drunk and she don't like it. So I go charging in there. I go right up to the guy, who is like six or seven inches taller than me. I've always been a bantamweight, but bantamweights are scrappy.

"Hey, man, stop fucking with my sister," I says to the guy. "Get out of her face!"

The guy turns toward me, and he's like one of them battle robots in the video games. I suddenly realize – too late – how big he is.

"Fuck you, man," the guy says, and then he rears back and cold-cocks me in the head – wham! – and I go flying through the air, all the way into the next room. That dude must have been ex-military or something. There's blood spurting everywhere, blood on the expensive Oriental carpets and the furniture and whatever. Patsy, my beautiful sister, don't normally get too worked up about shit. But she's a little bit loaded and she seen this big bubba attack her brother so she goes over and grabs some four-thousand-dollar vase or whatever and cracks it over the dude's head. Then we both leave the party, real quick (probably just as the cops arrive).

Patsy drives me over to Wayne General Hospital to get my face stitched back together, and I don't get home to my parents' house until, like, four in the morning. My face has been seriously rearranged and it's all bandaged up. I look like Jack Nicolson in that movie Chinatown. So that's how the weekend starts.

So then on Sunday, Patsy asks me to help her deliver some Christmas gifts to clients of the cosmetics company, Chelsea Cosmetics, that she's working for. Ironically, the gifts are all bottles of booze – Jack Daniels, Bollo wine, Valpocello and whatever. So I agree to help her, even though my face looks like a doctor lesson. So the next day, Monday, we go down to midtown Manhattan to deliver these Christmas gifts to Macys and Gimbels and whatever.

And after a little while Patsy is just – I dunno, she's going too slow. So I grab ten bottles of wine and two bottles of Jack Daniels and go upstairs at Gimbels and I say to some guy, "Hi, my name's Bob Perry, and this is a Christmas gift from Chelsea Cosmetics." And the guy gets all flustered and he says, oh, we can't accept gifts unless they're mailed, and I fight the urge to do some surgery on the guy's face with a bottle of Jack Daniels, and I get out of there just in time.

So I go downstairs to the street and I'm standing there on the corner of Avenue of the Americas and Broadway with a crowd of people waiting for the light to turn and I look over and here's this absolutely spectacular brunette standing there. I mean, there are plenty of fabulous women in New York but this woman is out of this world. She distracts me completely. Then the light turns. I step into the street. I hear her say to me, "Look out!" And the next thing I know, it's like a freight train slams into my body doing about sixty and I'm being dragged down Avenue of the Americas smashed into the bumper of a taxicab like a bug. I'm feeling a mixture of shock, surprise and unbelievable pain.

Finally the cab stops – it went almost from 34th Street to 33rd – and I vaguely remember all kinds of people come crowding around, including the beautiful brunette. (I didn't do this just to get your attention, darlin'!) I think the fucking cab driver would have driven away if it hadn't been for all those people. (New York!)

I remember drifting in and out of consciousness. I remember being unable to feel anything from the waist down. I remember terrific pain in my face, where the antenna of the cab had ripped my face open – for the second time in one weekend! And I remember a New York City policemen looking down at me. He throws a coat or something on top of me.

"This motherfucker is dead," he says.

I remember thinking, "I'm dead. I can't believe I'm dead."

Somehow or other, Patsy sees all the commotion and realizes it's me sprawled in the street, and she goes rushing over to the place where I'm lying on the pavement. She's hysterical.

"Bobby! Bobby! Bobby!" I hear her yelling.

I hear the cop saying, "Don't move," which is hysterical, because, like, how am I supposed to move? I've been whacked in the head by a wrecking ball and I'm completely paralyzed from the waist down.

Then I hear Patsy's voice, far away.

"Bobby, Bobby, Bobby!"

Then, at some point, I manage to throw the cop's coat back and yell out, "I ain't fuckin' dead!"

The inner lion that had come back over and over again in my life had just showed up.

I ain't fuckin' dead yet.

You asshole!

So an ambulance comes and drags my sorry ass off to Bellevue Hospital (the place they send the nutjobs, which happened to be the only hospital available). When I got there, I remember they loaded me on a gurney and this black guy pulls off my dungarees and I just screamed, the pain was so incredible (both my legs was busted up and broken). I remember there was, like, ten gurneys with bloody-looking guys laying there in the waiting area. These guys were handcuffed to the gurneys. One of them told me they were all there 'cuz of a riot at Rikers Island Prison. The guy tells me I look worse than any of them busted-up convicts. Boy, this has been a helluva weekend so far.

Patsy can't stop crying. She calls my dad's appliance shop and my dad is busy, so he sends over this huge guy who works in the shop. The guy is like six-six, and they call him "Thumbs." Thumbs can carry a Frigidaire on his back up two flights of stairs, but that don't do me much good now.

But what does do me a lot of good is when Patsy calls Debbie and she shows up in my hospital room, immediately, like an angel. And Debbie LaRusso comes to see me in the hospital every single day until I get out – 167 days later. This girl never missed a single day. I mean, wow. What a woman. Do I deserve that?

Absolutely not, but this is a story about a guy that always got more than he deserved.

Almost as soon as I got in the hospital, the doctors started giving me Percodan, a powerful, addictive narcotic. I guess they didn't know I was a junkie in training. And, of course, being a junkie in training, I never told them.

The cab had busted open the bone in my left leg. It ripped off the ligaments in my right leg. It ripped the shit out of my face. And all kinds of other stuff. But here's the worst part of it: I held the world responsible for what happened to me. As I would learn much later, in sobriety, it's your own attitudes and resentments that do the most damage, and it's only when you fix all them bad attitudes that you start to heal.

But I wasn't ready for that now. Now I figured, since the world done me wrong, it was fair when the doc gave me 60 Percodans for a month that I could eat them all in a week and ask for more. I didn't care if I was getting addicted to Percodan. It felt good, and God had done me wrong. I deserved it.

Uncle Raymond had a different explanation for what happened. He called me at the hospital the day after I got in there.

"So who hit you?" he says.

"Hit me? Nobody hit me. A cab ran over me."

"Yeah, right," he says. "You know everybody's saying the Bergen County mob done it."

"The Bergen County mob? Crooked-Eye Phil and Little Al and them guys? Raymond, you gotta be crazy. I got run over by a taxicab in midtown Manhattan in the middle of the day, with about a thousand other people standing there watching."

"Well, think about it. You had a dispute with them bastards over that little creep Chuck's debts. Basically, you told them you didn't owe nothing. They said you did. And that was, what, a couple of weeks before this cab thing happened?"

I had to admit, Uncle Raymond had a point. But I still thought what he was saying was ridiculous. I didn't believe that's what happened. What I believed, deep down, was even more ridiculous – that God hated me and was punishing me. And it wasn't until I got over that idea – years later – that I finally started becoming a whole person.

But for now, I had to take care of some business. Because Little Al and them guys would not back off. They couldn't find Chuck, so they were going to try to extort thirty grand out of me. It didn't matter if I was a fucking cripple. It didn't matter that I didn't have it. Finally I agreed to have a mob sit-down with these guys, in a restaurant owned by the Bergen County mob, on Route 6. I told these guys I was going to bring some friends, my Uncle Raymond and a friend of his named Bobby.

So I show up at this restaurant, a little early, on crutches, with both my legs in casts. It wasn't like this makes these guys any more sympathetic. Little Al gets in my face again, mocking me.

"So where's the fabulous uncle of yours? Did he forget about you?"

And just about then Uncle Raymond and Bobby Cabert walk through the door. And those two guys – I'm telling you – you could just look at them and know there was trouble coming. Uncle Raymond came through the door like a bull elephant, ready to knock something down. Bobby

Cabert was dressed meticulous, like he always was, wearing two-hundred-dollar pants, a beautiful sports jacket, a nice hat, with them aviator-type glasses he always wore. Nothing was out of place. I never saw Cabert do nothing crazy, like Joe Pesci's character in that movie "Goodfellas," that was modelled after Cabert. When Cabert did his business, nobody was around. But right now, when he walked through that door, dressed to the nines, somehow you just got the idea that you probably better tiptoe out of there.

"How ya doin'?" Little Al says, which is what everybody always says in New Jersey.

"Whaddya mean, how am I doin'?" Raymond says, real belligerent. "How do you think I'm doin'? Whaddya think I'm doin' here?"

Little Al looked over at Bobby Cabert, and he must have recognized who he was. Everybody knew who he was.

"Listen," Al says, "We didn't really realize – "

"Yes you did. What the fuck are you trying to do to my nephew? He don't owe you shit."

And then Bobby Cabert got in the guy's face, and then Uncle Raymond did, like a tag team. A few minutes later, when they left the restaurant, that thirty-grand debt had just gone away, like a soap-bubble that just popped.

A few days after that, Uncle Raymond tracked down Chuck the gambler and they had a nice little chat. Maybe they had tea. And after that, Chuck paid up.

That's how things worked, if you were connected to guys like Uncle Raymond and Bobby Cabert.

Meanwhile, incredibly enough, I had this angel, Debbie LaRusso, come to my room every day with unconditional love and sometimes flowers. At first I was worried that I would never walk again, much less bowl. But once the docs started to fix my legs, operating on both the left and right leg, I got transferred into a wheelchair.

Eventually I got these big ugly casts on my legs and was given crutches, and then one day I was released from the hospital, and Debbie moved into my parents' house with me, helping me climb upstairs and get around. Think about that.

The cab driver's insurance company paid for all of them months in the hospital. I hired some shyster lawyer down on 125 Broadway and he got me, like, $20,000, even though I shoulda got two million.

Now that I had been released from the hospital to my parents' house, I was a "new man." On a personal level, I felt more in love with Debbie than ever. Professionally, I felt I would soon be as good a bowler as anyone on the planet – about ready to become nationally known, just as good as anybody.

Physically, though, I was still on the mend, hobbling around on these crutches that the doctors led me to believe might be a permanent deal. They didn't say so, but it was obvious they thought I might be a crutch-monkey for good.

Awhile after this – maybe a year or so – I was in the bowling alley with my crutches. There was a guy named Duke Ballady, that I knew from school, a family friend, bowling this other guy name Larry Duke. Larry owned these sporting goods stores. And Duke Ballady, even though he was only 17, was really a fantastic bowler. But he was also a fucking loudmouth, and he was trash-talking Larry, big time. It started to really piss me off. Who did this kid think he was, disrespecting this older man? But the kid wouldn't quit. Then he turns to me. He's aware that I'm watching, and also that I used to be one of the most formidable bowlers on the planet.

"If you didn't have crutches, I'd bowl you now!" he says, in a very mocking, sneering way. And the next thing I know, I'm trying to throw my crutches away and put this little creep in his place. I didn't succeed – that happened a few months later – but the inner lion had come out again. When I was driven to it, I had this savage desire to succeed, to overcome adversities, to climb back into the winner's circle. When the lion came out, there was almost no stopping him.

When I got out of the hospital, I gradually shed not only the wheelchair, the crutches and the casts but also the whole idea of myself as a crippled guy. Now I was back on my feet, good as new. Unfortunately, that also meant that I slipped back into my old habits of staying out half the night, drinking and snorting blow. There was only one change: Now I had a new addiction, to Percodan.

For me, drugs and alcohol were like peanut butter and jelly – one went with the other. When I drank, I wanted to do drugs, and when I did drugs, I drank. I couldn't stop.

Was this any way to treat a good woman? No, especially one who nursed me back to health for 167 consecutive days. But this was not a matter of manners. This was addiction – in fact, multiple addictions. More and more I was becoming a slave to them. Even when I got back into my groove and started bowling real good, I'd sometimes win a ten-thousand-dollar purse... and within a couple of days, I'd be broke again. And trying to come up with some big lie to tell Debbie about how come I got home so late.

Sometimes we'd go into the city and I'd drop her off somewhere and tell her I'd be back in an hour and then I'd be gone all night. Things were getting worse and worse. We just couldn't get along. I have to say, looking back, that I can hardly blame her.

Debbie was a real good bowler and she liked the whole bowling world, and she really loved Bob Perry the bowler. She knew that I was a guy who could go all the way, become nationally known, win all the top tournaments, win a lot of money. But she could also see that, from time to time, I would make mistakes under pressure. It was like I was cracking, but slowly. She was watching me deteriorate myself. She was watching the drugs and booze obliterate me.

Then, finally, things hit absolute bottom. One night Debbie told me she was gonna make dinner, a meatloaf, and to be home by six o'clock.

But it's, like, eleven o'clock when I walk in the door of our apartment. I'm hammered, and trying to cover it up. That's my life: I'm one thing, but I'm trying to pretend I'm another. I'm bleeding from the nose but I'm pretending I'm not. Debbie is sitting there with black smoke coming out of her ears. She's fucking furious. Poor Debbie! Living with an alcoholic is making her old, and you can see it in her face.

"What are you so mad about?" I says, kind of innocent and surprised.

"Where have you been?"

"I had to take Raymond into the city."

"Bullshit."

"I'm not lyin', Debbie! Raymond had some business in Queens, in Ozone Park. The whole thing ran real late. Then we went to the track, he had to meet a guy over there. I tried to call you."

I knew she wasn't going to buy my story, but I stuck to it.

"I don't believe a word you say, Bobby. Every time you open your mouth, you're lying."

"Look, I told Raymond I would take him around tonight. Whatever it was he was doin,' it ran late. I can't help it! Whaddya, want me to tell Raymond to drop his business and come back here so I'll be in time for dinner?"

"Bobby, I made you dinner and asked you to be here at six o'clock. I wanted to sit down together, like a regular couple. Why can you never, ever do what you say you're going to do?"

"I told you! Raymond's business ran late! Why don't you ever believe me?"

And so everything kind of ratcheted up from there. When you're defending a lie, like I was, your voice tends to get louder and louder – as if, if you yelled loud enough, your story would be true. Poor Debbie. All she wanted was to have a nice meal with me at six 'o'clock, and here I was this raving, drunk lunatic in the kitchen screaming at her.

The meatloaf sat in the oven, getting colder and colder. Well, one word led to another and then the "F-U's" started. I was trying to defend an undefendable position and there was noplace to go except to a higher volume. Our little apartment was not that far from other little apartments, and I'm sure our neighbors could heard what was going on. It's possible somebody called the cops, I don't remember. Maybe the cops knocked on the door. I don't remember.

I just remember that this fight with Debbie kept getting worse and worse, in this tiny kitchen. Finally she pushed me, hard. I pushed her back, hard. And then she slapped me in the face so hard it felt like she broke my nose. When somebody hits or slaps you in the face, it makes you go kind of crazy. Then, next thing I remember, she'd picked up a knife. It wasn't no butter knife, neither – it was one of them big sharp kitchen knives like that you'd cut a turkey with.

"I'll fucking kill you!" she yelled.

And then, I dunno, I guess we both realized how bad this argument had got, how scary it was. It was actually the worst argument either one of us ever had. By far. We were about two seconds away from doing something we'd regret for the rest our lives.

I remember years later, when I was in prison, I was talking to my mom at the time the O.J. Simpson verdict came out.

"You think he killed those two people?" she said. "I know you know. 'Cuz you were there. Debbie told me about what happened that night. She told me how close it got."

But instead, kinda suddenly, Debbie and me both sat down, slumping into chairs at the kitchen table. We were both scared. We were both sad and confused. Then we both started crying.

"Look, Debbie," I says to her, pleading, with tears coming down my cheeks. "I can't live like this! We can't live like this!"

Then the remorse came up, like a big boiling flood. This was not a "dispute" – I was one hundred percent wrong. I was not right in any sense. I had thrown a bad blow into the woman I loved. My actions were terrible. This was one of the most major league awakenings I ever seen.

"Oh, God, I'm so sorry," I says. "I'm not going to be like that anymore. I promise."

But my promises didn't mean shit. And the next day, when Debbie told my sisters and her friends what had happened, every one of them told her to leave me immediately. They told her to move out of the house. And my two closest sisters, Patsy and Jeannie – both of them stopped talking to me.

A couple of days later, I found that meatloaf, stone cold and untouched, in the oven.

Heartbreak: That's what it is when the love of your life is leaving you, and it's all because of you.

Over the next few days and weeks, I was practically begging, trying to get Debbie to forget everything that went down. But no matter what I did, the addiction won. If I drank I drugged, if I drugged I drank, it all went to that. When I lay down next to my loved one at night, I was so happy to be there. But I stank of booze. She wasn't happy that I was there. She didn't tell me she was leaving, but I knew something was going to happen.

Meanwhile, I had an angry fight with Patsy over my drinking, and I punched a hole in her wall. My sisters had seen this anger in me, and by now they considered Debbie a part of this family. More and more, they considered me the outsider, the dangerous one, the guy that had to be thrown out to protect everyone else. The wolf.

"You get rid of him – you gotta get rid of Bobby," they kept telling Debbie.

And I kept begging her not to listen to them.

It was not too long after that terrible fight that I had to leave to fly out to Reno to the national championships. I didn't win the tournament, but I did pretty good, and then I remember there was this huge snowstorm, 24 inches fell, and I got stuck in the Denver airport for almost a whole day. On the way home I called Debbie from Chicago.

"I'm probably not going to be home when you get there – my mom and I are going to a show in New York," she told me. "Get somebody else to pick you up at the airport."

Things were not going well at that point. I tried to apologize to her for everything. She told me she was okay and everything was good and all that stuff.

So I called my friend Pepsi to come pick me up at the airport. He drives me back to the apartment in Paterson and I get out of the car and I can see Jackson, our dog, at the window of the apartment up on the third floor. That was kind of unusual. I didn't ever remember Jackson doing that. But I was eager to see Debbie.

Look: You gotta understand that by now not only was my relationship with Debbie on edge, my whole life was teetering on the brink. In the classic alcoholic, dope addict way, I was just completely in denial about what was going on in my life, or in the lives of people around me. I mean, I had no car, I had no money – I just spent everything I had on booze and drugs and partying – and everybody was mad at me. Even my own mother, who lived on East 26th Street, wouldn't talk to me no more. Too much lying, too much stealing, too many alcoholic blackouts. Once I had called her on the phone.

"Who is this?" she says.

"Bob Perry, your son," I says.

"Don't ever call this number again."

Click.

That was my life.

So I go bounding up the stairs to our apartment to see Debbie, carrying my little travel suitcase, and I unlock the door and bust into the living room and… it's completely empty. Jackson comes up to greet me, but there is nothing in the apartment except a mattress on the floor, a shower curtain, and a pile of my clothes on the floor. There's no food in the refrigerator, not even a toothbrush in the bathroom. All the utensils are plastic.

Debbie – beautiful Debbie! – has left me.

She's gone.

This sweet woman with the gorgeous body, who loves me to death – she's gone. She gave up on me.

There was no cell phones in them days, of course, so I go over to the neighbor's apartment to use the phone, but they don't answer the door. I go downstairs to the pizza joint next door to use the phone to call Debbie. She doesn't answer. I call everybody, but nobody answers. It turns out, everybody knew she was leaving me except me. Finally I called my sister Jeannie, and she picked up, but she didn't want to talk to me either. She said I should call my other sister, Patsy, who always gave it to me straight.

"Debbie left you – she moved out," Patsy says. "She's had it with your shit. Everybody else has, too."

These waves of loneliness just washed over me. I was devastated. Even now, over thirty years later, I can remember that empty apartment, and I feel devastated. Even now, I can't get that feeling out of my body.

Even so – believe it or not – it still wasn't enough to wake me up.

Even getting dumped by Debbie, the love of my life, was not enough!

I was heading down, and I had a long, long way to go before I hit bottom.

6 THE FULL FUCKIN' SKID

It's been more than thirty years since Debbie left me, but right now I can still feel what I felt in my body that night she told me to leave. The shock. The emptiness. The hollowness. The fear. When Debbie went out of my life, it suddenly made me realize how hollow I already was inside – I had a hole inside so deep and wide there was nothing that could ever fill it.

Except her.

And now she was gone.

Now there didn't seem to be no reason for living. It was just me, Jackson, an old mattress, some plastic forks and spoons, and a pile of hot-shit disco clothes from Mr. Stag's in a big empty room. I was lost. I never realized how much I depended on Debbie. I started talking to people in the bowling world, and I found out that there was a lot of sympathy for her, that people were helping her way more than they were helping me. Maybe I thought I was hot shit, the greatest, but other people seemed to have a different opinion. That made me feel even more alone.

About a week after she left me, I came around the corner at the supermarket with a shopping cart full of beer and I practically ran into her.

"Oh, hi," I says, very casual.

"Hi."

"You doin' OK?"

"Yeah."

"Where you living?"

"I'm back at my mom's."

"How's that goin'?"

"It's okay."

"Well," I says, real tough-guy, "you do what you gotta do."

We chit-chatted a little and then, realizing my heart was breaking and all that wiseguy stuff was bullshit, I just started begging. I practically got down on my knees.

"Look, Debbie," I says, "I'm so sorry for what happened. It's all my fault. I got no defense for what I done. But I promise you, if we ever got back together again I wouldn't do dope again, ever. I wouldn't stay out late no more. I'd earn money and not spend it, I'd bring it home. And you know what an incredible money bowler I am – the best. We could still have such a beautiful life together, Debbie."

She just stood there in the cereal aisle with all the Cheerios and Wheaties, with a look on her face that said, "I ain't buyin' this shit."

But for my part, I think I actually believed it when I said it. I didn't even realize I was lying like a rug.

A few months later, I had to take Jackson to the pound and give him away. I couldn't take care of myself, much less a dog. Debbie's mom didn't want to take the dog, either. So I asked Debbie to come with me to the pound and give him away. We both cried. There was no longer any home that was safe for a dog at all. The home Debbie and I had made together was gone.

For a couple of months I kept on living in that empty apartment, with no furniture except that old mattress, no TV to watch, no food except maybe vodka and chips. When I wanted to call somebody I'd walk three blocks up the street and call my old partner in crime Tommy Lorenzo. He'd help me out with a few bucks, and we'd go score some dope together and party. For a little while, everything seemed good again.

One day I went over to bowl on a team in Paramus, but it turned out they were all friends with Debbie and her mom and they threw me off the team. They were all couples bowling together in a league; they'd heard about me from Debbie, and that was enough for them.

Once or twice I called Debbie at her job at the insurance place. She'd didn't have nothing much to say, except that she didn't want to meet me. She said she was done. She was fine living back with her mother.

So then I gave up the apartment, along with Jackson. I couldn't pay the electric bill. I could still make a lot of money bowling – I even won a couple of big tournaments for five or ten thousand – but drugs and alcohol sucked it all up. Where did all the money go? I could barely afford food. Meanwhile, nobody was talking to me – not Patsy or Jeannie or anybody else. Even Uncle Raymond didn't seem to come around no more. He was such a powerful presence in my life that him not being there weighed on me, like a boulder on my back. I knew that he loved me, and I knew that him not being there meant he did not approve of my life.

The only person who would help me out was Tommy Lorenzo. Sometimes we bowled and I'd give him a lesson, sometimes we'd get in on the action bowling on a Friday night, or we'd go into New York after the action. But whatever we did, we'd always wind up in the city, seriously loaded on something or other. More and more, I'd wake up out of a blackout afterwards, someplace I didn't recognize.

I was finally able to talk to my sister Jeannie, and she let me stay at her house for a few weeks, but she started getting nasty to me, so I moved in with Patsy, but that didn't work either. So I moved into my mom's one-bedroom apartment on East Sixteenth Street. She apologized for being so nasty to me on the phone, and I apologized to her for everything I done. My mother still loved me then, and I loved her too, despite all the shit that had gone down. But by now nobody else in my family would talk to me, so mom's apartment was the closest thing to "home" I was going to get. One day she bet a hundred dollars and won five thousand, and recarpeted the whole apartment. My own life used to be like that: Magic, golden, easy. But now, somehow, I had turned into a thirty-year-old man waking up hungover in his mom's apartment, and all the big dreams of my life – a wife and family, fame, riches and national championships – seemed like stupid, busted toys.

Even so, I wasn't ready to give up. And the main thing I wanted – the thing I always wanted – was Debbie LaRusso. Now I decided to do everything in my power to see if I could get her back.

Maybe you can't believe this now, but when I was thirty and all pimped out in my disco clothes and blow-dried hair, I looked like the tits. In the bowling world, I was still famous all over the bowling world on the East coast. But the main thing I had going for me was my mouth. I could always talk my way into or out of almost anything. So I decided to try to talk Debbie into taking me back.

I'd get her on the phone, or sometimes even in person at the bowling alley, and I'd joke and beg and plead with her, promise her I'd do things, or not do things. I promised her I'd never do dope or stay out all night again. I wouldn't get fucked up. I'd straighten out and get better. I'd even go to rehab. I'd work hard to make money and not spend it all. I told her I'd saved up ten thousand dollars. I'd get us a nice apartment. Maybe I'd even learn to cook.

I don't know why, but Debbie finally bought it. About six months after we broke up, we moved into another apartment, this time in East Rutherford, New Jersey. It was nice. And for awhile I was really, really good. We had six or seven months of happiness together in that apartment. I didn't stay out late. I made sure I wasn't too fucked up before I got home. I was polite and sweet to her.

But the seeds of trouble were already there. That ten grand I told her I'd saved up? I made it selling coke. (I didn't say nothing about how I got it, but I think she suspected.) And I said I would stop doing drugs, that I would change, but the amount of effort I put into changing was zero. It was only a matter of time before the old, bad self, the junkie self, the hungry, empty self, would come back again.

And it did. One night I came home about four in the morning and I was shit-faced drunk and coked-up to the max. Debbie came stumbling into the kitchen and we had another big fight. I admitted to her, finally, that it was time for me to get some help. I realized that unless I got some help getting rid of this monkey on my back, I would lose Debbie for good. Finally Debbie had had enough of my shit. Actually, she was a saint for lasting as long as she did.

I remembered this old geezer named Billy, that I'd known for quite a lot of years from seeing him around bowling alleys. He told me he'd once been this terrible drunk, but now he was in this program of recovery. He never beat my brains in with it, but he told me this program would always be there if I ever felt like I needed it. Billy had been sober a long time, maybe 15 years or something. I never lost Bill's phone number – I'd kept that ratty scrap of paper in my wallet, when there wasn't nothing else in there. I'd run into Billy from time to time.

"You still in that program?"

"Yeah."

"Can I call you if I need to?"

"Yeah."

I thought maybe I'd call Billy, but the next morning Debbie made me call St. Joseph's Hospital, in Paterson, and they recommended this free detox program called Straight and Narrow. Debbie drove me over there that same day and I stayed there six days. I was a complete mess. My life was falling apart and I didn't want to lose her. It wasn't just that I couldn't breathe anymore because my nose was so fantastically stuffed up from cocaine. It was that the whole inside of my head was like a block of wood. But, more than that, deep down, even though I still looked fairly good and could talk a good game, I was a completely lost soul. There was just a lonely wind down a lonely road where a person should have been.

There was this thing inside of me that I could not get rid of, and would not understand until years later. All I knew was that if I took a drink I felt better, so I kept on drinking and doing blow until the next thing you know I was gone, in a blackout. I didn't know nothing about blackouts, I never heard of that. I just knew that more and more nights, I'd get home and not know what happened.

It was like my whole life was getting sucked down into a black hole, like one of them stars that sucks up all the light.

When I got out of Straight and Narrow, I felt pretty good. There was still shit draining out of my face, but I could breathe a little bit better and I felt kind of hopeful. But that wasn't good enough for Debbie. She insisted that I go to this 28-day program she found out about, called St. Christopher's Inn, which was part of this very woo-woo rehab place run by a bunch of Franciscan monks called Graymoor Spiritual Retreat Center. It was someplace upstate, far away from the city.

Debbie wasn't fooling around. I came back from Straight and Narrow and was in the apartment one night and then the next morning she drove me up to Graymoor. She seemed kind of happy, like maybe things would change. Like maybe there was a chance for us. I just felt sick and scared and desperate. I really didn't want to do this shit.

But when I got up to Graymoor, it was like walking into a different world. All the monks were wearing brown bathrobes and sandals, like from Bible days. Everything was real quiet. And them monks greeted me with open arms, because it turns out that my uncle, Father Benjamin McVey, had lived up there and was buried there. He was some kind of a big muckety-muck in the Franciscan world, so I figured these old gray-headed geezers would give me a break up there. It was going to be great. I had an inside track at this joint.

They gave me a bed and showed me the dining hall and the room where AA meetings were held. Part of the day you had to pray and part of the day you had to work.

So they gave me a little job in the intake area, checking in new people who would come through the door.

The first few days, I was trying to pay attention and be good, but after a little while the place started to really grind on my ass. The people who came in the door? They were pathetic derelicts and junkies and losers. They looked and smelled terrible. Almost all of them were homeless. What was I doing here? I mean, I wasn't like these people at all. I was one of the greatest bowlers on the East coast, maybe the whole country. Hell, maybe the world. I was one of the greatest action bowlers walking. I could make thousands of dollars in a night, easy. I had a great apartment in East Rutherford. And I had the greatest girlfriend in the world. I had never even been arrested for nothing (yet). I was just doing this because I didn't want to lose Debbie, that's all.

I went to a couple of them AA meetings, but they were total bullshit. I mean these guys – what a bunch of pathetic nutjobs. Spilling their guts, and probably lying through their teeth too. They talked about "The Steps," but I didn't know nothing about that and didn't want to, either. I'm sitting there in these rooms, listening to all this, and I haven't had a drink or a line of blow for twelve or thirteen days, and these people are driving me batshit.

There was this one old guy at Graymoor, maybe 40 or 50 years old, who they kept on as a maintenance man because he was too messed up in the head to be able to function outside. He was what they call a "wet brain" drunk, a toothless old guy who basically cooked his noodle from so many years of drinking. He was going to be at Graymoor for the rest of his life. But even though he moved real slow and had trouble understanding anything, he was loved by everybody around the place.

They called him Old Man John or some such thing.

But for some reason, Old Man John had it in for me. He kept coming around, bothering me, being nasty to me, getting up in my face. So I start being nasty back to him.

"I ain't like you, bro," I says to Old Man or whatever. "I ain't like you!"

Then I start yelling at him, belittling him, I guess just because I'm going out of my mind up there. And besides, he wouldn't get out of my face.

One of the monks, a guy named Brother Pious, overhears what's going on and comes in from the next room to bust my chops.

"Listen, Perry, unless you change your life, before you know it you're going to wind up like this man if not worse," he says. "If you don't change, you'll wind up in jail or dead or both. And soon."

It was complete garbage, of course. Horseshit. Brother Pious just didn't like me. Well, I didn't like him neither. The grizzle-headed old fuck.

The next day I was playing basketball with this kid from Brooklyn and he was being a little prick, pushing and shoving, trying to trip me up. I picked up the basketball and hit him with it. So Brother Pious calls me on the carpet again.

"There is no room for violence here," he says.

"You should see what this kid's been doing to me!" I says. "He's being a total jerk, he's acting out!"

"This boy has serious problems that you know nothing about," Brother Pious went on, his voice getting darker and angrier. "Go out and die on the street! You have no humility! You have no respect for anything or anybody! There's no room for you here. I should give your bed to somebody who could actually use it."

"I'm not like him or any of these fucking people in here!"

"You're worse than these people in here. Unless you change, there is no hope for you."

"Man, I don't belong here."

"No, you don't," Brother Pious says. And he hands me a bus ticket back to Manhattan.

When I got to the city I called Debbie and told her I'd done real good at Graymoor – so good, in fact, that they let me out early. When she came to pick me up she could see that I looked and sounded a lot better, since I'd been clean and sober a couple of weeks, eating good food and actually sleeping all night. She was happy for me, and happy for us. I called Uncle Raymond and he was real happy for the both of us, too.

It seemed like everything was turning around for me.

Then, two weeks later, I discovered crack.

The second I tried it, I knew I was gone.

Because crack was better than life.

There was this kid named Dennis who lived around the corner from us in East Rutherford, and he was the one who introduced me to the drug that was about to change my life forever. (This was around 1984, when crack was a brand-new thing.) I went over there one day and he showed me how you load these little white rocks of crack cocaine into a straight glass stem with a little bit of brillo stuffed into the end of it for a screen. Then you torch the crack with a butane cigarette lighter and – wham! – in a second that shit hits your brain like a freight train and you're gone. It's like sucking down 30 bottles of beer in one second, like the most perfect, most blissed-out you ever felt in your life. And then, after about four seconds, it starts to fade and all you want is to do it again. You'd sell your pet puppy, sell your girlfriend, sell your mother, to get more. And people do.

I was already a full-blown drunk, but crack escalated my drinking through the roof. It also escalated my lying, especially to Debbie, to cover it all up. And my hustling and stealing, because I had to pay for the shit somehow.

Because nobody could tell if you were smoking crack – it didn't have a smell, it didn't make your eyes red – I started thinking I could just do crack all the time and get away with it. The obsession started taking over my life. Then the paranoia and the weirdness started setting in. I became convinced that people were after me, following me, watching me, everywhere I went. More and more, I was turning into a creature of the shadows.

Joe Tolvay (Bob's bowling teammate): *"Bobby used to always think he was better than everybody else in the bowling world, and the thing is, he was. But then he got in with the wrong crowd and after awhile nobody trusted him anymore. He turned into a con man, a likeable con man. People thought he was just scamming them all the time, and I'm pretty sure he was. One time he came in with this Aiwa stereo system, must have cost a couple of thousand dollars, that he was selling for $200. I gave him the money, took the stereo, and the next morning when I came in, it was gone. That's when I knew he was in big trouble."*

At the same time, I started to hate the high I once loved. I hated the smell of the stuff, and especially the smell of all that butane you had to inhale to get high. It was disgusting.

(Some people smoked crack by setting fire to cotton balls dipped in 151-proof rum – that's why they sometimes call crack "151" – but I couldn't afford that.) Every time I went out on the street I would say, this is the last time, but I didn't do anything to change, so nothing changed.

More and more, I kept ending up in New York City at three in the morning, in places I would never have dreamed of going when I was just smoking pot or drinking vodka.

I'd find myself in some crack den in an abandoned building, looking over my shoulder, convinced somebody was coming for me. I used to be such a snappy dresser, but now I'd wear the same shit for days or weeks or months, first because I didn't care, and second because I couldn't afford new clothes — I was spending it all on booze and crack. I'd win a few thousand in a bowling tournament or in the action, but I could never manage to pay the rent. Debbie had to do it. I was completely financially dependent on her.

Meanwhile, my body was deteriorating. I rarely took showers anymore. I couldn't sleep. Sometimes I'd wake up at two or three in the morning, slip out of bed from beside Debbie, and drive into the city, into the middle of the apocalypse in the South Bronx, to cop drugs. I hated myself while I was doing this, but I did it anyway. I could easily have gotten shot or robbed or mugged in there. But I couldn't live with it and I couldn't live without it, so there was no real way to live at all.

It was inevitable, I guess. But finally, for some dumb reason, or maybe no reason at all, I smoked crack in front of Debbie at home. That was it. She told me to leave, like I knew she would, and I left without any fighting. I guess all the fight had gone out of me and I was just surrendering to a life of darkness and blackouts and death. I packed a bag full of clothes and I left on my reign of self-pity.

Now, once again, I started trying to patch together a series of couches to sleep on, since I no longer had a bed of my own. My sister Jeannie let me sleep on her couch for a few weeks, but I'd be coming home drunk at 7 or 8 in the morning and she hated the whole thing, so she threw me out. After that Tommy Lorenzo would get me one-room fleabag flats that you could rent by the week, but I never stayed longer than a month usually because I hadn't paid the rent. So then I'd move on to some other place to stay, just for a little while, until things went bad again.

Meanwhile, I always wound up hanging out at bowling alleys, either bowling for the action late at night, or just hanging out there because that's where I always felt comfortable, where I felt welcomed. Besides, I was Bob Perry the great bowler, everybody knew me and the bartenders would supply me with enough free booze to survive.

Believe it or not, I actually managed to get myself out to Las Vegas to the High Roller a couple of times during those terrible years I was living on the edge. I think it was 1985 or 1986 or something — it's all kind of foggy. Somehow or other I would hustle up the money to fly out there, I'd sleep on a guy's couch, sweet-talk somebody out of the entry fee, and then I'd step up to the line like nothing was the matter.

People that knew me said later, though, that they could see I was starting to come seriously unglued. I'd be wearing nasty pants and dirty shirts, with dirty, greasy hair. Me, the hotshot with the hot-combed hair and the Mr. Stag's disco threads!

I'd win my first couple of matches, and since the entry fee was $1100 that meant I was at break-even. And then the other guy would throw a lifetime best, or I'd have a rotten string of bad luck and I'd be knocked out. Or at least, that's what I told myself. I didn't tell myself: You're flabby, out of shape, undisciplined, drunk, homeless and it's a miracle you've even won a single match. I mean, I knew I could win if I could get straight, but I just couldn't get straight. Drinking always took me out of it.

So then I would react to defeat by drowning my sorrows in vodka and one long skinny line of coke that would have gone on forever if I could have afforded it. It was a good thing I bought a round-trip ticket, because otherwise I'd have been too broke to get back home. Yeah, "home" – a fleabag rented room, or somebody's couch like a 19-year-old kid, or, before long, 42nd Street.

I couldn't see myself at all: This sad raggedy man in his mid-30s, who was once a sweet-faced kid who dreamed of touching his inner greatness and winning a national championship but was now just a fading has-been.

I had become hopelessly, helplessly addicted to crack, and I would sneak away at every opportunity to make love to that little glass pipe. Finally, I went all the way. Over a period of two days, I smoked something like 500 vials of crack. (A "vial" is a little plastic stoppered bottle about two inches long, containing a couple of rocks of crack, that in those days sold for around $5. Yeah, that's a $2,500 high). I'm not sure I even knew this at the time, but it's obvious to me now that I was trying to kill myself. I wound up in Wayne General Hospital, in Wayne, New Jersey, where I was in a coma for ten to twelve hours. Then I was transferred to St. Claire's Hospital in Boonton, New Jersey, where I went through seven days of detox.

Amazingly enough, my sister Patsy was right there through this whole thing. How did I ever get so blessed with long-suffering women? And how did I ever turn into such a fuck-up? Brother Pious was right: I was on the road to a sad, pathetic ruin.

Once I got out of the hospital, I jumped into Alcoholics Anonymous the same way I did everything else: Way over the top. For 35 days, I went to three meetings a day. I was staying at Patsy's house and on my best behavior. Then somebody asked me to bowl in a big tournament, and I agreed. Then my old friend Tommy Lorenzo was betting money on the match and he gave me a ride to the bowling alley one night. He asked me if I wanted a line of coke and without hesitating one single second I said yes. And before you know it, there I was again: Getting loaded on coke and crack, swimming in a sea of vodka and orange juice, staying out half the night. Not too much later Patsy threw me out. And I was on the street again, sinking back into a permanent blackout so I wouldn't have to face what my life had become.

Mike Stella: *"It was absolutely incredible, probably the most amazing thing I ever seen in bowling. It's about 2:30 in the morning. My son Larry and I are at Lodi Lanes, in Lodi, New Jersey. Bob Perry walks in off the street. He looks like shit. Dirty clothes, dirty hair, just wearing gym shoes or whatever. He looks like he's a little drunk or stoned or something. He doesn't even speak to Larry and me. He goes over and pulls a ball off the rack, just the house ball. (The serious bowlers, of course, will come in with their own shoes and eight or ten or sixteen balls, for all kinds of lane conditions.)*

So Perry goes up to a lane on the bottom floor, and he throws a perfect game: 300. Twelve strikes in a row. Boom. Then he goes upstairs to the lanes on the second level and throws another 300. Boom! And then he goes up to the third tier and throws another perfect 300 game. Boom!

I mean, that's three perfect games in a row – a '900 series.'

Then he yells, 'I'm the greatest fucking bowler in the world!' throws his hands up in the air and walks out.

I think I practically fainted.

I mean, you got any idea how hard it is to throw a 900 series? It's practically impossible. In the whole history of bowling, with 70 million Americans bowling every year, somebody has bowled a 900 series only something like 23 times. And Bobby did it in crummy street shoes, with the house ball, drunk."

Larry Stella (Mike's son): *"Yeah, I saw that too. I couldn't believe my eyes. Bob didn't say anything while he was doing it, either. He just did it. Then he yelled, and he just left. I still can't believe it."*

But here's the kicker of that story: I got no memory of this happening at all. My whole life had become a blackout. Even throwing a 900 series in street shoes.

7 THE RAT AT THE BOTTOM OF THE WELL

I had no fucking idea how I got here.

I had no idea where I even was.

All I could see around me was a depressing sleazeball apartment, with two or three people passed out here and there, one of them a light-skinned black man. On the table there was a rubble of drug paraphernalia, crack pipes, matches, tin foil, empty vials, butane lighters. I looked out the window. This place must have been up on the 35th or 40th floor. It looked like the South Bronx down there – in other words, like hell.

And I was waking up out of a blackout. Again. I looked at my hands. They were covered with black grime and blood. I wiped my nose and the back of my hand came away with a long skid mark of fresh blood – my guts were seeping out through my nose. A flash of fear came over me: Did I have cancer in my nose or sinuses, after all these years of drug abuse?

I staggered over to the telephone and called my friend Tony, at Tri-State Telephone, in Manhattan. For some reason I could still remember his number.

"Where are you?" he says.

"The South Bronx, I think."

"What are you doing there?"

"I don't know, man. I don't know. Can you come get me?"

"Look, Bobby, I'm at work in the city. Why don't you get a cab?"

"I ain't got no money."

"Just jump in a cab and get over the GW Bridge and I'll come pay the fare when you get over here."

I walked out of the apartment and at the elevator there were some really ratty-looking people standing around, but as soon as they looked at me they moved away. They didn't get on with me. I rode the rattletrap elevator down to the "lobby," which looked like a shooting gallery or a bad alley. I walked outside. It was the Bruckner Expressway in the South Bronx, a real bad place to be, even in daylight.

I felt exhausted and sick. I needed something to drink, bad. Oh, my God. I knew I was hemorrhaging in my face – the inside of my nose and sinuses were all gone from doing crack and coke. My septum was totally shot. How long could I keep abusing myself like this and still live? Or had I already died?

I had gotten so worried about this nose thing that once (when I still had money) I went to an ENT doc and he says, "I'm not going to repair this because I can't."

"I'm not in here for that," I says, "I want you to check for cancer in my throat."

But he just says, again, "I can't touch that nose, there's too much damage."

All I knew was that everything was so raw in there, every time I smoked crack all those fumes and chemicals and butane just burned the shit out of the inside of my face. But I just kept smoking it anyway.

It was insanity, and I knew it, and I couldn't stop.

I walked out into the street and tried to catch a cab but once a cabbie got a look at me, in that neighborhood, he'd stomp on the gas and head for glory. I looked like a homicidal maniac fleeing a murder scene. Finally a cab driver who I guess wasn't paying attention pulled over and I climbed in the back. He was like Pakistani or something. He takes one look at my bloody, grimy face in the rearview mirror and he starts to scream.

"Don't hurt me! Don't hurt me!"

"I'm not gonna hurt you, man! I just need a ride to the other side of the George Washington Bridge!"

When we got there, I climbed out.

"How much?" I say.

"No, no, no! I'm going now!" and he goes flying off like a bat out of hell.

A few minutes later Tony pulls up in his big car.

"What the fuck happened to you?" he says.

"I have no idea."

Tony took me back to his office to get cleaned up, gave me 20 or 30 bucks, and dropped me at Tommy Lorenzo's house. But I was pretty sure that when Tommy came home, he wasn't going to be happy to see me. And if Tommy wasn't happy to see me, nobody was going to be happy to see me.

I knew Patsy had had it with me by now, and who could blame her? By now I was a guy living in hell, and everywhere I went I brought hell with me. I wasn't just destroying my own life, I was destroying the lives of everybody around me.

Joe Tolvay (Bob's bowling teammate): *"The things Patsy went through for Bobby! I was good friends with her, there is a special bond between us, Bobby and us being teammates, and her being an attractive woman. I remember that she promised God that if Bobby could get straight, she would dedicate her life to helping other people. And I believed her. But with Bobby, things just seemed to get worse and worse."*

I'd come to whatever crummy room I happened to be staying in at 5 or 6 in the morning, sleep a little, then get up and go hustle and bullshit to get a little cash for a drink or a vial. I didn't want to be in the day. It was all about existing, about making it through the next twelve hours. People? They were just ways of getting booze or dope. Meanwhile, I'd be coughing up blood from my nose, and now all my top teeth seemed to be rotting out. They'd started to get all discolored and loose. My body was falling to pieces.

Every day I'd say, "This is the last day, I'm not going to live like this no more," and then that day I would live like that. Again. By the end of almost every day I'd wind up in New York City, in the certain places where people do drugs, sometimes in abandoned buildings where the junkies shoot speed and heroin. Then when Port Authority closed at 1:30 in the morning and all the people I used to hustle were gone, I'd get a subway token and ride the train to Brooklyn and the Bronx. I'd ride it until 6 in the morning, kind of dozing, trying to forget my life. I hadn't looked at myself in the mirror in months, maybe years, but I knew I looked pretty bad because nobody would sit next to me. I guess they thought they might catch something.

Then I'd get off the train and go help a guy unload a truck for a couple of bucks, or push his hotdog cart ten blocks, always trying to figure out where everybody is, where I could hustle a couple of bucks off somebody to score a bottle of vodka or a couple of them sweet little rocks that were stealing my life away. Because realistically, I wanted what booze and dope did to me more than I wanted life. And it didn't matter how guilty I felt about it. I just kept doing it.

It was absolute hell, living like that.

It was hard to imagine that things could get worse.

But they were about to.

Because, even though it might have been shabby and depressing, at least I had a roof over my head. For awhile I was living in a room at the YMCA for $55 a week, but I had to leave because I never made rent. (What I mean is, I made rent but didn't spend it on rent.) Then I was sleeping on a series of couches – I was "couch surfing" before they called it that. Finally I wound up sleeping under my friend Dennis's laundry room. But, hell, it was a room. I was too wasted to notice it was a wet, nasty basement.

For awhile I had a job delivering beer (of all things) for the Pen Bottle

Company. I'd return the truck on Thursday night, get my $600 pay, go into Manhattan and wake up out of a blackout somewhere a few days later, dead broke. What kind of a life is that?

Dan McDonough (owner and publisher of The Sports Reporter newspaper, started by his father): *"Nobody was better than Bobby Perry. He was the best. Many times my dad said that if Bobby didn't go the way he did, if he would have stayed sober, he could have been the best ever. We all saw him going down, though. It was sad."*

The jump from that kind of life to being completely homeless is not much of a jump at all. I'd been getting closer and closer to the edge for years. In fact, in a way "homelessness" is a state of mind, and I'd been homeless for a long time before I was actually living on the street. I had no ability at all to create a warm nest that would be safe for a woman or a child, like a man is supposed to. All I knew how to create were nightmarish holes where I could hide away with my crack pipe and my bottle for a few hours, until I got kicked out. Again.

I started trying harder and harder to convince Jeannie or Patsy to let me stay at their house for awhile, that I'd be good this time, I wouldn't drink or smoke crack no more, that I was making all this money from action bowling and I could even pay them something. We had angry fights, almost to the point of somebody getting killed. But basically what it all came down to was, I was wrong, I was lying, I had no intention of quitting but I was telling them I would. As they say in the rooms, "Denial is not a river in Egypt," but I was denying, denying, denying.

Then, one day – I don't know which day it was, they were all the same – I had finally worn out my welcome with every single person in my life, even my beloved saintly sister Patsy, even Tommy Lorenzo and Tony and all my teammates and friends in the bowling world. Everybody. Nobody wanted to see my ugly face no more. Nobody trusted me. Nobody wanted to hear my line of bullshit no more, about how I had a big tournament coming up and I was gonna win so much money it should probably be illegal and I was gonna pay everybody back and all that. They'd heard it all before and they just didn't want to see me or hear from me anymore.

So I took the train back to New York City, where I knew my way around, where I knew how to hustle, where I could get crack and coke and booze and where I thought I could survive. I knew the places where people sold drugs, like the Queens-Midtown Tunnel on 34th Street.

I had my favorite bars: One on 44th Street, another all-night place on 42nd Street and Ninth Avenue, a couple of bars on Tenth Avenue, and some really dingy places by Port Authority. Midtown Manhattan has been really cleaned up since them days, but then that whole area was filled with sleazy strip clubs and bars and peep shows and other stuff any decent person wouldn't want to know about. That's where I lived.

Sometimes I'd stop at an all-night liquor store and get a bottle of vodka for a couple of bucks, get a paper cup with ice and orange juice and pour in the booze. It would be like a little campfire that would keep me warm on the street corner all night. Then all I had to do was find some dark place to curl up and sleep, hoping the animals wouldn't kill me, and get free of my life for a few hours.

Where did I get the couple of bucks for the bottle? Well, I never panhandled – I lived off the kindness and loneliness of strangers. I'd sit down at a favorite bar somewhere, get to talking to some lonely businessman from Cincinnati and figure how to get the next drink. The guy would tell me his sorrows, I'd drink and listen all night long. He would introduce me to some other guy – "Hey, meet my friend Bobby" – and we'd all tell our sad stories and drink while somebody else paid. That was my specialty: Getting other people to pick up the bar bill. Sometimes the guy would have some coke and we'd take turns doing lines in the bathroom, or he'd ask me to go score for him and I'd come back with some blow. It was all about existing. It was all about making it through the night. A lot of times, we'd sit there and drink and talk until the joint closed.

I'd be the guy's best friend for a couple of hours, until he got tired or had to leave, and then I would walk out of the bar and suddenly I would have to face my life. There would be nowhere to go. I'd hit this big wall of emptiness, like a faceful of icy air. If it was wintertime, I'd linger in the bar as long as possible, then the place would close and I'd have to step out there onto the street freezing to death. I never carried nothing, not like these homeless people you see nowadays with their shopping carts and whatnot. No bag, no backpack, no nothing. Most of the time I wore a ratty old winter coat my mom had gave me, with lots of pockets. And it's amazing how many people forget their gloves in a bar.

Maybe I didn't carry all that other shit because I wasn't really homeless. I was Bob Perry, the great bowler, just a little short tonight. Little did I know that "being a little short tonight" with no place to go would last for seven years, from 1986 to 1992. The truth is that during those years I was a homeless crack addict on the streets of Manhattan, and whatever great thing I might have done in the past, or hoped to do in the future, did not matter at all.

Winter turned to spring turned to summer turned to autumn, the years rolled on and I just got sicker, more pathetic, more desperate, my body more filled with death and disease. I started to look like a vampire, with discolored skin and scabs all over. I never washed. And, one by one all my top teeth got infected and pus-filled and loose, and I just yanked them all out. When I closed my lips, my mouth must have sunken in like a rotten pie, but I never looked in the mirror to see it.

I was just one cold winter night away from being an unidentified corpse in the morgue.

Without money, New York City is a very cold place, especially in the winter. If you go into a restaurant to use the toilet, they'll kick you out unless you buy something. So I figured out two places I could sleep (without ever admitting to myself that I was homeless). One was a kind of coal cellar under the sidewalk on 42nd Street – really, just a hole in the ground, where I'd curl up in the dirt like a rat. The other was inside one of them cubicles at a peep-show house, also on 42nd Street.

These peep-show houses were open all day and all night, and most of them were run by Indian guys, but the one I went to was run by two white guys named Freddie and Frankie. At 2 a.m. these places would be filled with businessmen, sick demented fucks watching porno, absolutely crazy sick human beings. I'd pay Freddie and Frankie a couple of bucks and they'd let me into this tiny room, almost a cabinet, where people watched porno, and I'd sit in a chair and put my feet up and try to sleep for a few hours. I was the richest homeless guy Freddie and Frankie knew, showing up almost every night at two or three in the morning. They'd let me in, and then a few hours later they'd kick me out, back onto the street, lots of times before it was even light yet. That was my home address: I was paying rent for a couple of hours a night at a peep-show house.

At the very beginning, before they knew me very well, Freddie and Frankie sent their bouncer after me when I walked in with a crack pipe loaded with a couple of vials of rock. That dude busted my face and I had to go the ER and get stitches. But I left the hospital AMA (against medical advice), and went back to the same place. I think the bouncer felt bad after he beat the shit out of me. After that we were friends, and he'd let me in. Him and Freddie and Frankie started calling me "Poppy" because I looked like I was a hundred years old, even though I wasn't even 40 yet. So that's what passed for my "home" and my "family".

All the peep-show houses had bouncers, and they had guys that washed the floors all night long. Otherwise they'd get too sticky, I guess. Not many people robbed them though, so even though it wasn't too comfortable or sanitary, it was fairly safe.

The worst time on the streets of New York is about four in the morning, a couple of hours before daylight, when most businesses are closed and the animals are on the prowl. And I mean animals. It's hard and heartless and dangerous out there. You've got to watch yourself, otherwise you could wind up knifed in an alley for no reason, or OD'd on some bad dope you just bought. And I knew from St. Christopher's that you can die from withdrawal, and I worried about that, too. That's why I tried to stay hydrated at all times. (That's a joke, kind of.)

Sometimes I would take the train out to New Jersey and go to Lodi Lanes, in Lodi, where everybody knew me and I could get all the booze I needed to survive. I'd go there and for awhile I'd hardly feel homeless at all. There was a sweet lady who worked the front desk and the snack bar and she'd sneak me food. Sometimes I'd help clean the lanes, and she'd even let me sleep there, laying down on a hard bench with no pillow back in the corner. Well, at least it was warm and safe.

By now, though, I was starting to look permanently filthy, and it was hard to hide that I was living on the street.

I'd wear some old pants for months at a time. When it got cold I'd spend twenty bucks on a thermal shirt, socks and sweatshirt and wear them all winter. I'm sure I smelled like a sewer. Inside, I knew my life was wasting away. I wanted to die every day. I was dying constantly, throwing up all the time, sticking my finger down my throat to get the pus out. It was terrible.

Why didn't I try harder to get sober? Why didn't I beg and plead to be let into some rehab somewhere, to try to put my life back together? Why didn't I go back up to St. Christopher's and fall on my hands and knees in front of Brother Pious? Why, why, why?

There is no "why." Addiction has no "why." My life was insanity, I was living a life of endless death, but I couldn't stop and I guess I didn't want to. So I'd shuffle over to the dingy bar around the corner from Port Authority – "Poppy," wearing my nasty winter jacket even in summer – and go inside, looking to find a lonely guy to get me loaded for one more night.

I'd sometimes go to that disgusting men's room at Port Authority to clean up a little, but only my hands, because they were usually almost black with grime. I never washed my whole body, in years, because if you took off your clothes the animals would steal them. Like, what are they going to do with a homeless guy's nasty old winter jacket? Put it in a homeless museum?

I have to say, I was not totally without friends in those terrible years. There was a guy named Rob Collins, and his sister, that I'd known since I was a kid. They were a nice middle class family living in New Jersey and they knew I was having some really hard times. I had helped both of them with their bowling when they were younger. Their father, who was disabled, was a very nice man who loved to play cards. He used to go play cards in Lodi, which is where all them ethnic groups hung out. He knew all the wiseguys and bookmakers but he was a sweet, kind man.

Anyway, Rob Collins and his sister and father were always nice to me, and they'd invite me to their house for Thanksgiving. Can you imagine? I don't know how they stood the smell. But they acted like I was just another friend from the old days, somebody who had helped them when he was able to help. And I can't tell you how much I appreciated that.

BOB PERRY WITH STEFAN BECHTEL

Even so, it was totally obvious to me and probably everyone else that I was on the fast train to oblivion. There was no way I could live like this for very long.

With all my top teeth rotted out, I could only eat soft food, like hot dogs and pizza and scrambled eggs. There were all kinds of sores up inside my mouth and sinuses, and on my face. My bones ached. There was poison through my whole body. I still cough up blood to this day, more than twenty years later.

So one winter day in Manhattan, around 42nd Street, I ran into this guy named Homeless Louie. I'd seen him around, picking through garbage cans and whatnot. He looked like hell, like me.

"Why don't you come downstairs and see my room?" he says.

"Okay," I says, kind of curious to see what he's talking about. So he leads me into Port Authority, down some stairs, and down some more stairs, and finally he jumps over the rail and lands in the gravel beside the tracks. I follow him into this dark greasy chamber with big pipes overhead and then he leads me into this smaller chamber, almost pitch black, where he's got pieces of cardboard spread on the floor.

"See? It's my room," Homeless Louie says. "It's pretty warm, pretty safe, and it's free."

He lights a little candle stub and holds it up. Now I can see a couple of little cardboard Chinese food boxes. They're swarming with cockroaches.

"Hungry?"

"I don't think so."

"Want to see my pet?"

"Okay."

And Homeless Louie lifts the candle a little bit higher and points over into the corner. And over there in the dimness, scrambling around like a dirty dog, is an enormous sewer rat. The thing must have weighed twenty-five or thirty pounds, like a little pig fattened up by human garbage. It was one of the most disgusting things I had ever seen.

"Lemme outta here!" I yelled.

And I bolted out of the place as fast as I could run. My life had been coming unraveled for a long, long time, but somehow this was the absolute bottom. I couldn't go no lower. I had no more will to live any more days of death. I was going to end it, now.

I ran up onto the upper deck, up the big stairway and out onto the street. It was freezing cold, and snowing a little. There was a garbage truck trundling down the street, and I ran in front of it, hoping the death would be quick.

But the driver veered sharply away from me and collided with a power pole. He threw open the door and I heard him screaming after me.

"You dumb fuck! Whassamatter with you!?"

I went stumbling off down the street.
Bob Perry, the great.
I couldn't even succeed in killing myself.

8 THE ADDICT AND THE ANGEL

I don't know how many days or weeks it was after I tried to throw myself in front of that garbage truck outside Port Authority in Manhattan that I came out of a blackout and found myself sitting in some sort of a bowling center with a friend of mine, Jackson Gist. Jackson was this huge black guy, maybe six-three. I'd met him at the bowling alley when he was bowling around 144 average, and by the time I was done helping him, he was an over 200 bowler, and he won a lot of money. I really helped him, and he kind of owed me.

But now it was, like, eight or nine in the morning, a gray winter morning, a Sunday morning, and the bowling alley was closed and empty. (Much later, I figured out that it was March, 1992.)

And Jackson was in my face, yelling at me.

"Look at you!" he's yelling. "Look at you! You coulda been the greatest bowler in the world and you're just a bum! You're just a drunk and a dope addict! You smell like a dumpster, man. You make me sick! You're pissing your talent away, and there's nothing worse than wasted talent. What's the matter with you? What's the matter with you, man?"

Look: I was just coming out of a blackout, and I had no idea where I even was. In them days, I never "fell asleep," like normal people do. I passed out. If you fell asleep on the streets of New York, that's when you'd get robbed or beat up or killed. And I never "woke up," either. I just came out of a blackout. This was normal to me.

"Shut up," I told Jackson. "Go behind the bar and get me a fuckin' drink."

Jackson, apparently, had a job cleaning the lanes on the night shift; this place, it turned out, was Eclipse Lanes, a bowling center in Hasbrook Heights, New Jersey, about six miles outside the city. As my head started to clear and I looked around, I recognized the place. I'd bowled here lots of times before, probably made a lot of money here, too. Probably threw some 300 games, maybe even won some championships here. Whatever.

I was also familiar with Eclipse Lanes because that's where I used to go to meet Tommy Lorenzo, when he needed drugs or I needed some money. Tommy was in the family business and had an office about ten minutes from Eclipse Lanes and whenever I called him he'd be there right away. Tommy was the king of enablers, and when we got together we'd just feed each other's addictions – he'd give me money to pay for a few nights in a hotel or a bottle of vodka, and I'd go cop dope for him. Then we'd get wasted together. This is what we thought of as a good time.

Eclipse Lanes was also a good place for us to meet because it was right by one of them greasy burger joints. All they served was soft stuff, stuff a toothless guy could eat. I was like an eighty-year-old man, even though I was only 39. The joint was cheap, too: You could get four of them tiny little hamburgers, fries and a Coke for, like, three bucks. I used to call them "murderburgers," because they'd give you diarrhea for days. But that was the sort of stuff I lived on, whenever it occurred to me to eat something at all. You could say that the way I fed my body was the same way I was feeding my soul: Just cramming some cheap nasty shit in there, without really thinking about it.

Right now, though, I just needed some vodka, that sweet poison that was killing me. I needed to go back to sleep and black it all out again. Jackson went around behind the counter of the closed bar and fished me out a bottle of vodka.

"You gimme that bottle or I'm gonna take it from you," I told him, real threatening. And I would have, too, except Jackson just handed it over to me. I guess he saw that look in my eye and he gave up.

"Listen, Bobby," Jackson says, "you gotta get outta here because if Joe comes in, I'll get fired."

Joe was the owner, and he was a real nasty guy who hated me. Even though I'd once had a part-time job at the bowling alley, Joe had already said to Jackson more than once, "If I come in here and find that kid here, you're fired." Sometimes, if Joe showed up when I was there, I'd go hide in the ladies' room. Look: I was a drunk and a drug addict and he was afraid I'd rob his place, which was a reasonable fear. But I never robbed nothing from there. I was always just going there to meet Jackson or Tommy Lorenzo.

Now Jackson was telling me to get lost or he'd get fired. So, once again, I was getting pushed out onto the street because I was an unsavory character, unwanted, useless, dirty, unsafe.

Before I left the bowling alley I fished around in my grubby pocket and pulled out one whole quarter. God knows how it got there. Then I pulled out something else: A folded-up piece of paper with the name of a guy named Billy. That guy who told me to call him if I needed to. The guy in that program.

The pay phone was fifty cents, so I borrowed another quarter from Jackson and called Bill. Here I was, this big champion bowler, and I was so broke I had to borrow a quarter to make a phone call. Unlike anybody else in my own family, Billy picked up.

"Where are you?" Billy says.

"Eclipse Lanes, in Hasbrook Heights. Look, I need help."

"Don't go anywhere, I'll be right down."

So Billy comes right down, nine o'clock Sunday morning, to pick me up. He walks into the building and looks me over, standing there like something the cat dragged in. He could see that I looked and smelled so bad I needed to get cleaned up, at least a little, before anyone could even tolerate me.

"Get in the car," he says.

"Where are we going?"

"I'm taking you to your sister's house."

"I can't go there."

"I'm taking you to Patsy's house. Where does she live?"

Billy knew her from bowling, but not well enough to know where she lived.

"I can't go there. If my brother-in-law sees me, he'll kill me."

"Bobby, you've got to take a bath and change your clothes, man. Where does your sister live?"

"She lives in a different house now, on Mountain Avenue in Pompton Plains."

So Billy starts driving me to Mountain Avenue in Pompton Plains. I'm terrified. Patsy's husband, James, was not real crazy about the fact that the last time he and Patsy let me stay there I found $360 underneath some clothes in a dresser drawer and I stole it. This was their special stash of rainy day money or something. . James was not a real forgiving type guy. As far as he was concerned, I deserved the death penalty. I'm serious: If he found me in his house, he would literally have killed me. Not just for the $360 I robbed from him, but because he loved my sister and he could see that I had practically killed her over the years. I hadn't been invited to their wedding or nothing.

So we show up at Patsy's house. James was a guy who grew up in Brooklyn and Staten Island, who had a real good job running the lingerie department at Lady Esther in Manhattan. He and my sister had a big house in a nice neighborhood, with a big lawn. Coming over here from my roach-infested world on 42nd Street and the bathrooms at Port Authority was like taking a trip to the moon.

Patsy opens the door just a little bit until she gets a load of me.

"What are you doing here?" she says, real cold and angry.

"I'm with Billy here. He's from AA," I say.

"I don't care who you're with – get the fuck away from my house. James is going to be home in twenty minutes and if he finds you here he'll kill you. And you fucking deserve it."

She turns to Billy, who she didn't seem to recognize.

"Get this pig away from my house. I don't care where you go, but you better take him with you. I don't want him in my house or anywhere near it."

Then she says to me again, very hostile, "You're lucky James ain't here, he'd kill you."

I didn't back away, though. I kept trying to break through to my sister, who used to love me. But she kept getting angrier and angrier. Finally she threatened to call the cops unless I went away.

Then Billy broke in.

"Please, Patsy – he's not going to be here that long. He just needs to get washed up a little and get some clean clothes and I'm going to take him to an AA meeting."

I don't know why. She had no reason to do it. But finally Patsy gave up and let me in the house. She and I, we had a bond that went way, way back. Beneath all the cursing she was someone who had known me all my life, and really all she wanted was what was best for me. In her heart she was a saint. I had abused her, manipulated her, robbed her, taken advantage of her in so many different ways she'd reached the end of her rope. I couldn't blame her if she hated me. But now she decided to take a big chance for me – one of the many times in her life that she took a big chance for me.

"Look, you can come in and take a shower," she said finally, in a softer voice. "I'll get you some clothes. But you better make it quick before James comes home. If he shows up here, you're dead."

Yeah, I get it: If James comes home, I'm dead.

I came creeping into the house like a sewer rat, trying not to touch anything for fear of polluting it. She laid out some socks, a pair of pants, some dungarees that didn't fit and a sweatshirt. I don't know, maybe they were James's clothes, maybe my old clothes. I left my dirty old clothes behind. And, I dunno, I didn't take a shower – it had been so long, I might not have known how to do it. Maybe I would just melt in there. I also just wanted to get out of there. I didn't belong there in that clean, tidy suburban house owned by one person who hated me and another person who loved me and hated me. I washed my face, though, trying not to look in the mirror. When I came out of the bathroom there was a twenty-dollar bill laid on the kitchen table, and Patsy was gone. I think she left that money because she didn't want me to rob her. She'd done what she could do for me. Now she had to get away from me.

I came out of Patsy's house and Billy was standing in the driveway.

"What are you still doing here?" I says.

"I'm waiting for you."

I got in the car.

"We're going to a meeting," Billy says.

"Well, okay, but don't take me to one of them meetings where there's a lot of people," I says.

"Okay."

"Don't take me to one of them men's meetings."

"Okay."

"Don't take me to one of them step meetings."

"Okay."

"Don't take me to one of them speaker meetings."

"Okay."

See, I'd had some experience with this AA thing and I was pretty sure I knew all about it, from after I did those 500 vials of crack and almost killed myself back in 1981. I'd gone to detox for seven days at St. Christopher's Inn, before Brother Pious handed me a bus ticket back to Manhattan. For a little while I even had a sponsor then, a wonderful man, and he just kept trying to convince me to come back to meetings and say I'd been out on maneuvers, and get started again. Try to get sober again. "Progress not perfection" and all that. But I refused to do it.

"I'm not doing it," I told him. "I'm not standing up there and telling people I went out and got drunk. That I fucked up. I ain't doin' it."

Stubborn sonofabitch.

So I didn't do it. And what happened was, I went back out again, drinking and doing dope and all the rest of it. My life spiraled out of control, down into one great big blackout again.

But now Billy tells me he's taking me to a small meeting in Montclair, New Jersey. We walk into this huge church, I guess it was also a school, and there were two meetings, Al-Anon on one side and AA on the other side. There was some kind of celebration going on, maybe 250 people there, so Billy and I go to the back of the room and sit down way in the back.

A guy sitting next to me says, "Are you Bob?"

"Yeah, I'm Bob," I says. It was weird: I'd never laid eyes on the guy before. He hands me this card that says "Just For Today." The card was this whole list of spiritual tips, stuff like:

Just for today I will try to live through this day only and not tackle all my problems at once. I can do something for twelve hours that would appall me if I had to keep it up for a lifetime.

I leaned over and whispered to Billy, "Hey, look. This guy just gave me this card."

"Shut up," Billy says. Then he looks over at the chair next to me. "What guy?"

I look over to where the guy was sitting and he's gone. I mean, he wasn't even in sight. He was just gone.

Then the guy who's running the meeting says, "Do we have anybody here for their first AA meeting, or anybody who's coming back?"

"Stand up," Billy whispers to me.

"No," I say.

"Stand up."

"No."

"Stand up," he says, and he grabs me with one hand and just drags me to my feet. So there I am, standing in the back of this huge room like Ratzo Rizzo in that movie Midnight Cowboy. If you'd have saw the way I looked you would have been shocked, with my greasy hair, my infected teeth, bleeding from my nose constantly, the whole miserable package.

"My name's Bob and I'm coming back," I say.

I found out later that usually, when people say things like that in meetings, there's a big round of applause. But not too many people clapped for me.

I sat down and listened to the main speaker, a wonderful guy from Clark, New Jersey, named Frankie D. It seemed like everything he was describing had happened to me. I could relate to everything that he was saying. He'd been homeless, he'd been a bum and a dope addict, he'd had blackouts and all the rest. Drinking and drugging ruled his life, and he wound up on Skid Row. But now the guy had I think it was five or six years sober, which to me seemed like eternity, impossible. One thing that really stuck with me was that he said he read pages 86 to 88 of the Big Book (sort of the Bible of AA) every day. It was about beginning each day with a grateful heart, without selfishness or self-pity, and trying each day to ask God to help you. Boy, did I ever need that.

After the meeting, Billy told me to go get a copy of the Big Book and that he'd pay for it. I picked up a paperback copy, because it was cheaper, and stuck it in my back pocket.

After Frankie D.'s talk there was this big party with cake and whatnot and people milling around. I had sores everywhere and a bloody nose and I could tell that people were moving away from me. It wasn't like anybody was making some big effort to get to know me. But this guy Freddie D.: I wanted to ask him more about pages 86 to 88 in the Big Book. Also, you know, this seemed like a guy who could understand me and my story. Maybe even a future friend. So I go up to him.

"So what's so important on page 86 of the Big Book?" I ask him. "And could you give me your phone number?"

Look: I'm from New York. Some might say I'm a little pushy,

but I figured, you just go up to the guy and ask for what you want.

"Aren't you that guy that stood up in the back?" he says.

"Yeah, that's me."

"Well, that book's not going to help you," Freddie D. says, looking me up and down. "AA will not help you – you need to find another way. You're too far gone, man. You need to go somewhere where they can help you, like a psych ward or a detox or something."

I was absolutely shocked. Here this guy was, who'd supposedly led a life like I had, who'd been homeless, who'd been cast out, and I thought he was going to help me, but he only belittled me. I felt so degraded by what he said to me. I felt like I'd been assassinated. In fact, I carried around that hurt for years afterwards, maybe because I was afraid he was right: I really was too far gone, beyond hope. And I thought this guy was going to give me a miracle!

"Billy, take me out of here," I says to Bill. "I want to go back to New York."

I walked out of that stinkin' place, and away from that guy who could cram that Big Book as far up his ass as it would go.

"Look, Bobby, don't take that too hard," Billy says, following me out of the building, kind of begging. "You shouldn't go back into the city. You shouldn't do that."

"Just take me to the fucking bus stop."

"Bobby, please, let's try another meeting."

"Take me to the bus stop in Union City, that's the cheapest ticket to Manhattan – a buck-fifty."

"Bobby, you need to get better," Billy says to me, practically begging me on his knees. "If you don't, you're going to kill yourself, kill someone else, or end up in an insane asylum!"

"Yeah, well I'd rather do that than go to the rooms of Alcoholics Anonymous. Leave me the fuck alone!"

***

I got on the buck-and-a-half bus to Manhattan, headed for my old homeless haunts, the floor of the peep show on 42nd Street, the cellar on Eight Avenue, and all those other places I swore I'd never go back to. But I had my self-respect: I swore I'd never go back to Homeless Louie's rat and roach-infested "room" in the subway, and I didn't. But now the insanity of my situation was really taking hold. It seemed like one day would go by but it was probably a week; I had no way of knowing. Now I was dragging around the Big Book and reading it to myself and to other people, like some demented street preacher. I always wore this old jacket my mom had gave me for winter, which was by now ratty and nasty as the bottom of a dumpster, with my paperback copy of the Big Book stuck in my back pocket.

Here I was, this hopeless alcoholic and dope addict, reading the Big Book while I was doing crack. Here I was in a bar, reading the Big Book to some lonely, drunk commuter while both of us were getting wasted. The other drunk would be paying the bar bill, of course. Here I was in the peep show, trying to read the Big Book to some perv who had come in there to get off.

And that book was driving me absolutely insane. Because I knew it was the truth. It described my life completely, and I knew I had no other idea what to do. I'd reached the end of the road. I couldn't eat. I couldn't swallow. I couldn't breathe. I couldn't sleep. I couldn't wake up. I couldn't live. I know the book said suicide was not the answer, but I was constantly thinking of ways to kill myself. Yet here I was, sitting on the steps of the YMCA or on a park bench on 18th Street, by the projects, talking to other drunks and junkies and reading to them out of the Big Book. We'd talk together, we'd be philosophizing and reflecting, while our whole lives went up in flames all around us. Like, who gives a shit what a bunch of bums and crackheads have to say about the meaning of life?

So one day I called my sister Patsy again, collect, as always.

"Please, please don't hang up the phone," I says to her. "I need your help."

"I don't care, Bobby, goodbye," she says.

"Please, Patsy, please."

"Try praying to mommy and daddy," she says. (Both of my parents were dead by then). "Maybe they'll give you the answer. Don't call this number again."

Click.

Almost everybody in my life had tried to help me, even Tommy Lorenzo, in his twisted enabling way. But I had used and abused everyone, sucked them dry of everything I could get out of them. Other people were just ways of satisfying my own desires. They weren't really people at all. They were just scenery. Now they had all turned their back on me, even my own beloved sister, and I was alone. Uncle Raymond, of course, had been a fixture in my life for years, sort of a big brother and Godfather, but I'd broken his heart and he wanted nothing to do with me. Last time I saw him I'd robbed some money off him and promised I'd pay it back, but I never did. Uncle Raymond was out of my life now but it didn't matter. John Gotti and the mobsters, my "friends" – they were all long gone, too. (I learned much later that Uncle Raymond and my sister, at least, were praying that I was not suffering or dead even though I had no contact with them at all.)

So I prayed to my mother, a woman who had once loved me and who had sort of slowly seeped out of her body with Lou Gehrig's disease; and to my father, a humble Polish man who had worked various humble jobs his whole life and who had also once loved me, before I broke his heart. I prayed to them from the bottom of my heart because I did not know what else to do.

I was a dead man who could not die – a dead man who could not live.

And what came up in my prayers was the name of Graymoor and St. Christopher's Inn – that place I'd gone eleven years earlier and where I had acted like such a flaming asshole the monks had kicked me out after ten days.

The Graymoor Spiritual Life Center, in Garrison, New York, not too far upstate from the city, was a kind of religious retreat run by the Franciscan Friars of the Atonement – a bunch of priests who dressed like John the Baptist, with the brown robes and sandals and all. Graymoor was sometimes called "the holy mountain," because part of the 400-acre property ran up a wooded mountainside. I think they also called it that because supposedly miracles happened up there.

There was also a homeless shelter and 28-day rehab program called St. Christopher's Inn on the property. Apparently the Franciscans had been doing this work since around the turn of the century, offering to pick up drunks and dope addicts off the streets of New York City, cart them up to St. Christopher's for "a cot and three hots" for 28 days. They'd give you a bus ticket to come up there, give you clean socks and sneakers, underwear, sweatshirts, all donated by wealthy people, and your own little locker. You'd get a break from the streets, and food and shelter, for three weeks.

In the early days, of course, before AA (which got started in the late 1930s) that was about all they could offer; but now it was a twelve step-based rehab place. All kinds of famous people had gone there to sober up over the years. The owner of the New York Giants and other prominent people would donate all kinds of money to Graymoor every year.

The legend, supposedly, was that once a long time ago a little wobbly old man stopped at St. Francis Convent (which was there before St. Christopher's) and asked for a meal. The custom was that, in exchange for a meal, all the bums and homeless people who stopped there were asked to fill two buckets with water from a spring down the mountain. But the sisters decided this old man was too weak to fill the buckets, so they decided not to ask him to do it. When he finished eating and left, the sisters discovered that both buckets were full to the brim. So maybe it was a miracle or something. Anyway, after that, the sisters and the brothers started calling all the homeless people who came there "St. Christopher" (Christ), since it says in the Bible "Be not forgetful to entertain strangers: for thereby some have entertained angels unawares." That's how come it was named St. Christopher's Inn.

Well, I kind of knew this story because of my stay up there eleven years earlier. But at that time, I wasn't really paying much attention to all this spiritual shit. I was just trying to convince Debbie that I was dealing with my problems so she wouldn't leave me. But, you know, from Day One at St. Christopher's I had this bug up my ass about how my uncle was this bigshot in the Franciscan world. My sister's brother, Father Joseph Benjamin McVey, had actually gave a speech in front of the Pope one time. And he lived at Graymoor for the last part of his life and was buried there, in the friar's cemetery. So I thought this made me better than all those bums and losers and crackwhores in the homeless shelter. I was totally different than them, better than them – I was a world-champion bowler and all this other good stuff. In other words, I had a real attitude, and a real mouth on me too. I didn't go to any of them AA meetings they had up there. I thought they were stupid. Besides, I could see that all the things these people were asking me do in order to keep Debbie were really hard. They were asking me to actually change my life. And I just didn't want to go there. Fuck that.

So finally Brother Pious hands me a one-way ticket back to Manhattan and I'm happy to take it. Fuck them. What the fuck did they know?

But now, the second time I went to St. Christopher's, eleven years later, it was a whole different story. The first time, I may have been an arrogant know-it-all, but at least I had a home to go back to. I had a woman who loved me, or was trying to love me despite my behavior. I was still bowling in tournaments, winning lots of money. I still had Uncle Raymond and other people in my life. Both my parents were still alive.

But now I was a pathetic, beaten-down, homeless, filthy alcoholic and drug addict who had alienated every single person who had ever loved me or tried to help me. Now I was completely and utterly alone. All my top teeth were gone. I stank. I almost never bowled anymore – where am I going to bowl? 42nd Street? In fact, I had been beaten down to my knees. I was desperate. I had nowhere else to turn. Only later did I learn that being driven to your knees is a blessing – the beginning of recovery.

So I called Graymoor and asked for Brother Pious, who I had gotten to know pretty good the last time I was up there. He came on the phone.

"This is Father Benjy's nephew – Bobby Purzycki," I says.

"I know who you are," Brother Pious says. He was obviously not real happy to hear from me. "What do you want?"

"I need help, Brother.

"I can't help you."

"I've been living on the street for six and a half years."

"I can't help you – we don't want you here," Brother Pious says. "You're not allowed here. Don't you remember? We tried to help you years ago, and you wouldn't listen."

"Father, I'm ready to listen now. I'm desperate. I'm dying out here. I want to get better. I need your help."

There was a long pause on the other end of the line. I didn't know if Brother Pious was about to hang up, or falling asleep, or what.

"When was the last day you drank?" he says.

"When was the last day I was allowed?"

"Thursday."

"Okay, it was Wednesday."

I'm not stupid. I'd been there before, and I knew the ropes.

"When was the last time you did drugs?"

"When was the last time I was allowed?"

"Tuesday."

"Uh, I think it was Monday."

"Well, I'm sorry. I don't have any beds available."

"Please! I don't think I'll make it!"

"I can't help it if I don't have any beds."

"Please!"

Another long pause.

"Okay, be here Monday morning at 8 a.m. and don't be late, because if you're late I'll give your bed away. And don't show up drunk."

"What do I do until Monday?"

"If you've been on the streets for seven years, two more days won't hurt you."

Those Franciscans were real religious and all, but they could also be very hard-assed. Well, they had to be. They had probably listened to more junkie lies and bullshit than you could imagine. And Brother Pious was absolutely right to be skeptical of me: Eleven years earlier, when I was up there, I wasn't exactly "applying the principles of AA in all my affairs," as the Big Book says. In fact, I had basically told AA to kiss my fucking ass.

So what do I do when, for practically the first time in my adult life, a little ray of sunshine appears – some faint hope of survival and recovery and healing? When John the Baptist himself actually opens the door to me, even though I don't deserve it?

Well, I immediately call Tommy Lorenzo, my best friend, partner in crime, and chief enabler. The guy who always came through for me, helping me out with money, food, a hotel room, dope, booze, whatever. I was totally insane. I didn't want to live no more. I was dying as I was standing there. I figured within two or three days I'd be dead and that would solve everybody's problem. And as I look back on it now, I don't know why I didn't die that weekend.

I don't know what was going on with Tommy Lorenzo in the middle of all this – he was a guy who kept feeding my addictions, and his own, for years. He could see that I was killing myself, but his way of helping me was giving me money to buy more booze and dope. It was nuts. I know now that Tommy had his own inner demons. It turns out he was gay but tried to hide it from everybody. Anyway, this friendship with Tommy Lorenzo was an incestuous relationship that kept us both permanently sick and addicted, even though, at the time, I think we thought we were having a good time.

Believe it or not, my behavior had gotten so whacked out in them days that finally even Tommy Lorenzo wouldn't answer my phone calls no more. But at least he picked up the phone when I called him that day to tell him I was going into treatment at St. Christopher's on Monday. I told him I needed a place to stay for a couple of nights, and I needed some money for, you know, entertainment. So Tommy came over to where I was and we immediately went out to the liquor store and bought a couple of them liter bottles of vodka, the big ones with the handles, then we went out and scored a bunch of coke. Tommy rented a room at the King's Inn on Route 47 in Wayne, New Jersey – a semi-dive kind of place where people pick up broads and rent a room for a couple of hours. Then he and I got started knocking back all that booze and dope, and when he left I just holed up in that ratty hotel room and drank and did drugs all weekend, trying to die before Monday came.

Before he left, Tommy Lorenzo told me he couldn't drive me up to Graymoor by 8 a.m. Monday morning. So I called my sisters, Jeannie and Patsy, but neither one of them would pick up the phone. Not that I blamed them. So I called Billy. And Billy came through, like he always seemed to. He showed up at 6 a.m. but he seemed kind of alarmed at my appearance. I was stone drunk, and totally filthy, even though there was a bathtub in the room.

"Listen," Billy said to me, real earnest, "for the first time in your life you got to do what's good for you. Forget about what everybody else says. It doesn't mean a thing. You got to do what's good for you, Bobby."

Billy drove me up to Garrison, New York, where Graymoor was. I felt terrible. My life was a complete pile of shit and I couldn't even succeed in dying. Once we stopped for gas and I went into the convenience store for doughnuts or whatever, and I noticed they had these little pint bottles of vodka for four bucks, so I bought one and drank it all within a mile.

Billy dropped me at St. Christopher's and I walked in there.

There was Brother Gregory. He wasn't stupid.

"You're drunk," he says.

"Hell yeah I'm drunk," I says.

"Do you want help?"

"Hell yeah I want help. I can't take this no more."

"The last time you came here needing help we extended our love to you and you rejected it. When was the last time you took a bath?"

"Maybe two years ago."

"When was the last time you changed your clothes?"

"About a month ago."

I looked down at my hands and I could see that they were black with grime. I was afraid to look in the mirror for fear of what the rest of me might look like.

"If we allow you to come into this program we're going to watch you very closely this time," Brother Pious said. "And if you get out of line, we'll hand you a one-way bus ticket back to the city – for the last time. No more chances."

"Okay."

"Okay," Brother Pious said. "Sign him in."

So I was in, even though I broke every rule they had about taking people in.

The first night they put you in a sort of intake area, like a quarantine. And in my case, they made me take a shower and then they sprayed me down with some kind of anti-louse shit, to get all the bugs off me and out from under my skin. They sprayed me on the head and hair and arms and legs and my whole body, and the bugs started coming out. They gave me a brush to brush my hair, and my hair was full of bugs. It had been so long since I washed that when my skin came in contact with water, it just kind of shriveled. And, of course, as soon as my body started waking up to the fact that I wasn't drowning it in booze, I started puking, and all this stuff came up in my throat. Look: Of all those addicts and drunks who came in there, I was the worst of the worst. I bet ninety-nine percent of the people who came in there in the condition I was in, died.

I went and found a nurse and told her I wasn't doing too good, that I thought I was going to die.

"We could send you to the hospital," she said very sweetly, "but if we do, you can't come back. All we can do for you here, medically, is to give you some aspirin and some lotion for the sores."

I called my sister Patsy collect, but she didn't answer.

I called Billy collect, but he refused my call.

Finally I crawled into the bed they came me, with crisp white sheets, but I was scared shitless. Every time I fell asleep in New York the animals robbed me blind or fucked with me. And a bed felt so strange I could hardly sleep at all. The nurse gave me some pills so I could go to sleep.

The next morning I called Billy again, and he picked up.

"Bill, I think I'm gonna die," I told him.

"You're not gonna die," he said, even though there was a good chance he was wrong. "I told your family what's happening, that you've gone into treatment up there. But to tell you the truth, they don't seem to care."

The next day, they sprayed me down and made me shower again. Other guys near me complained that they were getting bugs from me. You know, somebody who's living the good life makes a positive impression on other people. I was just giving people bugs. I was given my own bed, which was the top bunk of a bunk bed. There were a total of 110 drunks, addicts and homeless guys in a fairly small area, with 22 bunk beds in each room. I was shaking so bad that the guy in the bunk bed beneath me started complaining that I was keeping him awake.

Brother Pious started to get real concerned.

"Look, I'm not sure I can tolerate this," he told me. "You are quadrupally addicted and detoxing." (I don't know if this is a medical term, but I sure was homeless, helpless, useless and worthless.) "You need to be in the hospital or a psych ward, and I'm thinking of putting you in there anyway."

But I guess I gradually started returning to the land of the living, or at least the half-living. As my strength started to return, so did the sense of guilt about my life. The guilt was killing me. I wrote a letter to Uncle Raymond from St. Christopher's saying,

I'm in a treatment center trying to save my life and hopefully someday you can forgive me. I don't know if I will ever see you again, I am getting better, I am not dying on the street, please forgive me.

Uncle Raymond didn't write back. Nobody answered any of the letters I wrote from in there. But the fact is, there was no reason to answer them because it would only interfere with my getting better. If Uncle Raymond forgave me, I wouldn't be helping myself as much as I needed to. Even so, it was a lonely feeling. Nobody was calling me up and telling me to come home.

Nobody.

I came into St. Christopher's on a Monday, and by Wednesday, I was still waiting for a bed outside the quarantine area. I had to kind of hang around the intake area in case a bed became available. So one day I was hanging around there and I walk to the top of this hill which is, like, the beginning of the holy mountain. I sit down on this bench up there. I was still just getting adjusted to this place – I still didn't know what I was going to do because everybody had to be assigned a job. You were supposed to work three hours a day in this 28-day program, but I couldn't functionally do anything. The only things I really knew how to do well were drink, smoke crack, manipulate people and bowl. It's not like I had anything useful to contribute to society, or to any other person.

So this priest sits down on the bench next to me. He looks like all the other priests up there, brown robe, sandals, about sixty, balding, no beard, but with some little tufts of gray hair on the sides of his head. Actually, he looked a little bit like my uncle, Father Benjy.

"How are you doing?" he says.

"Not too good, Father. I still don't know if I'm going to die or not."

"What's bothering you?"

"What about all those people I hurt in my life?"

"It doesn't matter."

"What about all those people I robbed?"

"It doesn't matter."

"What about the lives I ruined – Debbie and my sister Patsy, who stuck by me until she couldn't stand it no more? What about my whole family? Nobody is ever going to talk to me again."

"It doesn't matter."

"Then what matters?"

"God helps people who help themselves."

"That's it? That's your big advice?"

"I understand you were a bowler at one time," the priest said, very gently.

"Yeah, I was a famous bowler. How'd you know that?"

"I just found out. And what you need to do is to take all that talent you had from bowling and apply that to the task of getting sober. You have to understand that there's a reason you have to get sober. It's really, really important that you get sober."

"Okay," I says to the old guy. "I'll see you later."

Then I get up from the bench and walk to the bottom of the hill. And I see three old black dudes standing there, patients at St. Christopher's I guess. And they're laughing their asses off.

"Brother, what you so happy about?" they say to me.

"I got hope," I says.

"Where'd you get that?"

"From that brother up there."

They all double over, laughing.

"You weren't talking to no brother up there – you was talking to a tree! There's something wrong with you, bro. There's nobody up there!"

9 JACK COMES BACK

Not too long after I walked up the holy mountain and talked to that priest up there, another guy who was staying at St. Christopher's, an old guy I'd run into last time around named Old Man John, came up and sat down next to me. He was very rough-looking, like he'd lived on the streets for a long time. He told me that he'd seen the whole thing – watched me go up to the top of that hill and talk to a tree, and come back with hope.

"What's the problem?" Old Man John says.

"I don't know what to do," I says. "I had this great life, a great family, a great girlfriend, tons of money, a big career, and I wind up here. I'm broke, I'm alone, my body is fucked. I have nothing."

"You want to know how to get better?"

"Yeah."

"You truly, truly want to know how to get better?"

"Yeah, sure."

"Shut up. Don't drink. Go to meetings."

"You're kidding me, right?"

"No, I'm not kidding."

Not too long after this, Brother Pious comes up to me to have a confidential conversation or something.

"Bobby, I have a problem," he says.

"What's the problem?"

"I know you've been telling people about going up the mountain and having some conversation with a priest who wasn't there. I don't want to hear about this priest anymore. If you continue to talk about the priest, I'll be forced to transfer you to the psych ward."

"Yeah?"

"Yeah. Look: I'm not denying the reality of whatever it was that you experienced. I'm just asking you to keep quiet about this."

"How come?"

"Because I don't want to have to send you to the psych ward. People in detox have delusions. When you came in here, let's face it, you were pretty far gone. You're getting better. But I just don't want you talking about this."

"Okay," I says.

For some reason, even though Brother Pious was my own Uncle's nurse when he was dying at Graymoor, I don't think he liked me. He was hard on me. He wouldn't take no shit from me. The other people here might be getting their 28 days and going home, but as it turned out, the Brothers kept me at St. Christopher's for 67 days. Maybe other people were breezing through in four weeks, but I was setting up a program to get a life. I didn't realize at the time that I was the lucky one.

"There's an AA meeting tonight at eight," Brother Pious goes on. "I think you should go."

"I don't think it will help."

"I think you should go. And please, just don't say anything more about what we talked about."

So I went to this AA meeting at 8 o'clock that night, on the grounds. The speaker was a guy who was an "alumni" of St. Christopher's. He looked right at me and he said, "I once sat where you sit. I looked like you look. I felt like you feel. And finally I walked into the chapel here and asked God to help me and I haven't had a problem since."

So I started to pray. Every day. All the time. I was still in heavy withdrawal from alcohol and shaking like an earthquake. The guy in the bed underneath me said the bed was going to collapse if I didn't stop shaking, but I couldn't help it. And finally I went to the chapel, got down on my knees and asked God to help me.

"I can't live like this no more," I said, practically crying.

No beam of light came down. No Red Sea parted. But for about three seconds, for the first time, I felt like I was going to be okay.

***

That Saturday night I was at a meeting and for the first time I shared about what I was going through. Afterwards, a guy walks over to me.

"Hi, my name is Jack," he says. "I'm an alcoholic and I'm from New Jersey. How ya doin'?"

If there was one person who was critical to my search for a new life, it was Jack, my first sponsor, a guy I came to consider one of my angels. Jack was a guy who spent thirty years driving one of them magazine delivery trucks, just dropping off bales of magazines at newsstands or wherever. No fancy job or nothing. He talked very slow and to the point and looked straight at you. He never had no problem with the bottle. His problem was heroin. He was a bad heroin junkie for many years until he finally stumbled into the program. (I don't know why he didn't go to Narcotics Anonymous, but he didn't – and AA sure worked for him. When we met he was 30 years sober.)

Jack had an older brother, George, who was also sober a long time and they were both tight with Billy, the fireman who took me up to Graymoor in the first place. Sometimes Jack would come up with another old guy, Doc. These guys – even though they looked about as ordinary as the guy who comes to unclog your toilet or fix your tire by the side of the road – they were saints. Because one thing you learn pretty quickly in the church of Alcoholics Anonymous is that it don't matter for shit what somebody looks like. When you go to meetings, down in some dingy church basement somewhere, you'll see some raggedy beat-to-crap old guy who looks like he's been sleeping in a car (and maybe he has) and he won't say nothing for a long time, but then he'll say something, short and sweet, that will just knock your socks off with the spiritual wisdom he has to share. If the whole world blew up and we were all struggling to survive in the rubble and ashes, you'd want that guy – or any of a thousand other people in the program – on your side. Maybe the reason why a lot of the people in the program look so beat up is that they've already lived through the end of the world (like I did). And if the end came again, they'd be the ones that came up to help you.

Without these guys, and especially Jack, I would never have succeeded in getting sober. No way. I'd be dead, and nobody would have come to my funeral, either. I was what they mean when they talk about a "low-bottom drunk" and I think Jack knew what he was in for when he first met me. He and a friend of his had come up to St. Christopher's from his house in Whippany, New Jersey, which is like 90 miles away, because they had made a commitment to speak once a month. It wasn't Jack who spoke that night, it was his friend. So after that meeting, Jack comes up to me.

"Hey, your name's Bobby, right?" he says. He'd heard me share in the meeting, talking about my personal situation, which was my favorite subject.

"Yeah."

"How ya doin'?"

"Not too good."

"Yeah?"

"Yeah, I got no family no more, no friends, I wore out the welcome mat wherever I went. I robbed everybody, I ruined women's lives, my family disowned me, I got nobody asking me to come home. I been on the streets seven years and I lost everything. I even lost my fucking teeth. My mouth is fucking killing me."

This guy Jack – he's listening and looking at me very earnest, as if he actually cares about what might happen to me. Not like the way I listened to people, which was just pretending to be listening, waiting for my opening so I could start hustling them for food, money, dope, whatever. People weren't really people at all. They were just a way to get what I wanted.

"You've got to stay at St. Christopher's until your time is up," Jack says. "Don't leave here early. I know it's bad. I been there. But things will start getting better if you stick with this program."

"How do I do that?"

"You do it one day at a time. Isn't there a meeting here every night?"

"Yeah."

"So go every night. How long you here for?"

"I'm here for four weeks – I got two weeks and five days left. But then what? Where do I go after that? Go back to the streets? I got noplace to go after this." I was practically crying, listening to my own sob story. (Little did I know I was already two days into my life as a sober man.)

And Jack started coming to see me every Saturday, and he stuck with me for fifteen years. He became my sponsor. He helped me understand the Big Book, which I had read about two hundred times (about half of the time shit-faced on vodka or coke or something else). I met his friend, Doc, who still sponsors me today, over twenty years later.

Things gradually, gradually, gradually started to change. I wasn't worried about dying anymore. I wanted to learn how to live. And, if I learned only one thing, it was that I could only do this one day at a time.

"God will supply your needs," Jack says. "Just believe this, and you'll be taken care of. The important thing, Bobby, is you need to focus on today, on this one day. Can you do that? Just this one day? You know, like the next 24 hours?"

"Yeah, I think I can do that. So?"

"So you don't have to use the word 'never' – like 'I will never drink again,'" Jack says. "No drunk can do that. I don't think anybody can do that. Just say, 'I won't drink or drug today.' That's it."

"Okay."

"And avoid 'people, places and things' that will lead you back into drinking and drugging. That'll be easy for you – you're in here, confined. So take advantage of that. Okay?"

"Uh, okay."

"When you find the answer, you'll begin to live in the answer, and then your problems will start to disappear. Okay?"

"Okay."

"Okay, so I'll come back and see you here at five o'clock next Saturday night. Okay?"

"Okay."

"Look: I don't want you to call me collect, it's too expensive. I live 90 miles away. But will you trust me to come back next Saturday night?"

I'm standing there looking at this guy I just met, this old beaten-down delivery truck driver who's lived through the end of the world, and for some reason I trust him. I thought about that thing in the Bible where it talks about "entertaining angels unawares." What the hell. What did I have to lose? I already lost everything.

"I'm going to give you an assignment," Jack says. "What I would like you to do, if you can do it, is whenever you're sitting around, not working, just get a piece of paper and write down everything that's bothering you. I want you to keep clearing your head out, writing your thoughts down, and then setting that aside. Can you do that for me?"

"Uh, yeah, I guess so."

"Don't read what you write down. Just put the pieces of paper in a cardboard box. It's a 'God box' – when you put the papers in there you're giving your problems over to God. Later on, we can burn the papers or flush them down the toilet. Whatever. They're not your problems no more."

"One other thing," Jack says. "Don't call nobody on the phone. The phone is a booby trap. If somebody listens to you and maybe even says they forgive you, you'll want to call them back, but they don't want to hear from you no more. That will just keep you from doing the work you need to do. Okay?"

This really hit home to me. I had called Patsy and told her I was sorry a hundred thousand times. But I wasn't really sorry, at least not sorry enough to change my life. I just wanted money to get high again, or at least a little bit of forgiveness so I wouldn't feel so bad and guilty about getting high again. Asking her to please, please, please forgive me was just my way of not doing anything. It was my way of staying the same.

"Okay."

"So I'll see you here next Saturday night at five o'clock," Jack says. "You smoke?"

"No."

"You like candy?"

"Yeah, sure."

So Jack buys me some candy, almost like I'm a twelve-year-old kid – and actually, inside I am about twelve years old, because when you start drinking and doing dope like I did, your emotional development just stops at that age. Your body ages, but you don't. I was basically a 70-year-old 12-year-old.

Then Jack and the other guy leave the building.

For the next week, I just do what Jack told me to do. I don't try to run my own life, I don't try to tell everybody else how to run their life, or what pathetic fuck-ups they are, or none of that. I just do what I'm told. It's a brand-new experience for me, because after all, for most of my adult life I'd been acting like I was God, conducting the whole show right down to the weather. And look where it got me. Yeah, that worked out real well!

I go to at least one meeting every day. And I start writing down everything, all my regrets and fears and sorrows, everything I shouldn't have said or done, all the lies I told Debbie, all the lies I told Patsy and Uncle Raymond. In the morning before work and in the afternoon after work, I sit on these benches outside in the hot sun and I'm scribbling away like mad. I keep asking the guy at the front desk for more paper – I use up, like fifty or sixty pages, all the shit that's bothering me. Forget about it! Everything's bothering me.

But one day I go to a couple of masses and a meeting and then I realize around bedtime that I have actually gone through an entire day without wanting to leave this joint. This is incredible to me. (At St. Christopher's, the brothers made it very clear that you were free to leave at any time – they'd hand you a bus ticket back to Manhattan the second you asked for it. I knew, because that's what I'd done last time I was up here. But I didn't ask for no bus ticket this time.)

One day Brother Pious sees me sitting there on these benches in the sun writing away and he asks what I'm doing. I tell him what Jack said, and about how he promised to come back.

"Don't get your hopes up," Brother Pious says. "Honestly. Nobody ever comes back."

But I just keep on writing. For one thing, it helps me to keep my mind off the pain. My teeth and gums are killing me from where they're all infected and stinky. The sores on my body hurt. I am just learning to take showers again, and it still feels strange to have hot water pouring down over my skinny, wasted, junkie body. It hurt. It seemed like everything hurt. Even my heart hurts because I can't drink or do drugs and have to begin confronting what I look like in the mirror, and what I have done to my life and all the people in it.

When Saturday night rolls around, I'm waiting in the room where they have speakers come. Five o'clock comes, and Jack ain't there. Five-oh-one. Five-oh-two. Five-oh-five. And then Jack and his friend come rushing in, just like Brother Pious said they wouldn't.

"How ya doin'?" Jack says, very calm, very slow, very direct.

For the rest of the time I was at St. Christopher's Inn, he would drive those 90 miles, each way, just to come up and see me. Can you imagine that? Me, the thieving junkie who threw away a chance to be one of the biggest Somebodies anyone ever saw. Just for me.

And Jack keeps coming back for me for the next fifteen years, until the day he dies.

10 YOU ARE FORGIVEN

I started working the intake desk, where new people would come to check into St. Christopher's in all kinds of conditions, all of them bad. Confessions were held in the chapel at four o'clock on Thursdays, so one day I hear the bell for confessions and I get up from the intake desk and go into the chapel. And who's sitting there but the priest I talked to up on the holy mountain that day. I slipped into the pew beside him.

"You're getting me in a lot of trouble," I says to him. "Bless me, father, for I have…"

"Stop, stop with all that," he says. "Let me ask you one question: Did you ever kill anyone?"

"No."

"You are forgiven, and you can forgive yourself."

"Okay."

"And you are forgiven for what that guy across the street did to you when you were a kid."

"Okay."

It was weird: I don't know how he knew about this, since I had never told anyone.

"And you need to forgive that kid who blinded you in your left eye when you were twelve."

How did he know this stuff?

"But most of all, you have to forgive yourself. And remember what I told you: Take your talent from bowling and apply it to the task of recovery, and I guarantee you'll make it."

So I'm coming out of the chapel and I run into Brother Pious.

"How come you're not at the intake desk?" he says.

"Well, I heard the bell for confession and I went into the chapel and I saw that priest again – the guy from up on the mountain."

Brother Pious looks at me funny.

"There is no bell for confession," he says. "Bobby, I'm afraid I'm going to have to send you to the psych ward tomorrow. Pack your bags and get ready to go in the morning."

But, for some reason, Brother Pious never came for me.

Jack came up to see me every week. I could call him collect, and he'd pick up the phone, which was progress. I wrote a couple of letters to Patsy, hoping that someday she, too, would pick up the phone. And from time to time I caught a fleeting glimpse of the mysterious priest from the holy mountain around the grounds. As far as I was concerned, he was as real as you or me.

***

Even though the rehab program at St. Christopher's was supposed to be your standard 28-day "three hots and a cot," just a month-long break from the streets for a few of the homeless drunks and junkies out there, I actually wound up staying there for more than three months. There were a couple of reasons for that.

First of all, even though the priests didn't actually really want me there – who would? – they had no choice but to take me because my ride left. Billy just dumped me off at the door and took off. So, by their own rules, they were forced to take me. Just their luck, huh?

Second of all, the way the whole system worked was that if you were a resident of New York State, you qualified for a welfare program that would pay for a more long-term program after your 28 days was up. But I wasn't from New York. I was from New Jersey. (Even so, I couldn't prove it – I had been on the streets so long I had no ID whatsoever. Driver's license? Credit card? One of them cutesy little grocery store cards? Forget about it. All I had in my pockets was lint.)

So the priests didn't quite know what to do with me. They knew that I was so far gone, if they sent me back to the streets of New York I was pretty much guaranteed to wind up at the city morgue with a tag on my toe. So they started trying to work the angle of my Uncle Benjy, the Franciscan bigshot, to see if, being that I was his relative, I could qualify for some kind of special Franciscan grant or something. I guess they sort of looked on me as a member of the family, a bad-boy prodigal son coming home or whatever.

I think part of the reason I wound up staying at St. Christopher's so long was that the Brothers were trying to find me a much longer-term rehab to go to, like eighteen months to two years, and it was difficult to find one that had space available. They tried to get me into St. Joseph's, in Saranac Lake, New York, but there was no room at the inn. No luck at the Salvation Army, or a couple of other places either. I started to get increasingly frantic that they wouldn't be able to find me a place to go, and they'd just be forced to discharge me back to the street.

In the meantime, though, I stayed on there at Graymoor, working at the intake desk, watching these poor dazed-looking bastards come in the door straight off the streets. (Of all these guys, though, there was only one other guy that looked as bad as me. I was one sick puppy.)

And from time to time I kept seeing the mysterious priest, the one that nobody else seemed to see. I've thought about him a lot over the years, of course, and I can tell you this: He didn't look like no "ghost." He looked just as real as you or me. And altogether, according to my count, I seen him six separate times.

At St. Christopher's there were groups and meetings every day, and – since I've never been somebody who knows how to keep my mouth shut – I kept talking about my Higher Power and also about this mystery priest, this "angel" or whatever he was that was helping me learn how to get sober and begin to live a real, actual life. The one who told me to take all the talent and focus I had from bowling and turn it into the personal power it would take to begin living a new life.

Gradually, though, I started to realize that the other drunks and junkies at St. Christopher's were beginning to look at me like I was a nut job. Like the whole thing was a joke. Like I was a joke.

"Look at that dude, man – he's a crazy motherfucker, bro!"

I'd hear somebody say in a sort of stage whisper behind me, as I was walking down the hall.

"He sees people that ain't there."

"Yo! Seen that priest of yours lately, man?"

Even so, I didn't feel like shutting up about it. I didn't care what those guys thought. Fuck those guys. I wasn't crazy. I seen what I seen. And, after all, if you needed "proof" that the priest was real, how about the fact that he was the main reason I was on the road to betterment, that I had been lifted up to the mountaintop, after that despicable sick terrible life I'd been living on the street? My own awakening was all the proof I needed. What was happening to me was a miracle, and the miracle was real.

The priest had showed me that I needed to use my fierce inner drive to win at life, when winning isn't bowling a perfect game or a new car or a pair of $500 shoes. It's waking up every morning and not being addicted to a person, a place, or a thing – being free of the obsession to drink alcohol or do drugs, or any of the hundred other things people get addicted to. Spiritual victory – really, the courage to live – was waking up every morning and being free.

Well, anyhow, so one Sunday morning when I was still at St. Christopher's I went to the 10 a.m. Mass. All the residents there were required to go, all 106 of us. We must have made quite a sight, traipsing into that little chapel, which was actually kind of old and beautiful – this crowd of tired, beat-to-shit faces, all these misfits and losers and bums, dragging all our failures and mistakes and regrets behind us, like pets. At least we were all freshly-showered and had clean clothes on, because there was some kind of a special event going on. There were wealthy donors there wearing nice suits, and ladies wearing dresses. And there was us drunks, who had to look good even if we looked bad. There was also a special speaker giving the sermon that morning, a visiting priest from Brooklyn. Me and another drunk – Old Man John – walked right down to the front of the chapel and slipped into the front row. I always sat in the front row. That was my general approach to life: Get right in there, don't miss anything. Old Man John looked about as rough as they come. He'd had a couple of five-year stretches of sobriety, but he always wound up coming back here to give it another try.

The guest speaker from Brooklyn was a big jolly black guy, a very powerful Catholic missionary. He was huge: Maybe six-five, with a booming voice. His message was a message of hope and Spirit and the nearness of God, very uplifting. I'm listening to him speak when I notice another priest up there, seated to the left of him – an old guy wearing a baggy brown robe and sandals, with tufts of gray hair above his ears. And – holy shit! – I suddenly realize it's the mystery priest, "my" priest. He looks as real as a loaf of bread; he wasn't no spirit flying off the ground. He was just sitting there like an ordinary person, apparently waiting for his turn to speak.

I jammed my elbow into Old Man John's ribs.

"Yo! You see that guy?" I whisper to him, pointing to the priest. "That's the guy I've been telling you about! Right up there! That's the dude, bro!"

"Yeah, I see him," Old Man John says, not very impressed. "So what? I always see him. He's around here all the time."

"So you see him! You see him!"

"Yeah? So?"

"So you gotta tell Brother Pious you seen 'im!"

"Shut up," Old Man John says. "I'm trying to listen."

I sort of slump back in my seat, so relaxed and happy that I ain't crazy and that somebody else has actually seen the guy. I can't wait to tell Brother Pious. I start listening to the black missionary priest giving his sermon, and out of the corner of my eye I'm also watching the mystery priest, sitting up there, real as a heart attack, right in front of the whole church. Then, after a little while, the black priest steps down off the low platform at the front the chapel and walks right up to me.

"Stand up," he says to me.

So I stand up.

"Have you ever seen God?" he asks me.

"Uh, no." I'm nervous that I got picked out of the crowd – from my experience, that was always bad.

"Yes, you have." And he puts his hand on my head. He's one of these real jolly, hands-on type of guys, with big damp hands.

"Uh, well I..."

"Your eyes are the windows to your soul. I can see that you've seen God. I have not seen anything like that in years."

Then he takes his hand off my head, walks back to the front of the chapel and I sit down. I mean, you know: What the hell was that all about? Then the black priest sits down and the other guy, the mystery guy, gives the whole Mass and the communion and everything. I sit there watching him and listening to him do it. I can't wait to get out of there to tell Brother Pious what I seen. So after the Mass, me and Old Man John go out into the vestibule where there's all these fancy people milling around and I go right up to Brother Pious.

"Brother," I says to him, "I can solve the problem with that mystery man, the priest I keep seeing around here."

"You can, can you?"

"He just did the service for the Mass in there! And Old Man John here seen him!"

Brother Pious kind of pauses a minute, giving me the once-over with his eyes. Then he turns to Old Man John.

"Is that true? Did you see him?"

"Yeah, I seen him. So?"

Just then a youngish-looking priest, maybe 40 or 50, in a brown baggy robe, walks out of the chapel. I'd seen him around before – it's a guy they call Brother James.

"That's him," Old Man John says, pointing to Brother James. "That's the guy that gave the Mass."

"That's who you saw up there?" I says, incredulous. "But that's Brother James!"

"Yeah, that's the guy who was up there. That's the dude that gave the Mass."

"But that's not the guy I'm talking about! The guy who was up there wasn't young like him – he was an old guy about sixty, with little tufts of hair above his ears. It was a different guy! It was the guy I been seeing around here!"

And all of a sudden I realize that Brother Pious, Old Man John and several other people who are standing there are just staring at me, with their eyebrows raised. Like, "what's up with this shit-for-brains?"

"Please be in my office tomorrow at 8 a.m.," Brother Pious says to me, very clipped and businesslike, as if I'm in trouble again. But just then the black missionary priest from Brooklyn comes walking up, and he puts his hand on my head again.

"This is the guy I was telling you about," he says to Brother Pious. "Look at his eyes. His eyes are filled with Spirit. His eyes are cleansed. He looks like someone who has seen the Light."

Me? I'm just standing there, fresh off the streets of the Bad Apple, the guy who's been sleeping on the floor of a peep-show house on 42nd Street, with no teeth, no money, no home and scabs all over my body. Yeah: Like I'm really a guy who's "seen the Light."

But in a weird way, in a way I couldn't explain, I think I knew what he was talking about.

I showed up at Brother Pious's office the next morning at eight o'clock sharp. But it was pretty obvious from the second I walked in there that the poor guy didn't know what the hell to do with me.

"Look," he says, "I don't know what to make of all this. But I do know that all your talk about some mysterious angel or priest or whatever it may be is starting to annoy people around here, including people who are struggling to get sober. It's getting to be a joke. People are making fun of you behind your back. And it very well may be an ordinary delusion of a recovering alcoholic. So I'm going to ask you to put a lid on it. Just don't share these stories anymore, don't mention them to anyone. Please. God loves us and wants us to do His will. But he doesn't very often send down a personal angel to help us along the way."

Well, I didn't know nothing about that. All I know is what I saw. And what I saw was as real as anything I've ever seen or felt in my life.

It was so real it was in the process of changing my life.

***

In the end the Brothers let me stay at St. Christopher's for 67 days instead of just the usual four weeks. So I just stayed there at the Christ motel, and every Saturday night Jack would drive all the way up from Whippany to see me. Ninety miles each way, once a week. Like I say, he was a saint, as well as my sponsor, which is about the same thing.

Strangely enough, one of the other few people who was talking to me now was a guy named Tony. And Tony just happened to be the last guy I robbed. I could call him collect, and he'd pick up. Tony agreed to pick me up when my time at St. Christopher's was done, and take me to wherever I was going next. Eventually it turned out that a place opened up for me at a hospital rehab called St. Claire's Riverside, in Boonton, New Jersey. So a way had opened up, and I'd be leaving in a few days.

So anyways, not too long before Tony is coming to pick me up, I'm walking down the road to the friar's cemetery, to pay my respects to my Uncle Benjy and thank him for everything he done for me. I'm walking up the hill and a car pulls over. The door opens. It's Father Paul, the guy who ain't there.

"Get in," he says.

"No," I say. This is just getting too weird for me.

"Get in."

"No."

"Robert, get in this car, please."

"No."

"Where are you going, brother?"

"I'm going to the friar's cemetery."

"Where is that?"

Then I just stop and stare at him, an old guy in a baggy brown robe, almost like a pajama robe, with his little tufts of gray hair and his piercing eyes, staring at me out of the car.

"Who are you?" I says to him.

"It doesn't matter. What matters is that you do what I have told you all along — that you focus all that talent you have, all that intelligence, all that drive, on getting sober. It's very important that you get sober."

Then he closed the door and drove away.

Look: Am I telling you I seen a ghost driving a car? Well, I'm just telling you what happened. I don't know any more than that.

After Father Paul drove away, I walked up to Uncle Benjy's grave and stayed there quietly for awhile, thanking him. When I turned around to walk away, my foot scuffed something in the dirt, and I leaned over to pick it up. It was a Miraculous Medal, one of these little gold coins made to celebrate the time when a lady named Bernadette actually seen the blessed mother, at a place in France called Lourdes. They say that if you put this medal in the hands of somebody who's dying, they go directly to heaven. And that's the medal I later squeezed into the hand of my friend Michael Defino, when he was on his deathbed. All I know for sure is that when you get a spiritual gift like that medal, you've got to give it away. That's how you get it back. I've heard that called "the divine paradox," and maybe that's what it is.

***

Right after I had that strange meeting with Father Paul (which would turn out to be the sixth and last time I ever seen him), I told Jack about it. He listened to me in his slow, quiet way. He didn't tell me I was fucking nuts to be seeing a ghost driving a car.

"Why do you think they call it the 'holy mountain'?" he says. "Lots of crazy shit happens up here."

He was much less interested in ghosts and angels than he was in making sure I stuck with the program. That I do it day by day, and not try to lay out some grandiose plan for the whole rest of my life. Doing it that way was guaranteed not to work, he said.

After a little while we started working on the Twelve Steps of Alcoholics

Anonymous, which is where you kind of really put the program to work in your own life. The really, really hard work I had never been able to do.

The first step, Jack told me, was absolutely critical to everything that would come later. Like all the steps, it was simple:

Step One: We admitted we were powerless over alcohol – that our lives had become unmanageable.

"Powerless"? "Unmanageable"? Forget about it. The main thing I knew was that my life had become unbearable, unlivable. If I didn't change, I would die. So for the first time in my adult life I began to look at my life honestly, to confront all the damage, to lift the veil on all the lies I'd told all those years, to other people and to myself, just to survive. All of it, everything, was a lie. All I really cared about, all I ever wanted to do, was get wasted, and then get even more wasted. That was it. That was my whole life. Everything I told Debbie, everything I told my sister, everyone – it was just a cover story so that I could get money to stay high and not have to think about anything, not have to take responsibility for anything.

I heard the saying, "alcoholics love their childhood so much they want to take yours," and in a way that summed it up. I took advantage of everyone around me just so I could stay in the happy self-centeredness of childhood, just satisfying my own desires. And only now was I beginning to face all the damage that caused. It was more important to me to get drunk or stoned than it was to work, have a family, have a relationship, reach my potential, have financial stability, help other people or anything else.

There's a saying in the rooms that "I took a drink, then the drink took a drink, then the drink took me." That's what people mean when they say somebody "got drunk" – the bottle drank them. They were powerless.

Was I aware of this at the time, when I was doing all this stuff? Yeah, kind of. But I didn't give a shit. I just went ahead and did it anyway. Uncle Raymond used to say, speaking mainly of bad stuff, "it only turns into experience once you stop doing it." In other words, if you just keep drinking and lying and doing dope, you're not learning anything, you're not aware of anything, you're doing the same bad stuff over and over. Only after you stop doing it do you kind of wake up to what's happening.

Well, now I'd stopped. Even though my life was in ruins, and my physical health was almost destroyed, at least I'd finally stopped. And that's when the burning pain of self-awareness and shame and guilt started to kick in. Just because you stopped drinking doesn't mean you're "sober" – becoming a genuinely sober person is a long, slow, painful process, and the Twelve Steps are the key to it. Jack told me that the First Step was so important we spent almost that whole 67 days I was at St. Christopher's on that one step. He said I couldn't get much further unless I was absolutely clear on this. He told me that I was in a good position to begin this work – I was sober, if only for a couple of days; I was in confinement; I had the time; there were meetings every day; and the Brothers were there to help me. "I don't know how long it will take," Jack said, "but it will probably take a long time. You need to get the First Step in you, or else you can't go any further."

Every morning I would go to mass and all us drunks and junkies and thieves and liars would sing the St. Francis of Assisi Prayer (what's also known as the Eleventh Step prayer):

Lord, make me an instrument of your peace.
Where there is hatred, let me sow love;
where there is injury, pardon;
where there is doubt, faith;
where there is despair, hope;
where there is darkness, light;
and where there is sadness, joy.

Because I had so much time on my hands, and because it was so quiet there, I had a lot of time to work my First Step at St. Christopher's. I could sit outside with a prayer book or the Bible, or walk up the hill to that bench where I first seen Father Paul. I prayed. Other times, I just got sick of the whole thing and started thinking, 'Man, I gotta leave this fucking joint.'"

One day Jack shows up when I'm in one of those moods and he just explodes at me.

"Man, I'm driving 90 fucking miles up here to see you, and if you're not listening, or doing what you gotta do, you're wasting my time," he says. "There is a big change you have to make in your life – it has to be done. If you're not willing to do the work, I'm not coming back. I've got better things to do. But I'll tell you one thing: You go out there again, and you'll probably wind up dead."

Then I start begging and pleading for him not to give up on me, not to leave. Everybody in my life had left, except Jack and Patsy. Even up here at St. Christopher's, where there was the biggest collection of crackheads, dopers and losers you ever saw, even here people kind of gave me a wide berth because of the way I looked. The only person who didn't treat me like I was nuts was Jack (and Patsy, when she came for a visit). And here he was, about ready to leave.

So I promised Jack I would ask God to help me find my way to a new life, a new way of living.

I wanted to get off the last train to oblivion. And Jack promised that he would give me another try.

"When you really start to change, other people will see it — there will be no reason to tell them about it," Jack told me.

I was waiting for that day to come, but at least so far it seemed like it never would.

11 THE SECRET

So, anyway, I wound up spending more than two months at St. Christopher's Inn, at Graymoor, until the priests found me another long-term rehab at this place called St. Claire's Hospital, in Boonton, New Jersey. They had a seven-day detox followed by a 28-day rehab. This was just kind of a rest stop on my way to a longer-term "behavior modification" program called Freedom House, in Glen Gardener, New Jersey. I guess the priests recognized that my shit was going to take some industrial-strength medicine to change. (Good luck with that: Can you imagine anything powerful enough to "modify my behavior?" I'm telling you: The only medicine strong enough was God and his personal messenger, an old guy in a baggy brown bathrobe.)

So I got transferred to St. Claire's. When I showed up there I was still crazy, even though I had a string of several weeks of sobriety, the first in memory. This was a hospital-based program so at least they could deal with the nasty infections in my mouth. There were meetings and classes almost all day long, and I started gradually adjusting to the fact that normal people sleep all night, get up in the morning and have coffee, make friends, have normal conversations, take responsibility for stuff and all that. It was weird.

So one day about halfway through my stay at St. Claire's, I'm in the kitchen making coffee for the group and I have my back turned when I hear a visitor come into the room. Then I turned around and saw her.

It was Patsy.

"Hi," she says, kind of shyly.

"Hi," I says.

And then she starts crying.

"Oh my God," she says. "It's really happening."

"I told you I'm getting better," I says.

"I can see it."

"How you doin'?"

"I'm doin' okay. You know you can't come home."

"Yeah, I know."

She asked me if it was okay if she brought Jeannie and I said, sure. I'd love to see her. So the next Sunday Patsy came with my other sister, and Jeannie saw me, and she believed it. I was really, actually coming back into myself after all those terrible years. Patsy later said that all she ever wanted was for the Bobby Purzycki that she knew was in there to come out again. And it was happening. It was almost like Lazarus, in the Bible, getting raised from the dead.

"You know you can't come around us anymore," Jeannie said, repeating what Patsy had said and what I already knew.

I'd done this to myself. I knew I had. Now it was my job to take responsibility for my own life. Maybe someday I'd be allowed back into the circle of the family, but I had a lot of work to do before anything like that ever happened.

It was while I was at St. Claire's that something very scary and painful happened that changed my life. It later became known as "the pizza incident."

One Friday night, I just completely flipped out. I went nuts. I'm throwing chairs and tables, bouncing off the walls. People ducked for cover from all that flying furniture. What set me off was one of them tiny things that isn't tiny at all – those "little" things that set off bitter arguments, like the ones I used to have with Debbie. The sort of arguments that can get people killed.

What happened on the surface was that, on Friday nights, all of us patients in the program would pool our money and get pizza, and on this particular night I was put in charge of collecting the money. There was a woman named Peggy, a very hard, no-bullshit woman, who was in charge of that shift. She was the boss, and for some reason Peggy was on my case. She didn't like me, and more important, she didn't believe I would ever make it. She thought I was too far gone ever to get my shit together and become a responsible, sober person. She thought I had no shot at redemption. It was like I was already a corpse. I could feel that from her, and even though it was probably a reasonable thing for her to think, it fucking pissed me off. As a result, you know, there was bad blood between us.

So this particular night, after I'd collected the money and given it to her, she accuses me of slipping a little bit into my own pocket.

"This money doesn't add up, Bobby," she says, very stern, counting. "Where's the rest of the money?"

"Are you accusing me of shorting the money?" I says to her. "Bullshit! I didn't steal a penny! Look in my pockets!" And I pulled my empty pockets inside-out to show her.

Look: Nobody else in that room was willing to collect the money for the very reason that handling money was a very loaded issue for a lot of these people. We'd probably all been accused of stealing money before (and with good reason). But I had decided to take on this job because I was trying to take responsibility, and now I'm getting treated like a fucking sneak-thief. But even though what Peggy was saying was not true, she persisted. She really got in my face. She wouldn't back off. And neither would I.

"You're just in my shit because you think I'm a loser and I'll never make it!" I yelled at her. "Well, look at you! Making five bucks an hour at some crap job on the drunk ward!"

"You're a thief, and you know it, Bobby! Give that money back, or I'll bring you up on charges!"

And that's when the explosion hit: BOOM! I just went off. Shit flying everywhere. I turned a bed upside down. I knocked over a desk. I just absolutely flipped out. To be unfairly accused like that, and also to be treated like someone who could never get sober, never get well, a homeless addict who would always be a homeless addict — well, it blanked out my brain, it made me so mad.

Obviously, Peggy could have called the front office at St. Claire's and threw me out of there after this incident. I was being violent and scary. But she didn't. Maybe it was partly because, after I started to calm down, I started to beg.

"Please don't throw me out," I says to her finally. "Look: I'm sorry. I lost it. It won't ever happen again. I promise."

I guess Peggy had calmed down too, so she backed away from a bigger fight and we ordered the pizza. (Later on, believe it or not, Peggy and I became friends and we corresponded for years.) But the thing is this: Like most arguments, it wasn't about pizza, or money, or any of that.

Earlier in the day, another therapist named Judy had about 12 or 18 of us sitting in a circle for a group session. She said you were "only as sick as your deepest, darkest secrets," and we were going to explore some of those. (She had a degree in psychology or some such thing.) Then she hypnotized us, or tried to, I don't know how that works. Didn't feel like much. But before you know it, I was waking to some ancient, ancient memories and they were scaring me shitless. In a way, the therapist tricked me into this. I wasn't prepared for what happened next.

I had gone all the way back to when I was 12 years old, a skinny little Polack kid growing up in Paterson, New Jersey, and starting to show all this amazing promise at the bowling alley. But I was still a scared kid who was beat up and bullied. I was not a fighter. I just got pounded down. Then I got busted in the eye and went half-blind. But that wasn't the scary part.

Right about this same time, there was this older kid who lived across the street, named Vinnie. He was, like, eighteen years old or something, five or six years older than me. And whenever his parents weren't home and nobody was around, he would call me across the street.

"Hey Bobby, come 'ere," he'd say. "I got some candy!"

I mean, I liked this kid. I admired him. Then he'd lead me into the house. He'd take me downstairs. And then he'd do these sex acts to me, disgusting things, things I never heard of. I had no idea what was happening. I just knew I was being kidnapped and forced into hell, and there was no way I could get out of it, and nobody I could ever tell about it. When it was over, Vinnie would tell me that if I ever told anybody, he'd make me pay. He'd kill my whole family. He'd kill my mom, my dad, and all my sisters. If I told anybody, I'd be a murderer.

So I just put these disgusting memories in a box and decided to bury that box way down deep inside where it could never be found. I just stuffed it. (Much later, when I seen parts of the Jerry Sandusky pedophilia trial, at Penn State, on TV, I started to relive the whole thing. When I listened to the testimony from Victim Number Four, I heard this kid say Sandusky had threatened him with the exact same words Vinnie threatened me. I knew that kid was telling the truth, because he was telling my story. I felt so sorry for that kid. I know how alone and messed-up he felt inside.) There was one time, though, when I actually screwed up the courage to tell my dad about it, even though I risked killing my whole family. "Are you sure? Are you sure?" I remember my dad asking me. I could see his face getting red. I was afraid he was going to go charging across the street and rip that kid's lungs out. I actually remember asking him not to go over there, because of what might happen.

Instead, he called the police and they came to the house to interview me. But, I don't know, when they asked me what Vinnie done to me, it was too embarrassing, and I couldn't really describe what it was anyway. I didn't know nothing about sex – I was twelve years old. I didn't know what it was. Besides, if it got out in the neighborhood that I'd been messed with like that, I knew it would give the other kids one more excuse to beat the shit out of me. Why would the victim get blamed? Because that's the way it worked where I grew up. So in the end, I finally just told the cops, you know, "forget about it. It never happened." I just wanted it all to go away. The police left and nothing ever came of it.

Eventually, Vinnie's family moved away and I never seen or heard from him again. But yet, for all those years, I had carried that secret box, with all those secrets, hidden inside. I had tucked it away so deep I didn't even know it was there. And when the therapist brought it all up at St. Claire's, I just flipped. I went nuts, not because I was mad at anybody, but because I didn't know what to do with the shame.

Patsy: *"When I found out about this later, it really made sense to me. I actually suspected that something like this might have happened. It's my belief that a lot of Bobby's later problems came from being sexually abused and never talking about it, and also being injured in the face like that. He was traumatized. I see these men on Oprah that have been abused and they have no self-worth, can't do anything with their lives – it's so similar to what Bobby went through. He goes from extreme to extreme – he is either the greatest who ever lived, or worthless, nothing."*

So Jack would come to meetings at St. Claire's every Thursday. We began working on Step Two and Step Three of the Twelve Steps. We actually kind of worked these two steps together, because Jack said they were so related.

Step Two: Came to believe that a Power greater than ourselves could restore us to sanity.

Step Three: Made a decision to turn our will and our lives over to the care of God as we understood Him.

Unlike a lot of people in the rooms of Alcoholics Anonymous, I never had no problem believing in God. I grew up Catholic, I had accepted Jesus Christ as Lord and Savior when I was a little kid (though nobody would have known it). But most importantly, I had had a direct experience with God when I was twelve years old and I was blinded and raped. When I was lying there in that bedroom with my right eye covered in patches, not knowing if I would ever see again, I prayed to God to restore my sight, and he did. Same thing when that creepy little pedophile Vinnie across the street was raping me – I prayed, and God answered my prayers.

Look: I'm not really a religious guy at all. I didn't trust the priests at Catholic school – they were mean as shit, they beat me with a paddle. Instead, through AA, I was becoming a spiritual person. I've heard it said in the rooms that "religion is for people who don't want to go to hell. Spirituality is for people who have been in hell." Yeah, that's it.

Even so, the whole process of "turning my will and my life over to God" was a major, major change. Basically it was like firing my old employer (me) and hiring a completely new one (God).

Jack gently led me to the understanding that I had caused such hurt and pain to the people that I loved, like Patsy, that there was a good chance I would never see them again. He also led me to the understanding, in a fundamental way, I had never even learned to take care of myself, that society had no place for me, and that once my life underwent a dramatic spiritual change from working the steps, life would still be hard for me. Basically, I'd fucked it up almost beyond belief. Even so, very gradually, I realized my heart was shifting from a feeling of complete uselessness to a sense that I might be useful, not only to myself but to other people. That I could make a positive difference in other people's lives. That I didn't ever have to go back to the streets, or to the nightmare that my life had become. That my life was being transformed because I had met God or his angel, one or the other, and that whether Father Paul was real or not real, I was learning to use the talent I had as an athlete to become a sober man living a useful, spiritual life.

Jack told me that, if I stuck with this, he guaranteed I'd make it.

12 THE GOD BOX

Most people have just one sponsor, but I kind of had three – Jack; his older brother George; and my friend Billy, the guy who always showed up. These guys were my little community, my back bench. It's quite possible I needed three people because I was so fucked up. Or maybe I was just lucky. Or maybe that's the same thing, in some strange way. I mean, the luckiest thing that ever happened to me was getting into AA, and I never would have got there if I hadn't been driven to my knees.

The program that Jack was leading me through now was pretty simple, actually. Some people say you can boil it down to six words:

"Quit drinking. Clean house. Help others."

The "cleaning house" part is the twelve steps. That's it. Sounds simple, but it's some powerful magic, that's for sure. And if you do it right, it hurts. Sometimes people will do the steps two, three, four times or more, because every time you do this work, you hurt more, and you feel better, as you do the hard work of cleaning up your house. Nobody's perfect, that's for sure. Like it says in the Big Book, "we are not saints…We claim spiritual progress rather than spiritual perfection."

So it's a program for people who have failed, people who have been humbled, people who finally had to admit that they were "powerless over alcohol."

Now I started working on the fourth step:

Step Four: Made a searching and fearless moral inventory of ourselves.

Oh, jeezus. Like, I'm actually supposed to look at that sick twisted vampire in the mirror, at everything I had become, at everything I had been running from all those years? I am supposed to actually come clean about all the people I done wrong, everybody I'd cheated, lied to, robbed or stolen from? The whole idea of beginning to start cleaning up the mess I'd made of my life made me feel exhausted, scared, panicky, freaked out, sad, angry, and every other bad feeling you can think of. It also made me desperate for a drink or a line of coke or a little glass stem of crack. But I couldn't do it. I could not do it. If I did that, I knew that I would go right back to the place I was before, and not long after that I would be dead. And I'd make a pretty scrawny, pathetic-looking corpse.

Jack tells me that now is a good time to start using the "God box," and just throwing shit in there – things I done wrong, things I was embarrassed about – and giving them over to God. It was a relief not to have to carry that shit around no more. I wrote and I wrote and I wrote, laying out all the stuff I regretted (at least, the parts I remembered), and putting it in the shoebox for God.

Jack pointed out to me that if I was going to stay sober for the long term, I was also going to have to avoid the "people, places and things" that I associated with getting drunk and doing dope. Unfortunately, at least for now, that included bowling alleys. Alcohol was so much a part of the sport that at a lot of bowling alleys it was literally built in, with cup holders in the tables right by the lanes. My friend Irene had told me that she had quit bowling for this reason, so I decided to do the same, at least for now. Even though bowling had played such a critical role in my life and my sense of myself, my sobriety was a whole lot more important than bowling. (It would be two and a half years before Jack felt it was okay for me to bowl again. And even then, he strongly warned me to be careful about setting foot in a place that was so loaded for me.)

After Jack felt that I'd gotten a handle on the fourth step, he told me he was going to lead me through the fifth step. Here's what it is:

Step Five: Admitted to God, to ourselves and to another human being the exact nature of our wrongs.

But before we got into that, Jack said, he said he was going to take me down to a meeting in south Jersey where he had a speaking commitment.

"Who's speaking?" I says to him. "You?"

"I don't know," he says. "It ain't been determined yet."

So me and Jack and George and Billy drive down to Red Bank, New Jersey the next night. It turned out, it was a huge meeting – there must have been 300 people there – and Jack was leading it.

After the preliminaries Jack says, "I brought along some friends of mine, George and Billy and Bob. And our first speaker tonight will be Bob P."

Holy shit, man. I never spoke up at no meeting before. I was just a beginner at this. I was shaking all over. But I started speaking anyway.

"Hi," I says, "My name is Bob and I'm an alcoholic. I've been sober since May 6, 1992, and for that I am eternally grateful."

And I start telling people the whole story, getting raped and blinded when I was a kid, growing up to be a champion bowler, Uncle Raymond and John Gotti and Bobby Cabert, falling down the black hole of addiction, life on the streets, Brother Paul and Graymoor, and now my first attempts to claw my way up out of the darkness and into the Light.

Jack told me later that his original plan was to have each of us talk for about half an hour. But, I don't know, I just kept talking, pouring out my heart, pouring out my story, and when I finally finished I realized the time was almost up. Jack told me afterwards that I had talked for an hour and twenty minutes. Through that whole thing, I could see and hear that the other drunks and druggies in the room were listening intently. I'm sure that in many ways I was telling their story, too.

Anyway, when we were climbing back into the car after the meeting, Jack says to me, "Congratulations. You just done your fifth step."

"You're kidding," I says. "Really? That was easy!"

"Well, that's the way we do it in New Jersey."

Next came the sixth step:

Step Six: Were entirely ready to have God remove these defects of character.

Now we were starting to move into the realm of miracles – the realm of Father Paul. How am I supposed to remove my own defects of character? I can't, really. I can only ask God to do it, or to help me do it. In this process, I used the power of the pen every day, scribbling down these defects of character, putting them in the God box, and asking God to take them away. And gradually, I began to change. When somebody got up in my face with me, I began to learn not to get nasty back, not to bring up that angry, small, pissed-off alcoholic behavior. To try to step back into a place of calm and serenity. (Is this easy? Hell, no! In fact, without God's help, it's impossible!)

"Look," Jack says to me, "you gotta do this step work in AA, because in the future, if you get into a tough situation, it will work for the rest of your life. This is about fundamentally changing yourself, not just putting a bandaid on a problem."

I started to learn how to do basic life stuff like making commitments, planning ahead, showing up on time, keeping my word. Before, I'd hand you a whole shitload of promises, almost all of them lies, about what I was going to do or not do next week. I didn't realize that making commitments and sticking to them, just like showing up on time, was a matter of integrity, a matter of character. (Character? Integrity? In my former life, I had no idea what those words even meant.) But now I could say, simply and honestly: I commit to going to five meetings a week. To making coffee before the meeting. To joining a home group. To bringing a meeting to St. Claire's on the first Monday of every month. And of course, not picking up a drink or a drug.

My new, changed life also began to appear in other ways. I started trying to be completely honest, which was about as easy as learning to speak Chinese. Helping other people. And of course, no robbing, stealing or manipulating, which in my former life came as naturally as breathing. That, in fact, was a pretty good job description of what I spent most of my time doing. Now, everything had to always be on the up and up. I started paying attention to my own cleanliness, to taking care of my teeth, to going to doctor's appointments. As usual, I sometimes got carried away: I'd sometimes wash myself 30 times in a day, because of all those years on the street. It was like I couldn't wash myself hard enough, or often enough, to wipe away that feeling of shame and degradation.

Then came the seventh step:

Step Seven: Humbly asked Him to remove our shortcomings.

Again, this is all about miraculous stuff here. Now, instead of waking up someplace with a hangover and almost no memory of what happened last night – but this vague feeling of dread that it was probably pretty bad – I was waking with a sense of actual joy in my heart. At least, some or even most of the time. Just because you're sober don't mean you have no problems anymore. Far from it.

For a lot of alcoholics, getting sober means waking up to the fact that the life you've created is a huge unbelievable mess, that you owe people money, that you've got all kinds of physical problems or injuries caused by drinking, that your liver is fucked, you're in trouble financially, that various people hate you (and for good reason) and all the rest of it. The difference is that you're now confronting all this as an honest, sober, spiritual-minded person and not as a thieving drunk and a liar. Now, my greatest joy was thinking of ways that I could help other people without them knowing I did it. (And if that ain't a miracle, I don't know what is!)

The eighth and ninth steps kind of go together, Jack said, so we worked on them almost like a single step:

Step Eight: Made a list of all persons we had harmed, and became willing to make amends to them all.

Step Nine: Made direct amends to such people wherever possible, except when to do so would injure them or others.

Oh, man. This was painful. It filled me with shame and remorse to start making this list of all the people I harmed, especially the people I loved that I had harmed. But at least I felt shame and remorse. Before, I didn't feel nothing. I just saw a vague outline in front of me, not even a person, just a way of getting money to get high. If I had to lie, cheat or steal to get the money it didn't matter. Remorse? What was that? But now, when I wasn't completely numbed-out by dope or alcohol, I began to feel what I should have felt a long time ago.

Man, it hurt. And, one by one, where it was possible, I started making amends to people I had harmed. I'm sure were lots of people I'd wronged but I didn't even remember because I'd been in a blackout.

The biggest people I owed amends to, of course, were Debbie and Uncle Raymond. But I felt strongly it would be a bad idea to go back to Debbie – who was now married, with children – and bring up all this painful old shit from the past. Besides, her husband might have wanted to kill me. Later, I did happen to see Debbie across a crowded room, and she gave me a "dirty hello," like "hi, fuck you," so I knew there was a lot of unfinished business there. And Uncle Raymond – he wasn't looking for me no more, and I thought the best thing was to just stay away from him. So I wrote them all letters of apology, and then I burned them. Put them in the God box. Thank God for the God box.

Other people I was able to apologize to in person. I went to the owners of Eclipse Lanes, where Jackson Gist used to work, and apologized for all my bullshit and arguments and getting drunk during league play. I apologized to Joe Tolvay, a friend in the bowling world that I had borrowed a lot of money from, and then I paid him back. I apologized to Tommy Lorenzo, but he didn't seem to care. I apologized – or tried to – to Tommy's father, Rocco, but he didn't want to hear about it. I apologized to Gene and Al and the Lodi Lanes, for having to bar me from drinking and doing drugs in the bathroom, and all those noisy scenes with Debbie. I apologized to Adam Monks and my friend Tony, from Tri-State Telephone. There was a guy named Philly Pauchi, from Queens, who had been one of my chief enablers in the old days, but it turned out he was tremendously happy when I got sober. And on and on – there were so many people, actually, that I started writing it all down. (To write them all, I'd have to write another book!)

Then I started having to take care of all the driving violations I had stacked up. Amazingly enough, I didn't have no DWIs, just moving traffic violations, running red lights, and all that type of shit. But now that I was trying to clean up my own mess, I had to go to 16 to 20 different courtrooms. I had to pay, like, $20,000 in fines. But since I didn't have no money to pay them, the court took my license away for 5 or 6 years, until I could finish the payments.

I was also doing what is known as "living amends" – learning to live my life as a sober person, and doing right by everyone in my life, as I went along. My general approach to life became: I will stay sober every day and when the time comes to make some past wrong right, I'll make it right.

Later on, when I returned to bowling and started winning money in tournaments, I was happy to notice that nobody came after me to get the money I owed them after selling them some song-and-dance of I was dying of cancer or my mom was dying of cancer or whatever horseshit it might have been. Gradually, I was beginning to live a real life.

In the middle of all this step work, I went to Patsy's house. I wanted to make amends to her because she of all people was the one who never gave up on me, even though I dragged her through "the valley of the shadow of death." She was the one who loved the Bob Perry that was inside me, the one who had been lost and was now in the process of being found.

Patsy and I wound up starting the nonprofit that we called "Last Stop." It started out, actually, when I took this gig working as a volunteer drug and alcohol counselor at St. Claire's, in Boonton. I was doing the 2 pm to 10 pm shift, holding meetings, sharing how I got sober, trying to help people. I was also working at the intake desk, and every person I checked in was a mess. People who were freezing on the street, people dealing with fear, people out there detoxing (or not detoxing) all alone. We got a lot of low-bottom cases, and what they call "MICA" cases – mentally ill, chemically addicted, a lot of alcoholics from the street.

I guess you can understand why I was good at this job.

I noticed right away that a lot of people in treatment had lost their driver's licenses – if they had a driver's license at all – or they had other problems with the Department of Motor Vehicles. Since I'd had all kinds of problems with the DMV of my own, and had kind of started to figure out the system, my idea was to start a little nonprofit to help recovering alcoholics and addicts deal with the DMV. So that was the original idea.

But Patsy and I also noticed right away that a lot of these people had nowhere else to go, no next step, after they finished the program at St. Claire's. And they needed help, they needed information, about staying sober.

So we wound up renting an old train station in Pompton Plains, New Jersey, and set up shop. Our "business" – which didn't charge anything at all – helped recovering alcoholics and addicts find a referral to another, more long-term program, just like the Brothers at Graymoor had done for me. And we also became a nonprofit bookstore stocking recovery literature from all of the more than 100 Twelve Step programs in the country. We carried books not only from AA and NA (Narcotics Anonymous) but Overeaters Anonymous, Sexaholics Anonymous, Cocaine Anonymous, Crystal Meth Anonymous, Heroin Anonymous, Gamblers Anonymous,

Workaholics Anonymous, and all the others.

I worked at the store 40 or 50 hours a week, for nothing (except for fees from helping people get their licenses back). Over a couple of years, I bet I referred 300 to 500 people to rehabs and treatment centers. The only reason I could do it was because by this time I had a legit job that was paying me around $3,000 a month (more on that later). But the main reason was that I was trying to give back the spiritual gifts that had been given to me.

Patsy loved working at the store, and the people loved her. In fact, they loved her more than they loved me.

"Hey, where's your sister?" they'd say.

"Sorry, it's just me today," I'd say. "What can I get for you?"

Patsy had an awful lot of wisdom to share with people about loving someone — a spouse, a sibling, a relative, a dear friend — whose body has been taken over by the evil monster of addiction.

Eventually, after a couple of years, the city of Pompton Plains came in and took over the building under eminent domain, so we moved into a church around the corner. But we lost 80 percent of our business because people couldn't find us. So we shut Last Stop down. But we'd had a real good run of it while it lasted.

Running Last Stop was part of my step work, part of my recovery. Now, over time, me and Jack worked through the last three steps on the list.

Step 10: Continued to take personal inventory and when we were wrong promptly admitted it.

"Old habits die hard," as they say, and the job of changing into a new person, changing all my sleazeball junkie habits into the habits of a sober honest person would take a lifetime. But you can only do this work one day at a time, trying to pay attention to what you done wrong and correcting it as it happens.

No, it ain't easy.

Step 11: Sought through prayer and meditation to improve our conscious contact with God as we understood Him, praying only for knowledge of His will for us and the power to carry that out.

Step 12: Having had a spiritual awakening as the result of these steps, we tried to carry this message to alcoholics and to practice these principles in all our affairs.

Spiritual awakening? To my way of thinking, I had had a spiritual awakening before I even started the steps. I had had a personal encounter with Father Paul, who as far as I was concerned was God's messenger, the burning bush, the parting of the Red Sea, and every other miracle in the Good Book combined. He's the one that started me on the path to sobriety and to a new life. This book you're reading right now is a big part of the reason I got sober. My story only matters if it can help you, and I think it can. If nothing else, it shows you that if I can do it, anybody can. You don't need no angel – but if you're lucky, maybe you'll get one. Father Paul couldn't have appeared to a less-deserving person than me. But for some reason, he did. Who knows? Maybe it was because I was so undeserving. All I know is that I am blessed.

And I know you are, too.

13 WELCOME HOME

After St. Claire's, I got transferred to a behavior modification program in Glen Garden, New Jersey called Freedom House for, I think, six to eight months. When I first got there I had to work in the kitchen, and for the first 14 days I was in full blackout from society – no contact whatsoever. It was like: You're entering a new world, a new life. And I began the slow, painful work of trying to be honest with myself, trying to come to terms with the mess I made of things, trying to be sober.

Now, for the first time, I also started getting some of the medical attention I'd needed for a long time. One of the directors at Freedom House, a wonderful man named Frank, really started to focus on my nightmare dental problems left over from life on the streets. He arranged for me to go to a medical center where they gave me enough antibiotics to kill the infection in my mouth but not enough to kill the pain. It turned out that the infections in my teeth and gums had spread into the bone. So they had to crack the bone and pull the roots off the top of my mouth. It took 90 stitches to sew my gums back up again. Sure: They gave me Novocain and whatnot, but the pain was unbelievable.

After my bones and gums healed (it took months), a lady dentist spent a few more months molding a partial denture to replace my missing upper teeth. And once that was fitted, for the first time in six or seven years, I was able to eat regular food again, without too much pain.

Even so, while all this was going on, I'd sometimes get a chance to bowl. I went bowling one Sunday afternoon and bowled eleven strikes in a row, for a 279, but then I had to quit because the pain was too much. It was like: That old lion inside, the one who had been asleep for so long, was starting to come back.

During them early days of sobriety, there was one other person (besides Jack) that really helped me a lot. While I was still staying at Freedom

111

House, I had a day job working at a dry-cleaning place called Turpok's Cleaners. I'd work in the back all day, folding sheets and towels and whatnot – they had a big contract to do all the laundry for local motels – and the person I worked with most of the time was this wonderful, beautiful, petite little old black lady named Marie. Marie was in her late sixties, semi-retired, and just a lovely, lovely lady. She had been through some rough times in her life. She had pain and regret in her life. She'd made serious mistakes.

But she also had eighteen years of sobriety and she had this passion for AA and the spiritual gifts it can give to people. Her passion was to share what she had, to give it away to me and anyone else who would listen to her. "You can only keep it if you give it away," she'd say.

Standing there folding those warm sheets and towels in the back room at the Turpok's, Marie talked to me all day long about the program and her experiences and what she had learned in sobriety. She became kind of my First Mother of sobriety and AA. She'd say these wise sayings, usually very quietly, that were so profound sometimes it took me a week to grasp what she meant. Like she'd say, "time takes time," and what I finally figured out she meant was that the mess I'd made of my life would take a long time to clean up, but that I had to be calm and patient and, most important, try to change my life one day at a time and not all at once. She told me that all the sadness and regret I had over my failed relationship with Debbie, all the ways I done them wrong, would all get straightened out sooner or later so long as I just stayed sober, did the steps, and kept going to meetings. It was so simple even I could understand it. I'd leave work every day feeling so good it was almost like I been to church. And I thought I was just folding sheets and towels from the Holiday Inn, in the back room of a drycleaners in New Jersey. One of the most amazing things to me was that Marie's life and experiences, as a drunk and a junkie and now as a sober person, were so similar to my own. Here I was this white smart-ass fallen pro bowler in his forties with all these mobbed-up friends, and there she was this little old poor black lady from Flemington, but yet we had both done all kinds of things we regretted, had woke up out of blackouts a thousand times, had lived lives of supreme self-centeredness, and now we were having to confront it all so that we would never have to go back there again. The story of addiction and recovery is actually an old, old story that's shared by millions of people around the world. Figuring this out helped me get past this idea that Bob Perry was some kind of unique creation – what people in the rooms called the idea of my "terminal uniqueness" – and was instead just a beautiful child of God, like everybody else.

My friend Marie was there folding sheets at the drycleaner's one day when I started feeling really faint and dizzy. I grabbed onto the edge of the folding table, but I just collapsed onto the floor. Marie was there when I hit that particular bottom. She called an ambulance, and it came and took me to Huntington County Medical Center, where I stayed for about fifteen hours. Turns out, I'd had a heart attack. A doc at the hospital told me he thought it might be related to my withdrawal from alcohol and dope, and to all the anxiety I was going through. He also said it might be related to all that poison from the infections in my mouth. A couple of days later, after I got out of the hospital, I went to a meeting at Freedom House, had a cup of expresso and collapsed again with another heart attack. They sent me back to Huntington County hospital again, and this time I had to stay there two and a half weeks, first in the ICU. They diagnosed me as having something called pericarditis. The docs told me they found black spots around my heart from all those years of booze, coke and crack. (How ironic that I had "black spots on my heart.")

Freedom House was only 20 miles from Jack's house, so I got to see him more often. It was while I was staying there that I went this huge AA convention called the Area 44 Convention. There were maybe a thousand people there, with 24-hour-a-day meetings, speakers, and the whole deal. So I'm walking into the dining room for breakfast on my first morning there and I practically run into a lady I had not seen in more than ten years. Her name was Irene and she had been one of the best women bowlers in the New York area and one of the best on the East coast. She was always a lot of fun, but she was also a heavy drinker – maybe even more than me. When she laid eyes on me, it was like her face just lit up.

"Oh, my God!" she says. "It's you!"

"Hi, Irene!" I says.

"Bobby! What are you doing here?"

"Well, I'm in the world of sobriety now. I couldn't live like that no more."

"How long are you sober?"

"Over a year."

I guess Irene could see that sparkle in my eye. Then she breaks down, crying.

"I never thought you'd make it! I could see it was getting really bad for you, and I prayed for you for years to be in here. And now my prayers are answered!"

Irene told me that "booze destroyed my life" and AA had saved it. She'd been sober for, I think, ten or twelve years, but she hadn't bowled in years and couldn't even go into bowling alleys anymore because of all the memories, and the fact that booze was so much a part of the sport.

"Where are you living?" she says.

"I'm at Freedom House," I says. "Thanks for praying for me, Irene." I wasn't exactly a Catholic altar boy no more. But I knew about the spiritual power of prayer, and the power of the program of AA.

***

Over the following weeks and months – years – through our work at Last Stop, Patsy and I began to renew the love and friendship we had once had for each other. The love that – incredibly – had never been lost. She even stood up for me when the guy who started Freedom House, a guy name Fred, started coming after me.

As I say, I'm not a guy who knows how to shut up about stuff, and in the groups I'd been telling people about my life, and how I was once this famous bowler. Well, the owner, Fred, didn't believe me. He thought I was lying. He thought I was having "delusions of grandeur," or whatever, and if I was being untruthful and living in this fantasyland, I could never get better. The only thing was, it was all true. So one day I'm going through some almanac or encyclopedia book or something, and here's this list of champion bowlers from recent years, and there's my name: Bob Perry. So I go take this book to show Fred.

"There's my name – right there," I says. "Bob Perry. Firestone Tournament of Champions."

"So?" he says. "That's not even your real name! Your paperwork says 'Bob Purzycki.' You're still lying!"

He'd heard of Bob Perry, he knew who he was, and I sure as hell wasn't him. I also told people that Tommy Lorenzo had a racehorse that he named Bob Perry. True story. But this guy Fred said he was going to throw my ass out of the program because I was a liar, because I was living a lie, and nobody can succeed in recovery unless they're standing in the truth.

I'd been on the streets so long that I had no form of identification at all – driver's license? Forget about it – so it was really hard for me to prove my point. So finally Patsy and Jeannie come to visit.

"I'm getting thrown out of the program," I says.

"Whaddya mean you're getting thrown out of the program? What for?" Patsy says.

"Because they claim I'm lying about being Bob Perry, the bowler."

"Well, how come they don't believe you?"

"I dunno. Maybe I don't look like a famous bowler." (Actually, I never did.)

So Jeannie and Patsy have a meeting with Fred.

"Your brother is living a lie, he keeps telling everybody he's Bob Perry, he shows people Bob Perry's name in the encyclopedia, he claims there's a racehorse named after him. He can't get well if he's a pathological liar."

"Why do you think he's lying? He is Bob Perry," Patsy tells the guy. "He's my brother. He's not lying. It's all true."

Eventually the guy was forced to back down, but I think he was embarrassed by all this and he kept being nasty to me. Hey, I couldn't help it if I was Bob Perry, the famous bowler. Or at least, I was Bob Perry, the famous bowler. And now I was becoming that person again.

Fred hated that. He really did. After I got sent to the Huntington County Medical Center for that heart attack, because I was indigent and maybe because I could pose a health risk to Freedom House (by dying), Fred didn't want to let me back in. I think maybe he just wanted an excuse not to let me back in. Then he suggested that, once I got better, maybe I could agree to give ten percent of my earnings to Freedom House, since the taxpayers were paying my way. But I told him that wasn't true – United Way paid $375 a week for me to stay there, they took half my pay, half went to Freedom House and half went to the bank (to create a kind of forced savings account) and I got twenty dollars a week for spending money. The taxpayer wasn't out a dime. So anyway, we had a dispute that never got resolved.

Before too long, Fred arranged to have my stay at Freedom House terminated. He put my stuff outside the building and I never seen him again, even though I owed him a debt of gratitude for the time I spent there.

Patsy came to pick me up when I left Freedom House. She'd agreed to take me back to her house in Pompton Plains and let me stay there a couple of days until I figured out what I was going to do next. When she let me in the front door of her house, there was her husband James, standing there. My pissed-off brother-in-law. The guy who had threatened to send me to an early grave if he ever caught me in his house.

"Welcome home," he says, reaching out to give me this huge hug. I mean, you could have knocked me over with a feather.

Then he sits me down at the kitchen table.

"I just want to say, I wish you the best," he says. "I'm here to help you."

This is the same man I robbed, cheated and stole from. And he was, at the time, a sick man. He had prostate cancer and he wasn't doing too good.

"I don't know what I can do to help you," I says to James. "I mean, I done you wrong. I almost wrecked you and Patsy's marriage, and I know you love her. If there's anything I can do to make things right, please tell me. Because I'm just trying to do the next right thing, trying to make up for everything I done wrong. I'm trying to live my life one day at a time."

And it's a funny thing – a really funny thing, if you think about it – but James later told me that the whole idea of "living one day at a time" was the greatest gift I ever gave him, since he was struggling to face the possibility of his own death by cancer. It really helped him. After all, the stuff you learn in AA is not just about learning how to quit living like a drunk. It's about learning how to live.

There's some line in a blues song that goes, "If thoughts could kill, we'd all be dead." But, by the grace of God, somehow or other, it's possible for people to be transformed by love and actually change. And if both James and I could change, anybody can. He turned out to be a wonderful man. I had gone to James and Patsy's house to stay for a couple of nights. I wound up staying for a year and a half.

14 THE ROAD TO HELL

Living at James and Patsy's house in Pompton Plains, with the nice lawn and clean sheets and all the comforts of home, was like getting a second shot at life. I was going to meetings all the time, trying to get my life together, and learning how to live with a "new employer" – God – running the ship.

I made contact with my old friend Tony, who had this business called Tristate Telephone, which was where they'd set up a whole telephone system for movie and TV sets for shows being filmed in New York. He had a production office at 57 Columbus Circle. Me and Tony were great friends so he gave me a job, basically as a gopher. But it was a brutal routine, where I had to wake up at 5 a.m. to catch the bus into the city, get to Manhattan by 6:30 or 7, work all day, come back to Jersey and catch an 8 o'clock meeting almost every night. And Tony was tough on me, too, even though he loved me. They'd have all this food laid out for the crews – we worked Law & Order and other big shows – and he'd give me a raft of shit if I touched any of it. For a recently homeless person, all them tiny hot dogs and pickles and cheese was practically irresistible. So after six months or so, I told Patsy I was looking for another job.

At some point I got back with an old bowling friend, Mike Foti, and we set what was then the world record for doubles bowling. (That means two guys bowling three games each.) I threw 267, 279 and 299, and he bowled 794. That stood in the record books for quite awhile. I mean, setting that record like that – it set fire to my old dream of winning the Super Bowl High Roller – the big kahuna, the biggest-money national tournament in the country, the place all the best bowlers in the country went to battle it out for the big cup.

"Hey," Mike says, "there's this guy I know in Union City who owns a bowling alley called New Bowl-Rite Lanes. He knows about you, of course

117

– he thinks you can help with his business, just by being around, being well-known, helping people bowl, whatever. He's a Polack – C.J. Egnosky. His wife's name is Annie Lord. Great people. They're having this doubles tournament over there, so why don't you enter? Get to know these guys a little?"

So me and my friend Adam Monks go over there to Union City to this kind of slightly seedy bowling alley called New Bowl-Rite Lanes, and we bowl in this tournament and we do okay. This guy C.J., he shows me all around the bowling alley, very interested in me and all. I hit it off with C.J. right away – a short, thick guy, a few years younger than me, who was really warm and funny. He showed me around his bowling business, which was very near to a pretty rundown, mostly-Latino area, almost but not quite a ghetto. It was only two blocks from Jersey City (this was before the yuppies started invading Hoboken). Most of the people in the bowling alley looked like Mexicans or Puerto Ricans, and some blacks.

"Whaddya think?" C.J. says.

"Whaddya mean, what do I think?"

"Well, would you want to work here? I can't pay you a lot of money, but I'd love for you to work here. I think your reputation, and your knowledge, would help my business."

I thought about this for a little while.

"I don't know if I can take this job," I says. "Look: I'm sober almost three years, and my sobriety is more important than bowling."

C.J.'s face kind of brightens up.

"I know all about that," he says. "I'm sober eight years. And my sponsor is my wife Annie's dad. He's got twenty-five years. How does $150 a week sound?"

"Well, that sounds all right. But you're going to get a lot of slack for hiring me – you know that, right?" I says. "I used to be pretty famous, but nobody has seen me in years. Nobody knew where I was. And I'd rather just skip the whole story."

"That's okay," C.J. says. "I can handle that."

So I went to work for C.J. and Annie, at the New Bowl-Rite Lanes in Union City, New Jersey. It was sometime during the winter of 1994.

***

C.J. and Annie were the most wonderful people I'd ever met. Not only were they sweet, funny and kind, they knew all about the disease of alcoholism, so I didn't really have to explain where I been. They were just the greatest friends a guy could find.

So I started working in the bowling alley, helping to run the pro shop, working the front desk, cleaning the lanes, whatever needed doing. And it didn't take me long to notice that C.J. and Annie, my great new friends, were getting robbed blind. See, a lot of it was cash business, because people didn't use credit cards much. So I'd see, say, the girl at the snack bar charge a guy five bucks for a hamburger, but only put three bucks in the cash register. She wouldn't ring it up. I saw the same thing happening all over, at the ball rental counter, at the front desk, everywhere except the bar, where a girl named Carol, who was honest as the day was long, was in charge.

I guess I noticed these things because, after all, I had once been a junkie and a thief.

So I go to C.J. and tell him what I'm seeing.

"Is everybody stealing from me?" he asks me.

"Yeah," I says, "Everybody is stealing from you. Everybody except me and Carol."

You could see C.J.'s face just fall. I didn't quite realize this at the time, but financially, that bowling alley had become a nightmare for them. They had already lost their home, and had had to move in with the in-laws. But they still had all this debt hanging over their heads, part of it left over from a previous business partner who had been stealing from them, too.

Why do the good people, the honest people, get targeted by the crooks? Because they're honest, and it takes them a long time to realize they're getting ripped off.

The long and the short of it was that C.J. and Annie owed something like $57,000 in back rent on the building, and the landlord had started getting heavy with them. He was a guy who worked for the Food Town grocery chain and owned a couple of buildings. Now he was starting to get nasty with my new friends. Finally he sent over a guy named Don Cardillo to be his hired tough guy. Don Cardillo was the owner's henchman, the manager of his buildings. He walked like a tough guy and talked like a wise guy. He started to get real threatening.

"You better come up with the money you owe, or else," he'd say to them. And Annie, she was just this little sweet-faced woman, probably didn't weigh more than 125 pounds, she'd just burst into tears. A lot of the back rent situation had to do with their deadbeat former partner, but the fact was, the rent was owed and Cardillo was gunning for them.

Finally one day he comes into the bowling alley and confronts C.J. I just happened to be standing there, and I saw the whole thing unfold. The situation sort of escalated, real quick.

Finally Cardillo just says, "I want all my money by Monday, or else."

And at this point, I just couldn't help but jump in. I'd seen guys like this all my life. I knew Gotti and Cabert and them guys. And this guy was just a fugazi, a fake.

"Or else?" I says to the guy. "What's the 'or else'?"

"I'm not talking to you, Jack," Cardillo says. "Who the fuck are you?"

"I'm their friend."

"Well, you need to be quiet."

"I'm not going to be quiet. What are you threatening my friends with?"

"Look: This here is none of your business. Keep your nose out of it."

"I work here. They're my friends. How about this? If you got some disagreement, that's fine. We can work it out. How about you come back here on Monday, and I'll bring a friend, and we'll work it out. Okay?"

Cardillo paused a couple of beats, thinking.

"Well, I don't give a shit who you bring Monday. You just get your ass here and bring me my money."

And Cardillo goes strutting out of there, like a little rooster.

C.J. and Annie were really scared. They weren't used to this. They didn't have the money to pay the guy – so they were freaking out.

"Look," I says to them, "I can help you. I've got an old friend who can help you."

"Yeah? Who's that?" C.J. says.

"My Uncle Raymond," I says.

To be honest, I had never mentioned Uncle Raymond – or John Gotti, Bobby Cabert, or any of them other scary guys – to C.J. and Annie. I never told them I was actually on pretty friendly terms with some pretty spooky people. I just wanted to help them. I was just trying to be a friend. I never really thought it through, which is what you're supposed to do when you're trying to be sober.

They say the road to hell is paved with good intentions. Well, I never really understood what that meant. But now, even though I'd stacked together three years of sobriety and was only trying to help a little old lady across the street, like a Boy Scout, my whole dark past was about to come back to haunt me, like mummies rising out of the grave in Night Of The Living Dead.

"C.J.," I says, "it's to time to go see Uncle Raymond.".

15 THE RETURN OF UNCLE RAYMOND

During those long dark empty years on the streets of New York, when I was a dead man walking, a vampire, "nothing but a chemical," as my sister later said, there was one person besides Patsy whose heart was breaking over me, who worried and wondered about me constantly, even though I never knew it at the time. That person was the man I knew as Uncle Raymond. Only me and Bobby Schumacher called Raymond "Uncle," because he did not have any children of his own and always treated the two of us as if we were his nephews. Really, more like his sons. You know: Bright kids with lots of promise who fucked up on a regular basis, and had to get our chops busted from time to time. Kids who wouldn't listen to their real fathers.

Raymond was a Polack (his Polish wife hardly spoke any English at all) and he liked it that I was Polish on my dad's side. In them days, of course, everybody was pretty much divided into ethnic enclaves in New Jersey, with the Polacks sticking with the Polacks, the Italians sticking with the Italians, the blacks with the blacks and the gangsters with the gangsters. Paterson wasn't no "big happy family" – it was a whole bunch of unhappy families that didn't really talk to each other much.

To everybody else except me and Bobby Schumacher, Raymond was known as "the fat man" or "fat Raymond." He wasn't fat, though; he was just stout, like a fucking oak tree, and strong as an ox. I once seen him tip over a full barrel that must have weighed two thousand pounds. (This was in the middle of the night, on some back road, unloading a truck for a "swag" job – meaning, moving stolen merchandise – but that's another story.) Just in his physical presence, the man commanded respect. All the connected guys used to use the word "weight" to describe someone who was powerful, who was feared. Well, Uncle Raymond was a guy who had weight, and he knew how to throw it around. Maybe they called him "fat

Raymond" not so much because he was obese but because he walked into a room like a fucking Mack truck. Uncle Raymond had a scary side, especially when he'd been drinking Manhattans with VO, but he also had a very sweet side, too. He loved to help people. There was this thing where you could pay ten bucks and get to write to a kid somewhere, and he spent hundreds of dollars, writing to them kids he didn't even know. He was in the trucking business, and if he came across some farmer that had a load of hay that needed to be moved, he'd do it for the guy for free. He loved doing shit like that.

He also looked after the people that were loyal to him, that belonged to him. People like me. Him and Cabert and Gotti: Their whole way of living was like something out of some ancient time, like maybe a thousand years ago, when all the peasants were protected by a local king or a baron or whatever, at the same time they feared the guy to death.

Raymond was 17 years older than me, so he was not so much like a substitute father as the big brother I never had. He had dirty blonde hair, wore glasses and smoked constantly. When he wanted to tell me something serious, something important, he would shove his glasses down to the end of his nose and peer over the tops of them at me. His eyes were like fucking laser beams.

"Perry!" he'd say, as if he were beating me over the head with a blunt object. "Listen to me!"

And I always listened.

Because Uncle Raymond was the smartest man I ever knew. Everything I ever learned about life, I learned from him.

At the racetrack, where he loved to be more than anywhere else, Uncle Raymond was like a goddam Rhodes Scholar. He and his crew – the small group of guys that hung around with him, like a school of little fish following a big fish – they were known as the best grass-race bettors anywhere. Raymond could consistently take short money – say, three or four hundred dollars – and turn it into ten or fifteen thousand, like magic. He did it by understanding breeding and genetics, things almost nobody understood at the time, by studying the Daily Racing Form, by watching and listening and understanding. He was a genius at the track. Back in them days, there wasn't too much horse-racing on TV, so you had to go to the track yourself. So Uncle Raymond and his crew would drive to the track – a guy known as Tom Bill, who was a cop from Bloomfield, New Jersey; a guy named Skinner; a schoolteacher named Anthony Margotta, Tony Margotta (who was actually Bobby Cabert's nephew); and me, the hotshot bowler, the kid.

When grass season came around, like in April in New York, Uncle Raymond and his crew would go to all the Jersey tracks, Garden State in Monmouth, New Jersey; Pimlico in Laurel, Maryland; Delaware Park in

Dover, Delaware; Philly Park outside Philadelphia; and then later, after it was built, the Meadowlands, in East Rutherford, New Jersey. Sometimes they'd even go down to Churchill Downs, in Kentucky, or other tracks down in Florida. One time, I remember, these guys actually won $365,000 at the track. I also remember that, except the money Raymond won, all that money was gone within a couple of weeks. (Uncle Raymond lived modestly, in a modest house, and was never extravagant about anything except fancy meals and booze. When he won big at the track, he handed the money over to his wife, whose name was a Polish version of Maryann that I could never quite pronounce. Then he'd start betting again, as if he hardly had any money at all. The whole thing was a big mind game for him, not a way to live fancy like a Mob guy.)

In some ways I was kind of a gopher for Uncle Raymond, picking up the Racing Form and delivering it to his house, going to the track if he couldn't make it to place his bets, and bringing back his money if he won. Later I realized that letting me handle the money like that was his way of testing me to see if I could be trusted. And I could be trusted, at least in them early days before booze and dope took over my life.

Another thing about Uncle Raymond, besides his brains, was his guts. He didn't seem to be afraid of anything or anybody. If you were in a war, you'd want him on your side. He was one of the few people who didn't even seem to be afraid of Bobby Cabert, a very connected guy who later became a made man in the Gambino crime family. Raymond was the only one who could calm Cabert down when he got all riled up and drunk and angry and dangerous. "It's no good to be angry," he'd say to Cabert, and then he'd just get up and fucking leave. He didn't care. He wasn't scared, even though Cabert – who was his best friend – could be about as scary as any human being can be.

When you "belonged" to Uncle Raymond, like I did, you knew you were being looked after, not just by him but his whole crew and all these other people who knew him – older men you might never even know were keeping an eye you, making sure you were safe. I felt loved by him (and, sometimes, dominated and controlled by him, especially when I was fucking up and he didn't like it.)

Uncle Raymond was a guy who grew up in New Jersey and had been in "the rackets" his whole life without once ever getting arrested. Being in the rackets just meant figuring out how to make money on the street, sometimes legally but usually illegally or semi-illegally, without getting caught or resorting to real serious violence like killing somebody. Yeah, sure: Cabert and other people Raymond knew were in the Mob. Shit, half the people I grew up with in New Jersey at that time were connected. Everybody knew who belonged to who – oh, Billy, Vinnie, Johnnie and Rocco, they're in such-and-such a crew, and all like that – but Uncle

Raymond was not in the Mob. He was a rackets guy, not a Mob guy.

What Uncle Raymond actually did for a living was run a trucking company that delivered stuff to foundries and scrapyards and dealers all up and down the East coast. But there was sort of a sunny side to this business, a legal side, and a shady side, and I think most of it was on the shady side. Like he'd run a truckload of scrap metal down to some foundry in South Carolina or Alabama or wherever. After he'd gotten unloaded he'd look around for something to carry back, so he wouldn't be running an empty load back to New Jersey.

"Hey, what's in all them barrels over there?"

"That's the scrap metal they scraped out of the furnaces," some guy would say.

"How about if I take those barrels off you for five hundred bucks?"

And if the guy agreed, they'd make a cash deal on the spot, no papers or nothing (since the guy didn't actually own the stuff, of course), Uncle Raymond would load up the truck and then he'd "run the road" all the way back to New Jersey – getting around all the way stations on the Interstate by taking back roads, which he knew like the back of his hand. Back in Newark or Hoboken, where he knew all the scrap dealers, he'd sell the load to some guy and triple his money because he bought the shit for pennies on the dollar.

Uncle Raymond always said there's a million dollars in junk – scrap metal, auto parts, even dirt – and he always seemed to be able to find it.

Uncle Raymond would also sometimes get these swag jobs and I'd sometimes go along to help, in the dead of night, on some back road somewhere. Raymond would pay me right away, in cash, of course, and I would immediately forget that any of it had ever happened. I had a really lousy memory that way. I knew what I was doing wasn't legit, but working for Uncle Raymond, I always made a day's pay, and good pay, too – a lot of times even more than I could make bowling. Raymond used to like to say he was in the iron and steel business.

"My mother irons, and I steal."

One time Uncle Raymond goes down to Arkansas or somewhere, and he needs a load of something to bring back. Turns out one of the big businesses down there is rice, so he winds up coming back with something like thirty thousand fucking pounds of rice. So he figures out a way to sell this rice to all these Chinese restaurants in Bergen and Hudson Counties for six cents a pound (after he'd bought the shit for two cents a pound or whatever). So one night I'm delivering this truckload of rice to this Chinese restaurant called Jade Fountain in North Arlington, New Jersey (one of Bobby Cabert and Uncle Raymond's favorite hangouts) when all of a sudden this black car pulls up in the alley behind the restaurant, where I got the truck parked.

Some guy jumps out, and I can see he's got a long gun, a rifle or a shotgun or something.

"You no deliver rice!" he yells, pointing the thing at me.

"What are you talking about, 'Me no deliver rice'? Listen, you don't know whose rice this is."

"Me no care. You no deliver rice!"

"Listen, man, you need to put that gun down," I says. "I'll be right back."

So I go inside where Uncle Raymond and Cabert are sitting in a booth, getting wasted on Manhattans made with VO, their favorite. (Half the time, he and Cabert would get so wasted at Jade Fountain they'd start having these vicious arguments, and then they'd have to call a cab to get them home.)

"Listen, Raymond, you need to come outside," I tell him. "I gotta problem."

"What problem?"

"There's this fucking Chinese guy looking to shoot me, OK?"

So him and Cabert come outside.

"What's the problem?" they ask the guy, who is not waving his gun around anymore.

"You no deliver rice to Chinese!"

"You know whose rice this is?" Raymond says. "It's my rice." Uncle Raymond is about twice the size of this little Chinese dude. "Who you work for?"

"Harry Moon, he the owner."

"Well, why don't we get Harry Moon and have a little sit-down over the rice." Uncle Raymond calms the guy down, and later everybody goes down to Canal Street in the city and meets with this Chinese Mob guy. "You not allowed to sell my people rice," he said.

"Why not?" Uncle Raymond says.

"Only Chinese sell rice to Chinese."

"Well, how about if I sell it to you, and not just to all these restaurants, and then you sell it to them," Uncle Raymond suggested. "I'll give you a good price. There's just one thing: You've got to buy it all."

The Chinese Mob guy takes a minute to think about it. You can just see the wheels turning in his brain.

"No problem," he says finally. "You give me good price, I take it all."

So next time Uncle Raymond takes a truckload of scrap down to Arkansas, he comes back with, like, thirty thousand pounds of rice. He delivers it to this Chinese guy in New York. A few weeks later, he comes back from Arkansas with another truckload of rice and delivers it to the guy. Then the next time, I get the job of driving this truck filled with fifteen tons of rice to the guy in New York. When I get there he comes out, and he's yelling at me.

"No more rice!"

"You said you was gonna buy it all," I says to him.

"No more rice! Tell your uncle, no more rice!"

The Mob guy had enough rice by now to last him three fucking years. And he'd learned the biggest lesson in the world: Don't make deals with Raymond, especially after you tried pushing him around.

***

So anyway, after all those years on the street, and during the first years of my recovery, Uncle Raymond had been gone from my life. Although I thought about him all the time, in all the years since my life disappeared down the dark hole of addiction I had seen Uncle Raymond only once and that time just by accident.

At the time, I was still living with Patsy and James, working for Tony in the city. One weekend I took the cheap bus to the Meadowlands, and I was walking along the rail down by the track and there was Uncle Raymond sitting there in the front row, wearing a Frank Sinatra hat, smoking, as always. This huge block of a man, full of power, with the Racing Form folded under his arm.

"Perry!" he yells, in that gravelly, growly voice. "How ya doin'?"

"I'm doing good, Raymond," I says, genuinely shocked and also happy to see him.

I was a little bit on edge, too, because of all the people I done wrong when I was on the street, and all them blackouts. I wasn't entirely sure I hadn't done Uncle Raymond wrong. He gets up off the seat – he's graying, and he's gained weight – and he walks towards me. He gives me this big hug, and then we chat it up a little. I told him, among other things, that I been sober three years already.

"If you need help, come and see me," he says, very close and earnest, just as we're parting. "I love you. I'm proud of you. Please let me know if you need anything."

I remembered that encounter at the Meadowlands when C.J. and Annie started getting in trouble at the bowling alley, and that's why I decided to go see "the fat man," a man I once loved more than my own father. C.J. and I drove over to Raymond's modest little house in North Arlington. I asked C.J. to wait in the car and knocked on the door. Uncle Raymond's wife, Maryann, answers the door. Maryann always loved me.

"Bobby here!" she shouts. "Bobby here!"

Then she reaches out and grabs my face in her hands.

"Oh, my God, you're beautiful!" she says.

I was clean and sober, dressed nice, and I even had teeth. It was great to see her after all I'd been through. Uncle Raymond had this downstairs room all fixed up, with an easy chair and a TV and all. It was like the lion's lair, nice and safe and cool down there. I go downstairs and there's Raymond sitting there like the Laz-E-Boy king. He'd gained enough weight that I guess he would have had trouble getting up the stairs. He beamed when he looked at me.

"Perry!" he says. "How ya doin?"

He always said that. We chatted it up, and after a little while I get around to the reason I came.

"I need to talk to you," I says. "I got a problem. See, I'm working in Union City at this bowling alley, owned by a couple of friends of mine, C.J. and Annie. C.J.'s a Polack."

"Yeah, I know – New Bowl-Rite Lanes," he says. Uncle Raymond always seemed to know everything, at least everything that was happening to people he cared about.

He seemed to have an army of Jackson out there.

"Well, this little sawed-off fugazi wiseguy named Don Cardillo is really leaning on them about a bill for back rent. It's like fifty-seven thousand dollars. They're shittin' bricks over this, Raymond. They don't have no money. They already lost their house. And the thing is, most of it is left over from a crooked partner they had, a guy who was robbing them blind."

Uncle Raymond is glaring at me over the tops of his glasses, just burning into me with his eyeballs. You can see his mind working, calculating.

"So the debt is legit?"

"Yeah. But it's not even their fault. C.J. is the best friend a man could have – he's eight years sober, and he's helping me save my life."

"So whaddya want me to do?"

"We just want you to tell this guy to back off. Get him to leave us alone."

"What do I get out of it?"

"You get to help me. And I think C.J. would pay you for your help."

"Why does this guy Cardillo or whatever it is think he's somebody?"

"This guy thinks he's everybody. He won't back off."

Uncle Raymond looks me over, considering. You know, he loved me, he considered me almost like a son. He was happy to see that I was cleaned up and sober. He could see that I cared for these people. And C.J. was a fellow Polack.

"OK," he says finally. "Bring this guy C.J. by to see me."

"He's waiting out in the car."

So I went out there and brought C.J. downstairs, and the two of them really hit it off.

Finally Uncle Raymond says to me, "OK, make the meeting."

"How about Monday morning, 10:30?"

"Fine. But I gotta go get somebody."

"Who?"

"Nicky the Plumber."

Nicky "the Plumber" was, like, seventy years old, a halfass wiseguy. He was about as threatening as, well, a seventy-year-old plumber. But he was part of Raymond's crew, a guy who was on the inside of Raymond's world, a guy who knew where all the bodies were buried (so to speak). I really don't know why Uncle Raymond wanted him to come along. But, unfortunately, the fact that he wanted Nicky the Plumber to come along reminded me of something I wasn't really admitting to myself. Look, let's face it: The only reason I had suggested that Uncle Raymond get involved at all was because he knew the guy who knew the guy who knew the guy. He was connected. He was scary. He had "weight." He could help C.J. and Annie, innocent parties, by threatening the shit out of this guy Cardillo, not personally, but through the guy who knew the guy. It was like Bobby Cabert once said to me: If the Mob comes after you, you'll never see it, and you'll never feel it. It will just get done.

Uncle Raymond wasn't going to off the guy, of course, but he was going to figure a way to put a hurt on him – maybe a big hurt – at a distance. But my dilemma was this: I had been sober three years. I had admitted that I was powerless over alcohol and dope, that I had completely failed to live my life without the help of God. I was walking on this new path, a path of honesty and integrity and helping others, a spiritual path. So what the fuck was I doing dragging in a connected guy to threaten somebody over an unpaid debt? By doing this, I was reaching back into my dark past. I was bringing all the old ghosts back to life. But now I was pushing all this down into the memory hole, the blackout hole, and trying to forget about it. I was just trying to help a friend, I told myself.

Little did I know I was about the begin one of the darkest chapters of my life.

16 THE DEAL GOES DOWN

So then the most amazing thing happens.

The deal goes down, and I wind up a hero. No shit! Uncle Raymond and Nicky the Plumber have a meeting with that little prick Don Cardillo in the bar at the bowling alley, at 10:30 that Monday morning. When Cardillo shows up, he's in a bad mood, and he don't want to hear nothing about how we're going to make no deals. He just wants his money or he's going to throw C.J. and Annie out on their ass. But then Uncle Raymond and Nicky the Plumber and Cardillo walk into the bar – it's got them swinging half-doors, like one of them old-time saloons in the wild west movies – and I can hear them talking and then the talking turns to laughing, and when they come out like an hour later it's like they're old Army buddies or some damn thing.

"How youse guys doing?" Cardillo says, all jolly, when he walks past me and another guy standing there at the front desk. I'd never heard him talk like that before.

"Uh – we're doin' OK."

"See youse tomorrow!" he says to Raymond, like Raymond was his long-lost chum, and then he goes swaggering out in that little sawed-off tough-guy way he had.

I was totally shocked. But it turns out, these guys all got along great. They had friends in common. They knew the same neighborhoods. They worked out a deal about how C.J. and Annie could pay back the debt, in small payments, over time, even though the business wasn't doing well and it would be tough and slow. But nobody was getting heavy or making threats or nothing. Everybody was happy. Cardillo was happy, C.J. and Annie were happy, Uncle Raymond was happy and I was happy. I felt useful. C.J. had a friend, and everything was going to work out.

Like I say, I was a fucking hero.

Or so I thought.
***

About this same time, in the winter of 1995, I ran into my old friend Tommy Lorenzo at the racetrack. At least, I seen him at a distance, standing at the rail with that good-for-nothing kid Steve that he was always with now. Steve and I didn't get along at all – I knew what he was up to, trying to suck up all Tommy's family money, and Steve knew that I knew. In fact, me and Tommy had had a big argument over Steve, and for awhile we weren't speaking.

I had also figured out that Tommy had a big secret (or at least, he thought it was a secret). He and Steve lived together, and they weren't just roommates. Tommy was gay. But I still loved him and cared about him, and it shocked me and saddened me to see that now, even at fifty yards, standing there in the broad daylight, Tommy looked absolutely terrible. He was only ten years older than me, but he looked old enough to be my father. It turned out that Tommy was dying of AIDS – in fact, he only had a few more months to live. That was Steve's gift to him. I felt really bad when I seen Tommy looking like that. I loved him. He had been my best friend.

Tommy and I had had a big fight over one other, more important thing, too. By then, I was three years sober, and I had tried to help Tommy get sober, too. One time I actually drove him up to St. Christopher's Inn, dropped him off, and he left that place so fast he actually beat me back home. Another time, I helped him get sober five days, and one other time he made it thirty days, but he always went back out. He just didn't have the heart for it.

"You gotta get sober," I says to Tommy one time.

"You gotta leave me alone," he says.

In the old days, of course, Tommy Lorenzo and I had been like Butch Cassidy and the Sundance Kid – two alcoholic addicts who were just thick as thieves, feeding on each other's addictions to booze, crack, coke, or whatever else we could get into. Then I sobered up, and Steve moved in with Tommy. And Steve didn't want me coming around no more. I tried to warn Tommy that Steve was no good, but he was sick and he wasn't listening. (He was just like me in the old days.) For awhile, we weren't talking at all. But as his death got closer, Tommy and I became real friends again. And we were still friends – real, true friends – the day Tommy died.

I went to Tommy's funeral with my sisters Patsy and Jeannie. Just as I was walking into the front room of the funeral home, I walked past my old flame Debbie, leaving the building with her husband Ron. I caught her eye for just a second and we just kind of nodded but didn't say nothing, because there was too much pain and longing and anger between us. I wished I could reach out and touch her, tell her I had changed so much since them days when I done her wrong, when we lived together in that little apartment with Jackson the dog, but I couldn't. It was like trying to reach across the Grand Canyon. She was such a great woman, and I lost her, along with all the other joys and treasures I lost. In that moment, it seemed like my whole life story was just a story of loss and regret and mistakes.

There was one other person I was afraid I might run into at the funeral home, and I did. That was Tommy's dad Rocco, who was very old, in his late eighties maybe. When he looked over at me from across the room, he might as well have been blasting my ass with a submachine gun. Rocco was a mean old nasty guy, and he hated me, because Tommy and I had gotten into such trouble together, and I think he also hated me because at the end Tommy was still doing drugs and I wasn't. But I walk up to him anyhow, sitting there in a chair with some other people in the family.

"I'm really sorry about Tommy," I says to Rocco. "You know, I loved him like a brother."

And Rocco gets right up in my face and snarls, "You're the reason my son is dead!"

"I'm the reason?" I says, genuinely surprised. "The reason Tommy is dead is right over there," I says, pointing across the room at that little whore Steve. "Your son was a grown man and he made his own choices. He was gay, and he got AIDS from that kid over there. I didn't have nothing to do with that!"

But Rocco wasn't listening. I guess he was kind of blind with grief.

"Get the hell out of this funeral home!" he snaps at me.

"OK, if that's what you want, I'll do that. But I loved Tommy, and I still do. I'm as sorry as anyone that he's gone."

And I left.

***

Well, after Uncle Raymond and Nicky the Plumber helped C.J. and Annie straighten out the mess their finances were in, Raymond came back into my life again. I loved having Uncle Raymond back in my life. I admired him more than any other person I ever met. To me he was part big brother, part mentor, and part God.

He and Nicky the Plumber would stop by the bowling alley almost every day, just to chat or have a couple of Manhattans at the bar and watch the action on the lanes. Uncle Raymond would sit there on a barstool in a cloud of blue cigarette smoke, this huge, powerful man, just surveying the world like Santa Claus, and Nicky would sit besides him, pretty soon drifting off to sleep. Nicky the Plumber was old and kind of feeble, and he was always nodding off.

Meanwhile, C.J. and Annie had asked me to supervise cleaning up the third floor of the building where the bowling alley was at. When they took over the place, they'd done some big renovations downstairs, where the lanes were, and in the process they had to store some big piles of lumber and shit up there on the third floor, which was vacant. So now they wanted it cleaned up.

I went up there and looked the situation over – this huge, dimly-lit room, like a cavern, with piles of junk everywhere – and I realized I'd need maybe four or five of them huge dumpsters like they have at construction sites. I'd need the big kind, the thirty- or forty-yard long ones. And I knew exactly who to ask. He was sitting there, nodding off at the bar.

See, Nicky "the Plumber" might have been old and about as scary as a chihuahua. But he was connected – big time. He'd been part of the New Jersey rackets, and the Mob, his whole life. Uncle Raymond was friends with Bobby Cabert, but Nicky the Plumber was best friends with Cabert. (Little Sammy was also best friends with Cabert, but Little Sammy was in jail.) Cabert and Nicky went way, way back. Nicky the Plumber really did know where all the bodies were buried – because, as it happened, Bobby Cabert was now in federal prison on a variety of convictions, including a couple of murders for the Mob. But he was also in there because of his involvement in the mobbed-up garbage business in New York and New Jersey. If anybody knew where to get a couple of construction-size dumpsters, it was Bobby Cabert. Nicky the Plumber was also part of Uncle Raymond's crew – part of his own little army. None of these gangsters worked alone; they worked as a family, an entourage. And Nicky was in the thick of it. So I asked Nicky the Plumber if I could maybe get a couple of them big dumpsters in here. He says, no problem, and he goes and asks Cabert about it. And before you know it, three or four giant dumpsters get delivered to the vacant lot outside the bowling alley – free. Normally these things rented for, like $400 or $500 apiece. But they just appeared, like magic, and so we started throwing shit out the third floor window into these dumpsters, and then the shit got hauled away, and the city never gave us no trouble at all. It was, really, like magic. Or so I thought.

Look: You gotta understand something. Part of the code of ethics of that place and time, and being around connected people, was that you never asked no questions. What am I, some kind of fucking novel-writer? You just had to know enough not to ask. You also had to be trusted not to say nothing, especially if you got arrested. Maybe that's why Bobby Cabert liked me – I could be trusted, I never asked no questions, and as an extra bonus, I could even make him some money as an action bowler (or at least, I used to be able to).

One time Raymond and I were talking about all our adventures, about me delivering a mysterious package to some guy at a junkyard, about swag jobs on back roads in the middle of the night, and Uncle Raymond says, "We oughta write a book!"

Then he thinks a second, and laughs. "Nah – they'd kill us!"

It was like that. The biggest virtue was: No questions. The second biggest virtue was: Shut the fuck up. (And by the way: The only reason I feel safe telling you this now is that all those other people are dead.)

So, even though I knew Cabert was really in the Mob, and probably had done all kinds of bad shit, all I really knew was that he was never anything but nice to me. I might have heard about stuff he supposedly did, but I never saw him actually do any of that shit and I could kind of push that away in my mind. Bobby Cabert was just Bobby. He was my friend. I helped him, he helped me. All the dirty details only came out later. It was a few years later that a guy named Salvatore ("Sammy The Bull") Gravano became the highest-ranking member of the Mob to rat out the Mafia. He was what they call an underboss, directly beneath John Gotti, who was by then boss of the whole Gambino crime family. Gravano had been involved in a whole bunch of mob hits, some of them ordered by Gotti, and he sort of blew the lid off the Gambino family and a lot of other people in that world. (Boy, if anybody needed the Witness Protection Program, it was that guy!) His trial, in Manhattan federal court in 1993, was all in the papers, of course.

And one name that came up repeatedly during his testimony was the name of Bobby Cabert.

According to a story in The New York Times on April 14, 1993, "Sammy the Bull" Gravano explained the mechanics of a Mob hit in Queens in 1988, during his testimony in federal court in Manhattan. The murder was a revenge killing of a man named Francesco Oliveri, who was held responsible for the earlier murder of a member of John Gambino's crew. Gravano said the hit was approved by John Gotti, the head of the Gambino organized-crime family.

"John Gotti told me to go on this hit, supervise it, get it done," Mr. Gravano told the jury.

Gravano testified that the five-man "hit team" included himself, two of the defendants in the trial, Mr. Gambino's brother Joseph, and Lorenzo Mannino, and two associates named Ozzie Stantini and Bobby Cabert. He noted that Gotti selected Bobby Cabert to be "the shooter" as a test before making him a member of the Gambino crime family.

After taking the entire hit team to Astoria, Queens, to survey the proposed murder scene, Mr. Gravano said, "I walked them through what we were going to do." He said he instructed them to get guns, walkie-talkies, two stolen cars and one "legitimate car." They knew that Oliveri moved his car each morning because of alternate-side parking rules in front of his apartment house, Gravano testified, so they plotted to kill him when he came out for the car. Their first attempt failed, he said, because they arrived after he had already moved his car.

A week later, on May 3, 1988, Gravano continued, the plotters tried again, starting out before dawn this time and assembling in Brooklyn. He said he and Mannino stationed themselves near the Oliveri house in one stolen car, and the three other men stayed in the second stolen car, with the legitimate car parked a few blocks away

"My role was backup shooter as well as supervisor of the hit," Gravano said. He added that he notified the others by walkie-talkie when Mannino saw Oliveri coming out of the house. "Bobby ran out and shot him a couple of times," Gravano testified.

The victim was shot five times, once between the eyes. After the shooting, he said, they sped away in the two stolen cars, then switched to the "legitimate car" and drove back to Brooklyn. Recalling that he reported to Gotti later that day at the Ravenite Club, the family's Manhattan headquarters, Gravano testified, "I believe I said that the problem was solved."

Much later, in December, 2008, Bobby Cabert died in federal prison, where he was serving a life sentence for various crimes including racketeering and first-degree murder for a mob hit he maintained to the end he did not commit. In a December 8, 2008 obituary in The New York Times, the paper pointed out that Cabert had been a childhood friend of the actor Joe Pesci, who had become famous for his portrayal of mobsters in movies like "Goodfellas." Pesci later said, in fact, that his portrayal of the mobster Tommy DeVito in that movie – an insanely violent, unstable hoodlum – was based on his friend Bobby Cabert. Cabert, Pesci said, was able to change moods in a flash, from being charming and funny to utterly frightening.

"The adjective for him is ruthless," Robert H. Cody, one of the prosecutors in his New Jersey trial, was quoted as saying. "The reason he was picked for the New York murder [the one for which he was convicted] was because they knew he was not afraid to walk up to someone in broad daylight and put a bullet in his head." In another obituary, this one in the New Jersey Star-Ledger, bearing the headline "Iconic 'Goodfella' Robert Bisaccia dies in Prison," a veteran organized-crime investigator was quoted as saying: "One minute he'd make you laugh, the next minute he'd have you crying and then he'd put a bullet in your head." But there was also some grudging admiration for the old mobster. Robert T. Buccino, chief of detectives in Union County New Jersey, who testified against Cabert for 28 days at the state trial, told the Times: "There aren't many left like him. You can count them on one hand. And one thing about Bobby Cabert, he never talked. He never would. Which is not happening much anymore. They get a wrong sentence, and they turn in a minute. Cabert would have taken a bullet rather than rat out a friend."

Loyalty: That was one big thing about Bobby Cabert. He was the most loyal person I ever met. If you belonged to Cabert, he would protect you no matter what. That's one of the reasons why, even after he went to trial and got sentenced to federal prison, I kept running little errands for him, making sure his mail got to him in prison and shit like that. He'd call me at the bowling alley collect, through a third party, thinking that would throw the feds off, but that was stupid. (In other words, Cabert would call somebody else and ask them to call me, and then I would talk to him through that third party's phone. He thought this would throw the feds off, but it didn't.) One day Bobby Cabert asked me to get this computer to his daughter and nobody knew where she was at but me, so I got it to her. I felt that there were times when Cabert helped me out, and I felt like I had to help him out. I could see he was in a terrible situation, facing life in prison. But eventually C.J. and Annie told me to stop taking Cabert's calls at work, I guess mainly because it was interrupting my job, and maybe because they knew who I was talking to.

But for all kinds of other reasons I finally just said to him, "Look, Bobby, I can't talk to you no more."

"I understand," he says. "But thanks for helping me anyhow."

I thought that was the end of it.

Actually, though, it was just the beginning.

17 RULE NUMBER ONE:
DON'T ASK NO QUESTIONS

So anyway, in the winter or spring of 1995, I have Nicky the Plumber ask Cabert to deliver some dumpsters to the bowling alley, and he does. Maybe I should have known better. Maybe I should have thought about the strings attached. But at the time, I just thought it was a favor from an old friend.

Right about that same time, Tommy Lorenzo's younger brother Ray walks into the bowling alley one day. I'd known Ray and Tommy's other brother, Ronnie, for years – they were a warm, close-knit family, and during my bad years I'd even spent a Christmas or two at their house. (In the bad years, there was no reason to go to my own house, because I'd just be thrown out.) I was also tight with Ray's teenage son, also Tommy, who I was teaching bowling. Ray had always been good to me, helping me, loaning me money and whatnot. But there was one other thing I remembered about Ray when he walked in that winter day in 1995: Tommy had told me several times never to trust his brother.

"I need to talk to you," Ray says to me.

"What's the problem?"

"My dad needs your help."

Like, I'm supposed to help Rocco, the guy who threw me out of my best friends' funeral?

"Well, you know that guy Dr. Richard and them? They're no good. You remember that fifty thousand my brother loaned them guys?"

I remembered the fifty thousand dollar loan, because Tommy had told me about it before he died. There was this sort of nut-job vitamin doctor named Dr. Richard (pronounced, very pretentious, "rish-ARD") who had supposedly come over from Europe with all these miraculous holistic medicines and vitamins, stuff that could cure Alzheimer's and also lameness in horses, and he had actually moved into the Lorenzo's house because he was trying to treat Tommy's mom, who had Alzheimer's, and also Rocco and Tommy's old Aunt Mary, who had helped raise the kids. It was a house full of old, sick people and this nutty vitamin doctor.

I was suspicious of the whole situation, but I wasn't too close to it, because at that point I was forbidden to go to the house because Rocco thought I was using Tommy to get drugs (this was before I got sober). But one day Tommy told me that the family had loaned this guy Dr. Richard and his partners fifty thousand to help start a holistic health and vitamin business in New York.

"Yeah," I says to Ray, "I remember Tommy telling me about that."

"Well, the guy moves out of the house, goes to New York, sets up this business, and now he's got a big successful vitamin business in New York, on Fifth Avenue and Twenty-third Street. But when my dad calls the guy to get the loan back, the guy just laughs at him. He borrowed the money seven fucking years ago. But he claims he paid the money back to Tommy before he died. You know, my dad's an old guy. It scared him. And he needs the money. He wants his money back."

It's not like I went around advertising it, but everybody around the bowling alley knew I had some very influential people in my life. People with connections, people with "weight," like Uncle Raymond and Nicky the Plumber and Cabert and Gotti and them. Ray knew I was close to all these people – people who could get things done, sometimes in broad daylight, sometimes in the dark of night. I figured that was why we were having this conversation.

"Could you help us, for Tommy?" Ray says, kind of pleading.

"What makes you think I can get the money?"

"I know you know people. Go talk to your people. See if they could help. We'd pay them for their help. And one more thing. My father says that if you help us, he'll forgive you for what he said to you at the funeral home. He's very sorry he said that to you."

"I'll see what I can do," I says. "I'll let you know."

So now I had a lot to think about. This was a complicated debt, not like the last one, which was just about money. Settling up this debt had to do with restoring my best friend's father's honor. It had to do with me getting Rocco's forgiveness, setting things right between us. It had to do with helping out Tommy's family, who had been wronged, and trying to set things right with them about all my past evil deeds. It had to do with doing a personal favor to the memory of Tommy, who I had loved. And, of course, it had to do with getting this phony-baloney quack doctor to pay back the fifty grand he stiffed Rocco for. Only it wasn't fifty grand no more. If you added ten percent interest for seven years, it was more like a couple of hundred grand.

But I think, really, what made me want to get involved in this situation was that Ray was laying a big guilt trip on me. I was so sorry for the mess I'd made of my life, and being thrown out of the family I once considered almost like my own, that the chance to make things right again seemed worth whatever risk there might be.

So I make a pilgrimage back to Uncle Raymond's house in North Arlington, get let into the front door by Maryann, who squeals something in Polish and grabs my face, and go downstairs to Raymond's basement throne room.

"Perry!" Uncle Raymond growls. "How ya doin'?" He's so heavy now he don't even bother to get up out of the chair.

By this time, I had a fabulous relationship with Uncle Raymond. We only lived a few blocks apart, and I'd see him all the time. I'd go make bets for him at the track and when he'd win, which was often, I'd go by his house and give him the money.

I would give him every penny of the money, because now I was trying to live in integrity and honesty. It was almost like all the lost dark years, the years of addiction and homelessness and spiritual emptiness, never happened. I was just Bobby, the talented, trustworthy kid from the neighborhood who loved to go to the track for his uncle.

So I explain the situation to Uncle Raymond. I tell him all about Tommy's brother's situation, and Rocco, and Dr. Richard – oh, excuse me, Dr. Rish-ARD – and the whole thing. Uncle Raymond just listens quietly – calculating, analyzing – while I lay the whole thing out. His eyes narrow. This was a man who had lived most of his life on the shadow side of the law, but who had never been arrested for nothing even once. He's so smart that suspicion had almost become second nature, like an instinct.

He asks a bunch of questions about the specifics of the situation, where this guy Dr. Richard lives and works, whether Ray and Rocco could be trusted to pay him if he collected the loan, and so on.

"Is the loan legit?" he asked, which is what he always asked.

"Yeah," I says. "I think so. That's what Ray says."

"How much money is involved?"

"Well, the original loan was fifty thousand, but the loan is unpaid for seven years, so if you add ten percent interest for that amount of time, it's, like, a couple of hundred thousand bucks."

Uncle Raymond stares at me, his eyes narrowed.

"Well, let me have a meeting with Tommy's brother," Raymond says. "I have to think about this." So a meeting gets set up at the bowling alley between Ray Lorenzo, Uncle Raymond and Nicky the Plumber. So these three guys meet at the bowling alley and go into the bar through the swinging doors, just like before. They have a long conversation in there, without laughter, that lasts a long time.

I stay outside, at the front desk, waiting.

Finally, they come out and Ray leaves the building without speaking to me. Uncle Raymond takes me aside. He seems a little troubled.

"I don't know about this. I don't know if I want to do this. Not because of Tommy – I loved Tommy. I just don't like the deal. I have to think about it. I have to talk to my brothers about this."

One of Raymond's brothers, Chet, was a hopeless drunk with, like, ten or twenty DWIs. Raymond spent a fortune trying to get him sober or keep him sober. His other brother was named Stanley, but Raymond called him "Stoshu," which I guess is some Polish thing. These two brothers – they were fat and skinny, Chet was fat and Stoshu was skinny, this tough little Polack. They were like Laurel and Hardy. Anyway, Uncle Raymond always consulted with his brothers whenever a deal made him nervous or didn't seem quite right. And I guess this was one of them deals.

I never asked no questions, of course. (Like, "what deal?") But afterwards Ray Lorenzo told me that Uncle Raymond had asked for a fee of five or ten grand for collecting the debt, and he wanted it paid up front before he sent his boys to collect the money. Ray got mad at this, but in the end he wound up agreeing to it. Uncle Raymond had also told Ray that, if anything happened – if anybody got arrested – he would pay the lawyer fees. I also knew, without being told, that Uncle Raymond would have to ask permission from whoever the guy was that "owned" the territory at Twenty-Third and Fifth. I really knew nothing more than that, and I didn't want to know nothing more. I only agreed to be the guy that collected the money. The bag man.

So sometime after that, Uncle Raymond and Nicky the Plumber paid a little visit to the nutty vitamin doctor's offices on Fifth Avenue. It was a Sunday afternoon. I don't know what happened. I wasn't there. All I know is that later that afternoon, Uncle Raymond walks into the bowling alley with a check for $6800, from Dr. Richard, made out to Rocco Lorenzo.

So a little while later, maybe a week, I get the job of going into the city to collect the next check. I decide to take this guy Binky along with me. Binky works in the bowling alley and he's this big hulking kid, a former high school football player. I wanted him to come because he was kind of intimidating. But he also wanted to go because, without being told, he was sort of putting it together that this was a mission to collect dirty money. And he was all starstruck about gangsters, like he was in The Godfather fan club or some shit.

So me and Binky take the train into the city, catch a cab over to Twenty-Third and Fifth, and take the elevator to the 19th floor. We come out into this sort of open office area, and there's a receptionist sitting there. I ask for

Dr. Richard, and he comes out from a back office. He don't look like no fancy-pants doctor from Europe. He just looks like an ordinary guy. But, I don't know, I been around Uncle Raymond long enough to be able to almost smell it when something ain't right. And something ain't right. Out of the corner of my eye, I'm noticing this guy sitting there in an easy chair, kind of pretending to be reading a magazine. And there's another guy on a ladder putting medicines or whatever up on a shelf.

"How ya doin'?" Dr. Richard says.

"Good. Have you got the payment?"

"Yeah," he says, kind of cheerful. "Who do I make it out to?"

"Rocco Lorenzo."

But as he's writing the check I'm thinking, This guy is entirely too happy about writing this check. When he's done, he hands it to me.

"I'll see you next week."

And me and Binky walk out of there. Well, the guy gave me the money, nothing bad happened, so maybe there was nothing wrong after all, I thought. Ray and Uncle Raymond were getting paid. Rocco was getting his revenge. The dude was coughing it all up.

Man, I felt like a big shot again. I was using my connections to come through for Tommy Lorenzo and his brother and his father. I was scaring the shit out of the bad guys, just like in the old West. But I knew I shouldn't be doing this.

I was supposed to be working on my sobriety, not turning into a gopher for the Mob.

I knew it was wrong. I just didn't know how wrong.

***

When I get back to the bowling alley, I hand over the check to Ray Lorenzo. And he gives me a hundred bucks for my effort. A hundred bucks to hang my ass out over the edge. No shit. But I was feeling worse and worse about this whole thing. It stunk, and I knew it. I opened up about it to my sponsor. Jack always put it to me straight.

"Bobby," Jack says to me, "You can't be in AA and be in the Mob."

Which, when he put it that way, was like, duh.

But by this time, I felt like I was in too deep to back out. I felt like I'd made a deal with Uncle Raymond and Ray Lorenzo and I needed to hold up my end of the bargain.

So a couple of weeks later, I go back into the city to collect the next payment from Dr. Nut-Job. But by now, the "wrong" bells are ringing all over the place. The night before, a Tuesday night, I had to pick up Binky over by the Lincoln Tunnel, and he's just bawling like a baby.

"Man, what's the matter?" I ask him. He looks at me like a scared rabbit, like somebody that just got caught at something.

"A friend of mine just died," he says.

Then a little while later I drop Binky off at the bowling alley, and I run into his mother, and she just looks at me and shakes her head. So the next day I have to go into the city to pick up the next check and I ask my friend Dominick, the cop, to go with me, but he says he's busy. So I call ahead to tell Dr. Richard I'm coming, take the train to Manhattan, catch a cab over to Twenty-third and Fifth, and go up to the 19th floor. When the elevator door opens, there's a sort of chainlink fence with a gate you have to walk through, like if there's some construction going on, but I couldn't see no construction going on. And I noticed that same guy, sitting in that same easy chair, like a store dummy, and that same guy, up on a ladder, putting medicines on a shelf. When Dr. Richard comes out of the back office, I tell him I want cash, but he says he only has a check, so he writes me a check and I leave – quickly. I get on the elevator but I only go down to the 15th floor. I get off, go over in a corner and rip up that check into tiny pieces. Then I walk all the way down to the ground floor. Something's up. Something ain't right.

Then I walk all the way down the stairs to the street. There's one of them little deli stands there, so I buy a banana and a Diet Pepsi. Then I walk toward the street. But out of the corner of my eye, it looks like when I take a step, the whole street moves with me. Then I walk across the street, and it seems to me like a whole bunch of people cross the street with me. It's like one of them Broadway musicals. On the other side of the street is a guy standing there, apparently trying to catch a cab, but he isn't trying very hard and when a cab stops he just motions the cabbie to keep moving.

"Don't you want this cab?" I says to the guy.

"Naw, not now," he says, which was weird.

So I open the back door of the cab and all of a sudden that guy and a whole chorus line of other people come to life. The guy and a couple of other huge guys slam me into the back side of the cab, and I can feel the barrel of a gun sticking in my ribs, another one at the base of my neck, and another one in my ass.

"Bob, if you move, we will blow your fucking brains out," a guy growls at me. "Where's the gun?"

"What gun? I don't have a gun!"

"Where's the gun? Give me the gun or I'm gonna blow your fucking brains out!"

"I ain't got no gun! I ain't got no gun!"

So then the cab driver, some little Pakistani guy or whatever, he starts to freak out.

"Don't shoot! Don't shoot!" he starts yelling. "Please, please! Don't shoot me!"

"Get that fucking cabbie outta there or I'll blow his fucking brains out, too!" yells one of the cops (or whoever they are).

Somebody yanks the freaked-out driver out of the cab.

"Bob, we know who you are," the cop says to me. "Your name is Robert Purzycki. We know all about what you are doing here. Now where is the gun?"

"I ain't got no gun, man!"

I can feel somebody snapping handcuffs around my wrist, behind my back. This whole thing, the vague fear and dread I've been feeling for weeks about this, all these suspicions I've been having, it's all come to a head. My whole life has come to a head in this terrible moment.

I'm spread-eagled against the cab, with cop cars everywhere and these huge guys sticking guns into me from all directions. Crowds on the sidewalk stop to watch, briefly, then they move on. It's New York. People are busy.

"My name is John Triolo," one of the guys says. "And this is my partner, Louie. We're from the New York office of the F.B.I."

18 THE END OF HOPE

"Where's the check?" this guy Triolo is yelling. Where's the check?" He and these other feds have me slammed up against the cab, stuck full of guns.

"What check?" I says. "I ain't got no check!"

"The check you just picked up from that office on the nineteenth floor. The check made out to Rocco Lorenzo for sixty-eight hundred dollars."

"I don't have no check – look in my pockets!"

But I knew these guys got me cold. I knew I was cooked.

"You have the right to remain silent," Triolo says, "but you're coming with us."

By now I was shitting bricks. The feds had me in handcuffs, and I had to pretend not to know what I knew. Then again, I did not actually know everything that had gone down. It was only later that I found out what had actually happened. Somebody – possibly Uncle Raymond himself or, more likely, somebody working for him – hung the nutty vitamin doctor out the nineteenth floor window of his office and threatened to drop him if he didn't pay.

"I'll pay! I'll pay!" the doctor yelled. Then they pulled him back inside. Then he changed his tune. Now he said he wouldn't pay. So somebody – whoever it was – stuck a .45 down the guy's throat and threatened to blow his brains out if he didn't pay. Just like in the movies. That's not just extortion (trying to extract money by the threat of force). That's extortion involving deadly weapons, with direct links to organized crime. And because I'd crossed state lines (from New Jersey to New York) it was also a federal crime.

That was about as serious as it gets.

So the next time somebody showed up at Dr. Richard's office – that would be me and Binky – the New York Task Force on Organized Crime had been notified and staked the place out.

I'd always been able to talk my way out of jams, but there was no talking my way out of this one.

The feds shoved me into a car and then they took the handcuffs off. And all of a sudden, they were nice as hell. It was like the FBI was my big brother. Triolo says, yeah, you're probably a little nervous right now, but it's going to be OK. They took me underground somewhere around the Brooklyn Bridge, a place called One Federal Plaza, down what looked like a private tunnel into some building. We seemed to be going way down underground. We got out of the car and they put me on an elevator back upstairs somewhere. Finally I'm in this windowless room.

"You can make a phone call," Triolo says.

"Okay."

"Who you gonna call?"

"My friend C.J., and my AA sponsor."

Jesus. How am I going to explain this to Jack?

"No problem," Triolo says.

So I call C.J.

"C.J., look, I've been arrested. It's a long story, but I'm in some kind of federal building downtown. Could you call Jack and just tell him what happened? And where's Patsy?"

"Patsy just left for Italy," C.J. says. "She told me she's gone 28 days. Are you okay?"

"Well, I'll let you know."

Click.

Patsy. She was the one person, through my whole life, who never gave up on me – even when she was telling me to get the fuck away from her door. She always believed in me, always remembered the kind, decent person who was down there inside me, no matter how much I might have looked like a drowned, toothless rat. Patsy, more than any other single person, was the one who always loved me.

But now she was unreachable for almost a month. (In them days, of course, there were no cell phones or Internet.)

So then Triolo starts going through my wallet. He pulls out card after card and holds each up one six inches from my face.

"Who's this? How do you know this person?" he says. "Who is this person? Who is this guy?"

One card is from a guy who owns Guess Jeans – I know him because he sometimes came into the bowling alley. Another is from the pro shop at Bowl-Rite lanes. On the back a name and phone number is scribbled: Paula Carter, wife of one of the greatest bowlers in the country, a guy I knew. But I'm sweating bullets now, because I'm pretty sure I've also got that card in there with Bobby Cabert's prison number on it, and possibly even John Gotti's. Finally, Triolo comes across Cabert's card.

"What's this?" he says. "This is a prison number. You gonna tell me whose prison number this is?"

I'm trying to think fast. But then I think, the feds are going to figure this out even faster. Why lie? (Later on, a guy in prison tells me, "When the feds arrest you, they've already put all the pieces together. If you're lying, they know it. So don't.")

"Bobby Cabert," I says. "Robert Bisaccia."

I have to say, these federal agents were terrific. They didn't rough me up or nothing, they were aggressive but polite. They walked a fine line. You don't have to worry that the United States government is not keeping you safe. But even so, it was obvious that I was in deep, deep shit. This wasn't going to end in ten or twenty minutes. I wasn't going home tonight.

Triolo makes a phone call, and pretty soon another guy shows up in the room where I'm getting hung out to dry.

"Do you know who I am?" the guy says. "I'm the guy that locked up John Gotti."

"What's that got to do with me?"

"That's what we're trying to find out."

Then he whips out a photograph. It's a picture of Bobby Cabert.

"Do you know this man, Robert Bisaccia? You may know he's now serving a life sentence in federal prison. He was convicted of being a hit man for the Gambino crime family."

He just stares at me, like his eyes are drilling a hole in my forehead.

"Mr. Purzycki, why do you have this man's prison number written on a card in your wallet?"

"Well, I knew him from Paterson, from the bowling alley. He wanted to know what was in the newspapers while he was in prison," I says. "So I'd mail him the papers."

I knew it was kind of lame. But it was true.

"Look, can I go home?" I says.

It's worth a shot.

"Yeah, if everything goes right, you can go home."

"I think I need a lawyer."

"Okay, we'll get you a lawyer."

So they escort me through these doors down this little corridor where there were seven cells in a row. They put me in the last cell, all by myself, and I sat there for, like, five hours. It was freezing cold. I just sat in there, freezing my nuts off, thinking about how bad this whole situation could get. I had three and a half years of sobriety and here I was in federal prison. I mean, this place was worse than Alcatraz — at least there, you could see the sky. Here there was no sun or sky. I was deep underground, like I was already dead and buried. It would take an atomic bomb to break out of this place. I looked down the long hall and I could see that the floors had been scrubbed sparkling clean. I suddenly realized why. It was because that was what I was going to be doing for the rest of my life.

***

Finally Triolo's partner, Louie, comes and lets me out of my little freezing cage and takes me down the elevator again, to an interrogation room or something. I might as well be ten miles underground. Then Louie brings me lunch, a turkey sandwich and two Diet Cokes. Man, was that sandwich good. It was the only good thing that had happened to me all day.

Then this public defender comes in.

"What's going on here?" he says.

"Can I talk to you?"

"Yes, I'm your lawyer."

"Look, this whole thing is about a debt, a legitimate debt. This guy owed a family fifty thousand dollars, and we tried to collect it. All I did was pick up the money."

"You got any priors?"

"I got one unpaid traffic ticket from Ocean Port, New York. By Monmouth racetrack. A hundred and twenty-five bucks."

"That's it?"

"That's it."

"Well, this looks really simple. We'll go in front of the judge. I don't see any problem with you posting bail. We'll call you after you're done eating."

Before I went in front of the federal judge, in a little underground courtroom like a bomb shelter, I got a little bit of good news. Somebody – I found out later it was Uncle Raymond – had hired me a lawyer, and a good one. His name was Allen C. Marra, and he was one of the most prominent, influential lawyers in New Jersey. (His office was in Montclair.) He was a medium-sized man, maybe five-eleven, in his early sixties, with black hair tinged with gray. He was wearing this tremendously beautiful suit. He didn't look like a mobbed-up lawyer, he looked like a business executive who demanded respect.

A U.S. Marshal leads me into the courtroom, in shackles, and sits me down beside Allen Marra.

The U.S. Attorney, a guy named Clark, says to the judge:

"I would like to hold Mr. Purzycki for three days – seventy-two hours, to prepare the charges against him," Clark says.

"What are they, in brief?" the judge asks.

"Your Honor, Mr. Purzycki is a capo for the Gambino crime family and I can prove it!" Clark says. "He is capable of ordering a murder with a snap of fingers – and that will happen almost immediately if you release him.

When he was arrested he had the prison number of Robert Bisaccia in his pocket. As you know, Robert Bisaccia is now in federal prison for nine Mob-ordered murders. His activities were recently described in testimony in federal court by Mob underboss Sammy The Bull Gravano."

Holy shit! This guy had me halfway up the ladder of power in the most ruthless organized crime family in New Jersey. I'm, like, stunned. And I suddenly realized – duh – that even though it wasn't true, I'd been living right on the edge of all that for years. I could see where somebody could make a case against me. Hanging around with Gotti and Cabert and Uncle Raymond had seemed glamorous and exciting. But there was a reason why I was never supposed to ask no questions.

"What say you, counselor?" the judge says to Allen Marra.

"These charges by Mr. Clark are preposterous. Mr. Purzycki is an upstanding member of society, he has an apartment and a job at a bowling alley in Union City, New Jersey, and has been a nationally-ranked bowler. His entire criminal record consists of a one-hundred-twenty-five dollar parking ticket."

The judge thinks this over for a little while.

"There are enough questions concerning your case, Mr. Purzycki, that it's easier for me to hold you than release you," he says finally. "You will be remanded to the Manhattan Metropolitan Correctional Center for seventy-two hours. This is not like jail, Mr. Purzycki. You'll be okay."

Leaving the courtroom, I happened to see Ray Lorenzo, surrounded by fabulous lawyers in expensive suits. I found out later his lawyer was Anthony Martone, one of the greatest criminal lawyers in the state, a guy who had represented Cabert. I knew very well that Ray had access to a lot of money from his family's businesses, and he was going home no matter what the bail was set at.

"You're going home, aren't you?" I says to him. "You're gonna make bail and go home?"

"I don't know nothing," he says. "I told the feds I didn't know you."

"What the fuck did you say that for?"

He was trying to lie his way out of this – pin it all on me. He wasn't owning up to what happened on his end. After all, the whole thing happened because I was trying to do a favor for him!

"You're gonna fuck me, aren't you?" I says.

He didn't say nothing, but I knew it was true. With all that family money he had, he was going to make bail and go home to sleep in his own bed. I got no money, and I was going to be stuck here in this eight-by-ten icebox, maybe forever.

When I get back to my cell, a guy says to me, "You make bail?"

"Nah. They're holding me for three days."

"Yeah, ha ha," he says. "You're never making bail. Nobody ever makes bail in here. Welcome to your new home."

Warrant for Arrest, Southern District of New York, August 15, 1995. United States of America v. Robert Purzycki, a/k/a "Bob Perry" a/k/a "Frank." [Sometimes I used "Frank" 'cuz, frankly, I knew I was doing stuff that wasn't exactly right.]

Docket No.: 95 MAG. 1672

To: United States Marshal or any other authorized officer. YOU ARE HEREBY COMMANDED to arrest the above-named person and bring that person before the nearest available magistrate to answer to the charges listed below.

DESCRIPTION OF CHARGES:

Extortion

So I'm transferred to what they call "MCC," onto cellblock Five North, in my baggy brown prison uniform, which looks a little bit like the one Father Paul always wore.

More shuffling around, in handcuffs, accompanied by a U.S. Marshal. When you're in federal prison, the U.S. Marshals own you. They'd lead me through doors that had to be unlocked when you walked through and locked again behind you. They took all my clothes, which I didn't mind. But what I did mind is that they also took the favorite necklace I had been wearing for years. It was just a piece of rope, like a shoelace, but on the end was the miraculous medal I had found in the graveyard at Graymoor. All I knew when I found it was that it looked incredibly old and beautiful and seemed kind of religious or something. But later Patsy found this book that had all about the meaning of the medal, and explained its history and power and whatnot. I put it on a string and put it around my neck and never took it off, just feeling all that power, like the power of Father Paul, the power that had changed my life.

Now I had to hand it over to some flunky at check-in at MCC, and maybe never see it again. As it turned out it, my clothes disappeared, but I did actually see that miraculous medal again, and I put its power to good use. Years later, an old friend of mine, Mikey Defino, got in a real bad car accident and they were getting ready to pull the plug on him. His mom called me and begged to come to the hospital before they let him go. She held off the doctors while I drove down from the Jersey shore. By the time I got there, Mikey was brain dead. But I remembered from that book Patsy found that if you have the miraculous medal on you when you die, you go straight to heaven. I took off the necklace, pressed it into Mikey's hands, kissed him on the forehead and walked out the door and he died.

Anyway, so I give the check-in the miraculous medal and he gives me this baggy brown outfit, one pair of underwear, two pairs of socks and these ridiculous blue boating sneakers. Like, I'm going boating?

"Is there anyone in this facility who would want to hurt you?" one of the Marshals asked, apparently trying to decide if I needed to be put in my own cell.

"No, I don't think so."

Somebody gives me a sheet and a pillow and ushers me into a tiny cell with a bunkbed, a toilet, a little small locker and a roommate – this huge, intimidating-looking black dude whose name, I later learned, was Tyrone.

"What you in here for, robbing old ladies?" Tyrone says.

I didn't say nothing. I'm trying to think fast.

"Whassamatter, you don't want to talk to me? I don't like fucking white people."

"Uh, no se habla Ingles. Me no speaka English."

"Hahaha – you funny guy!" Tyrone says. "You OK."

But I wasn't OK.

I thought: I'm never going home. I'm stuck in this sinking cell with this creepy dude forever.

I fall into this little routine, where every movement is watched by armed guards. There's a pay phone on Five North, so every chance I get I stand in line to use the phone, to try to figure out what's going on "out there." I talked to C.J. again, briefly, and he told me Uncle Raymond and Nicky the Plumber had been arrested; he also told them I'd been arrested.

The bad news was I got sent the charging documents – this big stack of papers laying out the state's case against me. I only had to read the first page to know things had gone from bad to worse. It didn't matter how polite John Triolo was, or how tasty the turkey sandwich was in federal prison. I was screwed.

And to think I had almost succeeded in breaking free of my life story! The encounters with Father Paul and my slow, steady return to the land of the living, to sobriety and integrity and a real, actual life. And now this. Sitting here in this cell on Five North with nothing but a bunkbed, a locker, my blue boating shoes, Tyrone and a charging document with all the details about how the United States government is throwing the goddamn book at me.

If I ever needed my Higher Power, and Father Paul, it was now.

19 "I LOVE YOU, YOUR HONOR!"

You hear people talk about "Club Fed," and how easy it is to serve time in federal prison. Well, forget about it. Those people don't know what the fuck they're talking about. It's the agony, the mental torment, that kills you. And security? Listen, this ain't like no Escape-From-Alcatraz type thing, where at least you see the sky through the bars. Here, you're buried alive, like you're in an upside-down skyscraper stuck underground. You might as well already be dead. In fact, in a way I already had a tag on my toe, like one of them unidentified corpses at the city morgue: It read, 857435757. My prison number. My new address, maybe forever.

The worst thing of all was the hopelessness. The believing that I would never be going home. That I would never sleep in my own bed again. All those guys in there told me I would never make bail, and I believed them. Whenever I tried to call my lawyer, Allen Marra, to find out about my case, he was busy or out of the office. He was basically telling me to fuck off. Nobody except Patsy would even take my calls.

I almost wished I could drink or do drugs again, so I wouldn't have to face the possibility that this was my new home, maybe for the next thirty years: Five North, at the Metropolitan Correctional Center in Manhattan, a stinking shithole which I shared with murderers, drug dealers, thugs and criminals of all kinds. And this place wasn't like no minor leagues of petty crime, like a state or local lockup. This place was the NFL of crime.

One of the guys who was behind the 1993 bombing of the World Trade Center, this huge Arab guy named Hussein, he was there. Guys from the Irish Republican Army were there, including one of its leaders, a guy named Peter McMullen, that I got to know pretty well. Supposedly there were quite a few guys in there who had killed more than ten people. And there were some big-time nonviolent criminals there too, like this guy Eddie who used to have a chain of discount electronics stores in the Northeast called

"Crazy Eddie's" – he had all these TV ads where he'd say, "His prices are insane!" – well, he was in there for owing 15 million in back taxes, or something.

And then there's me, Bob Perry, the kid from Paterson, Mr. "Money Bowler," the guy who couldn't lose. Me, Bob Perry, down here underground in a cell the size of a walk-in closet with nothing but two changes of underpants, an extra pair of socks and a roommate!

Gradually, I started to slip into the monotonous routine of incarceration in the federal system. Besides meals, there wasn't much to break up the boredom of "doing time" (even though, strictly speaking, I wasn't doing time, just waiting until my case came up). One thing was the "count." Every day at four p.m., all prisoners in the entire federal system nationwide had to be counted over a 30-minute period. So if you were working in the prison library or the infirmary or the kitchen, you had to return to your cell for the count.

Every once in awhile, there was also what they called "PC movement," meaning that a prisoner in protective custody was being moved through the cellblock. One of the Marshals would yell "movement!" and even if the prisoner was down on the first floor, and you were on the fifth (like me), you had to go to the back of your cell and not look. That's because people under protective custody – like, say, Sammy "The Bull" Gravano – were in serious danger of getting killed by people in there.

There are four levels of incarceration in the federal correctional system: "Camp," (for some white-collar guy who embezzles money at work); "Medium security," (for more serious crimes); "Maximum," (for really scary, dangerous people) and "Supermax" (where people like Gotti and Cabert got sent).

Not too long after I arrived at MCC, I got sent to another holdover facility, called Otisville Federal Correction Institution, about two-and-a-half hours upstate from Manhattan. Otisville was a medium-security facility. The big advantage of Otisville over MCC was that they had a prison yard where you could actually see the sky and the sun. The exercise area (which had a basketball court, a handball court and a track) was surrounded by a fifteen-foot barbed wire fence, with another fifteen-foot barbed wire fence outside that, that was electrified at night. There were also guard towers, with armed guards in them, staring down at you, just like in the movies. The guards watched everything you did. If you were out there sunbathing, you lost your privileges. If you were talking to too many people, you got reported.

Being in the yard was a long ways from "freedom."

But at least, a couple of times a day, I could get out there and smell the dirt and the trees and the rain. I kept clear of almost everybody in there. I learned not to talk to people. I'd just walk around and around and around

(25 times around the yard made a mile – in other words, it was a really tiny yard).

The best thing about Otisville was that, every once in awhile, I got a visit from Patsy. The bad part about Otisville was that if you were sent up there it meant your case was a long ways off. It was a holdover facility for people pending trial. They made you get a job or go to a GED class while you were in there. The rest of the time you were in your tiny cell, or released into a slightly larger cage where there was a pool table and a step. That was your life: The pool table, the step, the cell. Waiting, waiting, waiting.

But just in case you were getting comfortable with incarceration, the Marshals would do this thing called "diesel therapy." It was to break you down, drive you nuts, maybe make you talk. Say around 10 o'clock at night on a Thursday, a guy comes to your cell and tells you to pack all your shit up in a twelve-by-twelve box. You try to pack all your stuff in there, but you can't fit nothing much more in there but your underwear and socks. Then they take you downstairs into another bullpen, or holding area, where you have to wait until 12:30 in the morning. Then, one person at a time, you have to take all your clothes off, and another guy makes you bend over to see you haven't got a knife hidden where the sun don't shine, then you put on some different clothes and you get loaded on a prison bus for the two-and-a-half hour ride up to Otisville. When you get there, you get stripped and examined again, and taken to another cell. By this time, you've probably missed breakfast. You're held in this cell until ten o'clock at night and then some guy comes to get you and it starts all over again. And this goes on for days, until you're so exhausted you can't even see nothing.

Look: I had seen the charging documents, and I knew very well that the case the government was throwing at me was serious. Very serious. But did I really belong in here with these murderers and terrorists? I kept trying to get some answers from my lawyer about this, but he didn't return my calls. I couldn't say that I blamed him: I didn't have no money, like Uncle Raymond or Ray Lorenzo. I was just your average run-of-the-mill inmate in federal lockup, an unlucky guy lost in the shuffle.

From time to time I would get through on the phone to C.J., who told me that Uncle Raymond and Nicky the Plumber were out on bail. He said they'd been seen at the racetrack, like nothing ever happened. I found out they'd hired that same heavy-duty lawyer Anthony Martone, who later became a federal judge in Monmouth County, and he got them out on bail in a couple of days. Uncle Raymond had finally gone to prison – but for 48 hours or something. But I was still stuck here with the crooks and the creeps, staring out at the world through bars.

I wound up spending about half my time at MCC and half at Otisville. MCC was the worst. I'll be trapped there in my little coffin underground, where there was no daylight, no birds chirping, not even the sound of traffic, just the sound of some asshole on Tier Five playing bad rap music and the jangle of keys locking and unlocking doors, or jail cells clanking, or every now and then the sound of a cue ball cracking a rack on the little pool table which was the only thing inmates on Tier Five North were allowed to do to keep from going crazy. Part of the day, they'd open up our little area so we could crawl out of our cages into the larger cage. You couldn't get the newspaper. You couldn't exercise in your cell. You couldn't really do nothing except die. You couldn't even die fast, because you were constantly being patted down for knives or whatnot.

I did not know if I would ever walk free in the daylight again.

And sitting there in my miserable cell, C106, Five North, I had way too much time to think. And more and more, I kept thinking about Bobby Cabert, my old friend, a guy I once thought of as the big brother I never had. It was Bobby Cabert, I had come to believe, who was the main reason I'd wound up in this tomb out of reach of the sun. It was his prison number on that card in my wallet that helped the feds link the two of us together.

I thought about the first time I met Cabert, at a racetrack in New Jersey with Uncle Raymond. This was about twenty years earlier, in the early 70s. I was around twenty years old at the time, a real hotshot (or so I thought). And I thought the world Uncle Raymond was introducing me to at the time was fabulous. That was the word: "Fabulous." The fact that there was this shadowy world just beneath the surface of everything, all kinds of things that were never spoken, the fact that these men were powerful and influential and feared – I thought it was just glamorous and enticing as hell.

And Bobby Cabert, more than any other single person, seemed to personify the dark glamour of that world.

Little did I know at the time where it would all lead.

Wearing this baggy brown prison outfit and these stupid blue boating shoes, and where they keep the temperature so low you're always freezing your nuts off. In a federal holding facility they give you nothing but a sheet, a pillowcase and a pillow, a thin blanket and a towel. They also give you this crappy little locker and I had all my stuff in the world in there – one extra pair of underwear and a change of socks. Oh, and one other thing: Even though everything is slick as a whistle, in that locker there are roaches. When I reach into that locker to get my other pair of socks, the roaches go skittering away like criminals caught in the act.

Real glamorous.

***

It was December 21st, 1996 – four days before Christmas. I'll never forget the day. I had been in federal lockup for seven months (even though it seemed like seven years). It was a Thursday, like any other Thursday in the eternity of life behind bars. All that hope I got from Father Paul up on the holy mountain was almost gone. I was just trying to survive. Why, I don't know.

For the past seven or eight weeks, I'd been held in holdover upstate at Otisville. The big payoff was visits from Patsy, and a couple of hours of sunshine a day. A chat with Patsy and an hour of sunshine a day: that's what passed for Christmas in the federal correctional system.

So I called Allen Marra, and for once he picked up. (I had asked him earlier if I should call him "Mr. Marra," and he said, "No, call me Allen.")

"Allen, could you call the judge and ask her to keep me in Otisville for the holidays?" I says to him. "I gotta see my sister Patsy."

"No, I can't," Allen says.

My heart just kind of dropped. I was going back to the tomb.

"No," he says, "I can't keep you in Otisville."

"How come?"

"Because you're going home tomorrow."

It was like time stood still. I couldn't even breathe.

"What?" I says, figuring there was some mistake. "What?"

"I said you're going home tomorrow. You got bail. They gave us bail. Make sure you're on the list to come downtown, because you're going home tomorrow. Congratulations!"

When I got over having a heart attack and a nervous breakdown, I says to Allen, "What happened? What changed that all of a sudden we got bail?"

"Well, I have to say that it had a lot to do with a phone call from a friend of yours – Robert Bisaccia. Bobby Cabert. He was able to convince the U.S. Attorney that you don't belong in there."

"Bobby Cabert?"

"Bobby Cabert."

So it was Bobby Cabert, my old friend, the gangster, the guy whose prison number got me in here in the first place – it was him who was getting me out. Even though he was in federal prison for life for being a hitman for the Mob, he had achieved a kind of redemption by freeing me. He would eventually die behind bars, but now he was trying to do a good deed before he went down.

"How much was the bail?" I says to Allen.

"A million dollars, secured, Bobby. Your sister Patsy and her husband James put the deed to their house up. And both of them also signed a cash bond for about $200,000 each."

I could hardly believe what I was hearing. Since this was a federal charge, when you put up bail it ain't no ten percent, like for less serious charges. My sister and James had to come up with the whole amount, putting up $400,000 cash and putting their house at risk. If I jumped bail, they would lose it all. I knew James had a good job, but they didn't have that kind of money. Who did?

What they did have, despite everything I had done to them, was love for me.

Love!

When I hung up the phone, these indescribable feelings just swarmed over me. How could anyone love me that much? And, you mean... I wasn't going to spend the rest of my life in this hellhole? You mean... I was going to sleep in my own bed, in my little apartment in Union City, where my sisters had been paying the rent in the hope that I might come back? Like... tomorrow night?

One thing I had to remind myself: Keep this to yourself. Guys who are about to be released are a target in prison. If I blabbed about it, it wouldn't be the first time some loudmouth with his walking papers wound up knifed in the shower. So I didn't tell nobody except Peter McMullen, the Irish Republican Army guy, who I had come to like and trust. He was the one who had kept saying to me, "What the hell are you still doing in here? You don't belong here."

And I guess he was right.

So that whole day I kept checking to see if I was on the list, but I wasn't. I started freaking out. I called my lawyer back.

"Just tell them to keep checking," Allen says. "Don't get nervous."

It was a little while later, around 2 pm, that they told me I was on the list. Shortly afterwards I was taken by bus down to MCC in Manhattan and the next day, around noon, I was taken into the courtroom of federal judge Marion Cederbaum (who later resolved the baseball strike, and sat on Martha Stewart's trial).

And there, sitting in the courtroom, were my amazing, long-suffering, saintly sister Patsy and her husband James. Patsy! The one who cared for me so much that she could see through the horrible vampire I had become, and stuck with me all those years until my true self came back! Just sitting there quietly, with her whole financial future at risk because of me.

Judge Cederbaum explained the terms of my bail, which was that I had to stay in the Southern District of Manhattan and nowhere else without permission, and that I had to report regularly to my federal parole officer. The federal extortion charge was not being dropped, of course; I was just out on bail until the charge could be resolved.

OK, so I wasn't completely free, at least not yet. But in my heart, I could never remember being happier.

"Can I say something to you?" I says to Judge Cederbaum, after she finished talking.

"Yes, Mr. Purzycki?"

"I love you, Your Honor!"

"I love you, too, Robert," she says, laughing. "But you need to get downstairs and do your paperwork if you want to go home." Then she added, just as I was leaving, "Good luck, Robert."

"Thank you!"

20 GANG NIGHT

Getting sprung from federal prison is like being one of them cave bats flying out of the darkness into the middle of the day. You keep blinking, but it takes you a long time to get used to the sunshine. You don't trust it. You're not sure it's going to last. And usually, it don't.

Because the fact is, I wasn't really "free" at all – I was only out on million-dollar bail, like one of them old-timey prisoners dragging around a ball and chain, looking for some dude with a hacksaw. I may not have believed I had done anything seriously wrong – after all, I told myself, I was only trying to help out a friend. But in the eyes of the law, I was a guy with direct ties to the Gambino crime family, who had been involved in an extortion plot involving deadly weapons. I mean, that don't sound too good. My new lawyer, Maurice, had told me that I might be looking at three to five years in federal prison. And all for a hundred fucking bucks!

It's almost impossible to describe what living with this hanging over your head is like.

By now I was going on five years sober, but like a lot of people in early sobriety I found myself having to face the wreckage of my past life without the benefit of drugs and alcohol. There were lots of times when I was just about dying to get drunk or wasted, just to blank it all out. But by the grace of God, the fellowship of AA, and the presence of an old Franciscan friar who didn't even exist, I didn't go there. The main thing was that, if I broke parole, my sister and James – two beautiful angels that I did not deserve – would have been on the hook for a million dollars. I would have broken them, financially. I would never have forgiven myself (and they wouldn't have, either.)

So I stayed and suffered through it, trying to rebuild a real, actual life instead of a fake life built on lies, self-pity and self-seeking. I don't know what else to call that except a miracle.

Of course, you can't fuck up your life as bad as I done without consequences. The day after I got out of prison, I went back to see C.J. and Annie at New Bowl-Rite lanes in Union City. They had been some of the closest friends I ever had. C.J. was the best friend a guy could ever want. He was in the program eight years, so besides the fact that he was a Polack, we had always had a lot in common. He and Annie, who was this tiny little woman, maybe 125 pounds, with the most wonderful, sweet face – they had just welcomed me with open arms when we first met.

But when I came back from my little shoebox-size cell in the federal Big House, everything felt stiff and tense between us. Jokes kind of fell flat. Something was "off." But C.J. and Annie were nice enough to offer me my old job back, so I went back to running the pro shop, helping to keep the lanes clean and conditioned, working to build up the leagues and so on, but there was no getting around the fact that because of what I done, C.J. and Annie had had their whole world seriously rocked. I was different, too: I was older, sadder, more suspicious, and pretty close to broke.

When I was in prison I used to call C.J. quite a lot (you can only make collect calls from in there, and C.J. took my calls for quite awhile before he got fed up with it). Well, apparently the feds had the phone tapped. What they were really interested in was collaring the big shots in the Gambino crime family, like Gotti and them. They actually thought I was a capo in the Mob, when I was really just a pathetic recovering alcoholic bowler and former homeless crack addict who was doing somebody a favor for a hundred bucks.

So one day C.J. gets called down to the federal building in Manhattan to be interrogated by the F.B.I. He later told me he wasn't even really nervous. He was completely innocent, so what was there to worry about? (Believe me, even if you're totally innocent, if the F.B.I. wants to interrogate you, you should be really fucking nervous.)

So C.J. goes downtown and the feds get him in a room and they spread a bunch of photographs of these mobsters on a table – Gotti, Angelo Ruggiero, Joe Gallo and all them other guys.

"Where do you fit in this picture?" they say. "How high up the ladder do you go?"

C.J. couldn't believe it. Here he was this chubby Polack who ran a bowling alley in Paterson, New Jersey. Like, they thought he was Michael Corleone or some damn thing? It was a joke.

"You ain't got a ladder high enough!" C.J. tells them, busting out laughing. The feds don't think this is terribly funny, though. They start showing up at the bowling alley – two or three clean-cut guys, who would play three games of pool in four hours, maybe drink a Pepsi because they'd show up at a time when the bar was closed, and just kind of sit around looking to see who came in and out.

"Yeah, we had some more pool players in today," C.J. would tell me over the phone when I called in from prison.

"Look, Bobby," he'd say, more nervously, "I'm telling the feds everything."

"Go right ahead," I'd say. "I got nothing to hide."

I can understand why this really rattled C.J. and Annie's cage. And it was all because of me, because I tried to help them and instead dragged a bunch of mobbed-up thugs into their life and now they couldn't get free of them.

It was like my whole past life was a disease, and it had spread to their world.

The bowling alley had turned out to be a nightmare for them in other ways, too. The bowling alley was in a pretty poor, mostly-Hispanic neighborhood, not the ghetto but you could see the ghetto from there. Nobody had no money. The business was so slow that C.J. and Annie had to sell their house and go live with the in-laws to pay the bills. But there were still more unpaid bills, huge ones, I don't know how much money, but enough to hang over their heads like one of them science fiction monsters in the movies. Every time I talked to C.J. on the phone, I could hear the stress in his voice.

When I got out of prison and went to work at the bowling alley, I could tell that all this debt was eating away at him. But I also knew, from learning to live as a sober person, that sometimes taking on other people's problems as your own is a terrible idea. That's part of the meaning of the Serenity Prayer, that we say at every meeting: *God grant me the serenity to accept the things I cannot change, the courage to change the things I can, and the wisdom to know the difference.* It's about knowing where to draw the line of your own responsibility – this is what I am responsible for, and that is what I am not responsible for.

Even so, almost as soon as I went to work at Bowl-Rite, I began to notice that there was this crowd of kids, almost all of them Hispanic, anywhere from eight to their late teens, early twenties, who used to come into the bowling alley after school and just stay there until dinnertime or later. For some of them, I don't think there was a dinnertime. I guess a lot of places would have told these kids to scram. But I got to talking to them, and I could see that a lot of them were good kids who'd gotten a bum rap in life. A lot of them came from broken homes, the mom working long hours at some crummy job, maybe the dad in jail, nothing much for them to do after school except smoke dope and get in trouble.

I saw myself in these kids. I knew where they were headed. I knew what it was to feel unloved, to feel abandoned by the world, to feel lost, to be on the wrong road. So they'd come into the bowling alley in the afternoon and I'd let them do their homework there. Then I'd let them bowl a few games and give them some tips about the finer techniques of the game. Some of these kids had a real gift for the game, like I had. I felt that helping them gain confidence at something might even help to turn their lives around.

Helping these kids like that made me remember what it was like when I was a kid growing up in Paterson, and the bowling alley was about the only safe place in my world. It was also about the only place you'd see whole families – mom, dad, sis, junior, Fido, whatever. Well, at Bowl-Rite there might not have been whole families, but I wanted to make sure there was a clean, safe place for these kids to come. I wanted them to feel that same feeling of safety and security that I felt there, growing up.

I didn't tell these kids about my sorry history, being homeless, being in prison, and they never asked. To them I was just an older guy who showed interest in them, a kind of a father or uncle figure that they probably didn't have at home. I saw in them the children I never had.

I got real fond of a kid named Jeffrey Butler, who was half black, and whose dad was in prison. I took care of him and his brother Eddie like they were my own kids. Spanky was only five or six years old, being raised by a single mother, but he came to the bowling alley every day and I watched over him, kept him safe, kept him in line. Spanky was a great two-handed bowler at the age of six. (Much later, after he was grown, Spanky told me that if it hadn't been for bowling he'd probably have turned into a street kid.)

Then there was Havie, who was a tough gangster kid, but when you broke that shell, inside he was a sweet youngster who was actually extremely bright. And there was a good-looking Puerto Rican kid, an extremely bright kid, who went by the name Melrock. Melrock came to me one day and asked if he could have a job. "Sure," I says. "Throw that kid outta here."

So he throws the kid down the stairs.

Melrock was not only a good bouncer, he was also a fabulous graffiti artist. I had him paint a skyline of New York on the wall of the bowling alley, and it was so good that not too long after that we changed the name of the bowling alley to Skyline Bowl.

Then there was Paul Stamos and Dustin and a whole pack of others. As time went on, I hired more and more of these kids to work at the bowling alley – I must have had ten of them on the payroll at any one time, cleaning the lanes, being porters, cleaning the restrooms, working the front desk, whatever.

A lot of these kids, it turns out, had ties to the Latin street gangs, like the Latin Kings, the Ñetas, or the Vatos Locos. Then there were other kids with ties to the Crips and the Bloods.

But the thing was this: I knew these were basically good kids. And, once I started showing them how, it turned out a lot of them really liked to bowl.

So what happened was that I decided to start having Gang Night at the bowling alley. The rules would be that there were no guns and no fighting in the bowling alley. If you wanted to fight you had to go three blocks away. And I got the cops to agree that there would be no arrests at the bowling alley, either. It would be like one of those demilitarized zones in wartime, a bowling DMZ. A safe place where the kids could go at night. There was a cop named Dominick DiPinto who worked in the gang unit of the local police force, who worked nights at the front desk at Bowl-Rite. He had a real good observation post on what was going on, but the rule for Dominick and his cop friends was, hands off. Sometimes Dominick would take pictures of the kids, and the kids would just goof for the camera, like it was a joke. You were safe there, no matter who you were or what you had done.

Annie was a great promoter, and I met another lady in AA who was a marketing expert, so the three of us started really targeting the Hispanic community, who didn't usually bowl too much. We sent out coupons and postcards and promotions to Union City, Jersey City, Hoboken (where there's a lot of gangsters and yuppies) and nearby areas. I went out and talked to schools and camps, inviting all the kids to come.

The first time I put out the word we'd be having Gang Night at the bowling alley, more than 390 kids showed up. It was amazing. These kids came in and bowled 1400 games in five hours. All 24 lanes were filled all night.

But by a couple of weeks later, two hundred had dropped out. The reason was they didn't have no money. So I started letting a lot of these kids bowl for free. We offered them prizes, and had a little banquet at the end of the year. Jeffrey was a regular 12-year-old phenom, just like I was, and Dustin (who was C.J.'s son) bowled a 300 game when he was 14. So bowling, which in a way had been my downfall, became a kind of salvation for a lot of these kids.

Eventually, I moved out of my sister's house, scraped together a security deposit and rented a nice little studio apartment walking distance from the bowling alley, at a place called the Washington Park Towers. Now I had a decent place to live, and a job I liked, and people who needed me and depended on me. I even had kids, for the first time in my life. It was sort of like a multi-colored family. Things were looking up.

Financially, though, it was always a struggle to keep the bowling alley solvent, even though we were now the center of the universe to a whole bunch of semi-homeless Hispanic gang-bangers. I was working at the bowling alley all the time and doing everything I could to help the business pull up out of the shithole it was in. I walked to work from my apartment every day, and went to AA meetings after work almost every day. Every other week I went to Hoboken and took the PATH train into Manhattan to the federal probation department. Man, I'm telling you: I stuck to the terms of my probation like glue, because I had no intention of going down that road again. Even so, it still might not be enough to save me from serving more federal time in that eight-by-ten cell.

Then one day C.J. sits me down for a talk.

"Look," he says, "I want to make you a deal. Me and Annie – we're getting pretty burned out on running this place. How about if we just sell it to you? The sale price would be a steal: One dollar. We'd sell you Bowl-Rite Lanes, the whole schmear, for a buck. But, see, you'd also have to agree to take on everything, including the bad debt we got. You'd buy the business, good and bad. If you can turn it around, you could make some real money. That's the deal."

I thought about this overnight and the next day I told C.J. I'd do it. I just knew I could make it work. Now I turned my whole attention to trying to turn this damn thing around. I was well-known in the bowling world; I had a national rep. Maybe because of that, and because I did everything I could to build the business, build up leagues, have special promotions and so on, things started picking up pretty quick. People started coming into the bowling alley again. I was starting to reach into my pocket and find money there, instead of lint or a little sticky black crack stem, or a scrap of paper with a scribbled phone number for somebody I'd been trying to hustle, but now couldn't remember at all.

I even started attracting some celebrities. I got to know the U.S. Senator from New York, Robert Menendez, and his son, who would come in to bowl. Lawrence Taylor, who used to play football for the New York Giants, would come in. Ray Allen, a basketball player who used to play for the Celtics and the Miami Heat, he came in. And there was that MTV host, Downtown Julie Brown, who would also come in quite a lot.

C.J. went to work for another bowling alley, one of our competitors actually, and Annie decided to stay on as an employee, working for me. So now, for better or worse, I was a business owner – practically a member of the Chamber of Commerce. Me, the guy from cellblock Five North, was almost an upstanding citizen.

Being in charge of the left-over bad debt was like learning to be a grown-up, taking responsibility for mistakes. As business picked up I started making regular payments on the old debt, chiseling it down week after week. Because it was easier, I started paying the rent every week, and some months I'd add more than four weeks. Once I could afford it, I got C.J. and Annie health insurance, and I gave Annie a raise. And I told them both, if the business ever climbed out of the hole and got sold, I'd give them a piece of it. After all, they had helped to save my life.

By this time, all the mobbed-up guys who had once been so much a part of my life were gone, and they had also left my mind and my heart. They wound up where they belonged, I guess. Bobby Cabert, convicted of federal racketeering charges and sentenced to 40 years, would eventually die of cancer in prison (in 2008). I never spoke to him again. Tommy Lorenzo, my old friend and chief enabler, had already died of AIDS. The feds had finally nailed John Gotti, the "Dapper Don," after years of trying. He was convicted of murder, loansharking, bribery, tax evasion and a few other things and sentenced to life in prison. Now he was sick and dying in solitary confinement in the "supermax" prison in Marion, Illinois. Even so, I often thought of him and never forgot the times he helped me out. To this day, I remember his sweetness. I was just glad the feds never found his prison number in my wallet!

21 HIGH ROLLER

It was Christmastime, 1995, and I'd been out of prison for a year. I was sober, and an almost-respectable member of society. I'd been a business owner, and an employer, for the past seven months. I was even a mentor to kids. Imagine that! My past criminal history and links to a murderous crime family? It was nobody's business but my own. Look: there are plenty of people in America with a past they'd rather forget. But this is a country of second chances. So I figured I'd take mine.

The thing that had seized my attention now was the Super Bowl High Roller tournament in Las Vegas – the biggest-money bowling tournament in the country. The top prize was $100,000 (out of a total, record-breaking purse of $1,673,000). It was called the Super Bowl because it was the pinnacle of my sport. Ever since 1981, twice a year, in July and January (right around the time of the Super Bowl) the Showboat Hotel and Casino and the bowling equipment manufacturer Brunswick sponsored this glitzy tournament in Vegas that attracted all the top bowlers in the country. All the big bowling tournaments were in Vegas.

Because of the huge purse for winning, and all the other ways of winning money, the High Roller drew almost every single top bowler in the entire country – and from lots of other countries also. The incredible Mike Newman. Chris Barnes, a fanatical guy who bowled like, ten or twelve hours a day and was recently ranked number one in the world. His approach was smooth as silk. Pat Healey, the three-time World Cup Amateur of the Year. "Rudy Revs," from Long Island, who curved that ball better than anybody. Joe Vita, the great money bowler from Texas. David Haynes, Chris Hayden, Willy Willis, a tremendous black bowler. Mike Mullen, a leftie who bowled for St John's College and later became World Bowler of the Year. I mean, forget about it!

According to the rules of the tournament, these guys were all amateurs, but a lot of them would later go on to become the top pro bowlers in the country. Winning the High Roller was not just winning the biggest purse. It was winning the biggest honor in bowling. It put you in the permanent record books. The finals of the tournament were filmed on tape delay and broadcast nationally the next day on ESPN, Wide World of Sports and an affiliate of Fox Prime Sports Network cable sports show.

The main idea of the High Roller was simple: It was a tournament where, if you lost, you were out – no second chances, no second rounds, so long, see ya later. Since the tournament had a full field of 2,048 entrants, it was like starting out with two thousand gunslingers in the Old West. If you lost the duel, you were dead. And as the tournament went on, Main Street in Dodge City would get knee-deep in bodies. Anybody, even the greatest bowlers in the world, sometimes have a bad match. But in the High Roller, that don't matter. In order to win, you had to win all eleven of your matches in a row.

Actually, I was pretty familiar with the whole drill of going to Vegas for the High Roller, because I had entered six or seven times before. Back in my drinking and drugging days, I'd go out there, cocky as hell, with my hot-combed hair and major attitude, convinced I could win it all. And for the first few games I'd do great. There were lots ways of making money without winning the whole tournament, for example you could bowl what they called "sweeps" – two games together – and if you won them both you'd win a couple of thousand bucks. I'd go out there and win a few sweeps, almost as a warm-up to the big tournament.

Then I'd start drinking. Or, more accurately, I never stopped drinking, from the moment I got there to the moment I left. I'd get smashed out of my mind for, like, seven days straight. When I was younger, alcohol was like fire in my veins and I just became unstoppable, unbeatable. When I knocked back a few glasses of vodka and orange juice and stepped up to the line, I was like Wild Bill Hickok, scattering them pins with a hit dead square in the center, one strike after another. One time I won five thousand bucks the first day I got out there.

But whether I knew it or not, those days of wine and roses was long gone. Over time, I had turned into an old, slow, sloppy drunk, and I'd be drinking all night and all day long. I always had a drink in my hand during the whole High Roller, from day one through the whole tournament (or at least, as long as I lasted). I'd drink at the bowling alley, in the bars, in the casinos (where if you bet a dollar you got a free drink), at the craps tables, I'd drink socially and I'd drink alone. I'd wind up in my hotel room at three or four in the morning, drinking and puking.

Real glamorous.

Sure, there were some big-time bowlers who were falling-down-drunk alcoholics, and a lot of bowlers did dope, but I'm pretty sure I broke some kind of world record for alcohol and drug abuse – the Super Bowl High Roller of addiction.

Me and Vegas never agreed with each other. Alcohol jacked up my game at first, but then it destroyed it, and I'd wind up on the eastbound plane headed back to Jersey with a bad hangover and a dwindling stash of cash in my pocket, an early loser knocked out of the tournament before it even really got started. All this great promise that I had, or once had had, this chance to touch my inner greatness, this chance to reach my dreams – well, fuck it. You just flush the toilet, crawl back into bed, cover your head and try to forget about your life. Having big dreams only made you feel worse.

Maybe tomorrow would be a better day.

Except that it wouldn't.

One thing I didn't quite realize about all this was that my troubles were not exactly my little secret. I had become so well-known in the bowling world when I was younger that when I started my long, ugly downhill slide – and then vanished completely from the bowling scene for more than seven years – everybody in the bowling world knew about it. Everybody knew my story, even if I never told nobody nothing myself. Even the F.B.I. knew my story.

So anyway, that January of 1996, I decided I was going out to Vegas and I was going to win the High Roller. I wasn't just going to compete. I was going to win.

Sure, I'd been there before, but now this was a new day – for the first time, I'd be going out there sober, and focused. I put my head into the laser-focus of winning, however far-fetched that might be. I was convinced that I was capable of doing it. I remembered (as just one example) that time back in September of 1986 when me and Mike Foti broke the American Bowling Congress record with a team series (for three games) of 1639. I threw 22 consecutive strikes – 30 strikes out 36 frames – for a total score in three games of 845. Man, I was hot! And I knew I could do it again. (At the time, I'd been homeless, man!)

In my usual in-your-face New Jersey way, I figured I wasn't going to make no big secret about going out to win the High Roller, so I told everybody I was going out there to win and invited this whole entourage to come along. I told the league bowlers who came to Bowl-Rite on Friday nights – this was like 120 people – that I was going to buy them all shrimp when I won. C.J. and Annie and their son Dustin decided to come. Paul Stamos, Melrock, Chris Haden, Jimmy Mack and his brother Tim, all great younger bowlers in their twenties, they came too.

But my favorite kid that came was Jeffrey Butler, who was 11. Jeffrey was an extremely smart kid, and a really talented bowler. He and his mom lived right next door to Bowl-Rite, and he practically grew up there. His dad was in prison, his mom was raising him and his little brother, Spanky.

Jeffrey Butler: *"My mom said if my grades were all right, I could go. So I went. Man, it was surreal! Getting out of school and going to Vegas to watch the biggest bowlers in the country compete! I remember we all squeezed into a room at a hotel called the Stratosphere, that had a roller coaster on the roof.*

I think my mom understood that being with Bob, and hanging out at the bowling alley, was about the safest place I could be – and I'd be safe in Vegas, too. The neighborhood around Bowl-Rite (where my mom and I lived) was pretty rundown, and ninety-nine percent Hispanic. So the bowling alley was kind of a 'safe haven' for me. I was there every day, learning from Bob and watching what he did out there on the lanes. And he was amazing! I had heard all that stuff about him living on the streets, and being a dope addict and all. But I didn't care about that. To me he was just a good bowler, and a great guy."

Going out to Vegas with this whole entourage, even though a lot of them was kids, was almost like the old days when I came sweeping into that big money match against Ruby Red, down in Harlem, with John Gotti and Uncle Raymond and the whole mobbed-up crew. Except now I was sober, legit and nobody I was with knew a damn thing about the Gambino crime family except what they read in the papers.

Compared to all the other times I went out to Vegas with stars in my eyes, this time I had one huge new thing going for me. I was sober. If I sat down at the bar, it would be to have a club soda with lime, not five Manhattans.

I'd always been convinced that if I could stay straight, I could win the High Roller. Now, with more than four years of sobriety and constant contact with my Higher Power and Father Paul, I believed that I could succeed. I believed that I could make my dreams come true. This time, I don't know, I just had a good feeling about the High Roller from the very start. (Of course, there were two thousand other great bowlers who might have had the same feeling!)

But, realistically, I also realized that this would probably be my last chance to win this star-studded tournament, something I had dreamt about, and repeatedly attempted, for like twenty years. For one thing, I was in my mid-40s, and bowling is like anything else – you start to lose your chops as you get older.

Oh, and there was this other tiny little thing hanging over my head – a tiny little thing about the size of one of them 40-yard dumpsters Bobby Cabert sent over to the bowling alley. Patsy and James had posted a million-dollar bail to get me out of federal prison. But the extortion charges had been winding their way through the federal court system and were about to come before the judge. In fact, the way everything was working out, if I made it to the finals of the High Roller I might have to skip the championship round and hop on the redeye back to Jersey to face the music.

Maurice had warned me that I might be facing three to five years in prison. And if the judge gave me five years, by the time I got out, I'd be practically 50, and way too old to compete at this level.

So, bottom line: This was my last chance.

Then there was this other problem. Bowling, like golf, is a game of intense concentration. It all comes down to that instant when the ball is released, either from your fingertips (in bowling) or the club (in golf). It's like Zen: The whole thing comes down to one moment. But how was I supposed to beat all the other super-focused bowlers in the United States if half of my mind was worrying about going back to prison for three to five years, in my horrible little rathole in MCC or Otisville? How was I supposed to block that out of my thoughts?

When I got out to Vegas I met Eddie Baur, who was an old friend and director of the American Bowling Congress. Eddie had given me a free spot in the tournament (normally, the entry fee was around $1200 for three people). I'd introduced Eddie to Brad Edelman, who ran the High Roller tournament. They were glad to see me there, and they were nice enough not to mention what everybody knew: That I'd been way, way down and out, but now I was back.

Just before my big trip to Las Vegas to bowl in the High Roller, just before Christmas of 1995, a lady named Joan, who was one of the metropolitan sports writers at Bowler's Journal International magazine, came to me to do a feature story about me. She came to the bowling alley to interview me. And the last question she asked me was, "do you think you'll ever win again in bowling?"

"If I stay on the road, and stay sober, no doubt I'll win again, including the High Roller," I told her.

So this story, called "To Hell And Back," comes out in January, right around the time of the High Roller, and it looks like I'm predicting that I'm going to win. Which is a pretty ballsy thing to do. But I was pumping up my confidence, against all odds, like a prizefighter talking trash about his opponent. In a way I was just covering up my fear.

The only place in Las Vegas big enough to handle two thousand bowlers was the Showboat Lanes & Casino (which also happened to be the cosponsor of the event). The place was huge, with lanes 1 to 70 on the left side, by the casino, and 36 more lanes on the lower level. Before the tournament actually began on Saturday, I bowled a few sweepers to get a feel for the lanes. Jeffrey sat up as close to the action as he could get, just watching every move I made. He was like my right-hand man.

"Are you gonna win?" he'd ask me.

"What, are you kidding? Of course I'm gonna win," I'd say. "Forget about it."

"You don't look like you're gonna win," he'd say.

"Shut up, Jeffrey," I'd say.

I'd decided to use these new balls made by the Storm Company called Thunder (which was black) and Lightning (which was purple). In fact, these were the very first high performance bowling balls, not made out of rubber but some kind of synthetic material. This was the beginning of a whole new trend in bowling, synthetic lanes, fiberglass kickbacks, synthetic balls, that gave everything a big bounce and made a lot of noise.

Thunder and Lightning rolled really well, when I bowled a couple of practice games. I decided not to bowl any more sweepers, like the old days, because I had my sights set on winning the whole tournament, and I needed every ounce of concentration I could get. I wasn't going to be rolling up a few grand here and there by winning sweepers, then slinking off someplace to get wasted. I was going to blow into this place like Captain America and win the whole fucking thing.

On Saturday afternoon, I bowled my first match, and going into the tenth frame I was up by 18 pins. Still, if I threw a bad pitch, I could still lose. So I got up to the line and threw three strikes in the tenth, boom, boom, boom. The other guy, a great bowler from Ohio, was furious, because he knew he'd had a chance to win at the end but I stopped that.

Jeffrey Butler: *"Bob was very superstitious. You had to draw a lane out of a hat, so he let me draw the number for the first match, and after he won, he had me draw the number for the rest of the tournament."*

The second day of the tournament, Sunday, I didn't have to bowl, so I spent my time watching everybody else. Nobody had the "look" I had, which meant I was playing in the middle of the lane, and Thunder and Lightning were beautifully matching the lane. I won my second match easy.

That night I called Patsy back in New Jersey. Patsy, of course, was intensely interested in the tournament – she was praying constantly about it – but for some reason she never went to these kinds of things. We just talked every night on the phone, hoping that I would get far enough to where she could watch the finals on TV. (This was in the early days of Internet, I guess, but Patsy wasn't on there yet.)

I called her that night, and I suddenly started to get choked up.

"You know what, Pat? I think I could win this thing. I really do," I says.

"I know," she says. "I had a premonition. I think you're gonna win, too."

But now I could sense that a serious problem was developing. I called

Maurice, my lawyer, frantic.

"I'm doing great – I just won my second match," I says to him.

"That's great!"

"But I got a problem."

"What problem?"

"I'm supposed to be home Wednesday for the sentencing hearing on Thursday. But the finals are Wednesday night."

"Look, who's the lawyer, you or me?" Maurice says.

"You," I says.

"Okay, so relax and let me take care of it. I'll try to get the judge to delay the hearing. I can try to get a continuance. You just concentrate on winning."

"But Maurice – I'm really worried. I'm out on a million-dollar bail – if I don't show up on time, my sisters, my brother-in-law – all these people who helped me will lose a fortune!"

"Bobby, just concentrate on winning. Let me take care of the rest."

Meanwhile, I seemed to be getting some help from upstairs – way upstairs. I was in a constant prayer connection with my Higher Power. And I prayed to Father Paul, the old monk who didn't exist, with his long brown robe and his tufts of gray hair and his laser-beam eyes. Talk about a guy who was connected! He had told me that if I used all the focus and concentration and talent I had used to become a champion bowler, if I focused all that on my quest to become sober, I could succeed.

Now I prayed for the power to use that focus to win this national tournament, for the benefit of everyone who loved me and looked up to me. I prayed that I could stay in the moment. I had to bowl this tournament one frame at a time, just like alcoholics learn to live one day at a time. I prayed that I could keep everything "in synch," in the pocket, in the rhythm. I prayed that I could win.

Tuesday morning, I bowled a guy from Oklahoma who thought he was great. I figured it was going to be a tough match. Eddie Baur told me during practice to use Thunder, the black ball, so I did. I got a spare in the first frame, then I threw six strikes in a row and the game was over in the seventh frame. Mr. Oklahoma bit the dust.

That day, Tuesday, I had to win four matches to keep going. And by now, I was mentally moving deeper and deeper into the winning mode, praying to my High Power and to Father Paul to keep my focus.

I won my next two matches, boom, boom, and then, in order to make it into the top 64, I drew a guy named Mark Dyson, who was at the time one of the hottest amateurs on the planet. But this guy, he was a real loudmouth, and the night before the match I heard him running his lip about what a hotshot he was and how he was going smoke everybody out there (including me). I got up in his face about this – he just fucking rubbed me the wrong way – and we got in a pretty big argument about this. He was drinking a lot, and I seen myself in him – the trash-talking alcoholic, so full of himself he has no idea how he looks or sounds to other people. It's funny how the things that irritate you the most in other people are the same things you hate in yourself.

So there was definitely some bad blood between "the Diceman" and me before this match.

So I drew lanes 5 and 6, with Jeffrey's help. Jeffrey sat down close to me, in the settee area, which was this big half-circle of padded seats a couple of steps down from the main level of the bowling alley.

"Can you beat him?" Jeffrey whispers.

"Watch me," I says.

"You don't look like you can beat him."

"Shut up, Jeffrey," I says.

Eddie Baur had told me, again, to use the black ball, and I threw a strike in the first frame and a spare in the second. I made the sign of the cross before every frame I bowled. I don't know, maybe that was pissing Dyson off but on the third frame the guy got up and threw, and only clipped a couple of pins. It was amazing. Bowlers at this level never fuck up that bad.

In the third frame, I got up and I whispered to myself and to my Higher Power, "If you're ever going to throw good, do it now!"

I threw a strike, and Dyson was toast.

22 MANIFESTING A MIRACLE

Me and C.J. and Annie and the kids, Jeffrey, Melrock, Timmy Mack and them – we wind up staying at the Stratosphere Hotel & Casino, on the strip, because I know a guy there and he comps us the rooms. The kids are nuts about this place because it's, like, a zillion stories tall, brand-new, and up on the roof is this enormous tower and a crazy-ass roller coaster. The kids think this is the coolest thing they ever seen.

Whenever I finish my matches for the day I go back to my room at the Stratosphere and call Patsy. Calling Patsy is like touching home base in all that craziness. She's my center, my place of safety. But – it's weird – when I call, Patsy kind of seems to already know. She's thinking about me all the time, and praying for me like crazy. She's praying harder and harder. She tells me she had went to the cathedral to see the statue of Our Lady of Fatima and prayed to the Blessed Mother for a miracle. They say if the statue turns blue after you pray, your prayer will come true.

"Bobby," she tells me, almost crying, "The statue turned blue!"

When she tells me that, I almost start crying too. And I'm not even drunk.

"Patsy," I says, with my voice shaking, "I think I'm gonna win it! I can feel it!"

"I know it," she says.

The fact is, though, if I make it through the field of more than two thousand bowlers and get down to the final 32 or even 16, I'll be up against some of the best players in the world – top amateurs, a lot of whom will later go pro. Beating even one of them guys will take a sky-blue miracle. Of course, I got one big weapon that I ain't ever had before in all the times I come out to Vegas before: Sobriety.

I got a couple of other weapons, too. I got Patsy. I got my Higher Power. And I got Father Paul.

Patsy is kind of my positive therapist. She don't care what kind of hotshot bowlers I got coming up. She just keeps sending all these good vibes my way. They say big miracles can happen in the program, and we both are thinking, this might be it. This might be what we've been waiting for. The stage is set for something fabulous to happen.

It's so great to know that Patsy believes in me and is praying for me, and that I also have this back bench of supporters by my side in Vegas. Even so, look: This is the biggest bowling tournament in history, and there are so many accomplished bowlers out here that any one of us might win. It could be that the difference between who wins and who loses is going to turn out to be prayer. There is a side to this glitzy tournament – a side to life, I guess – that's all about the intervention of angels.

Meanwhile, the tournament begins, and over the course of two days I bowl five matches and win them all.

Four solid hours one day, five solid hours the next. Look: When you're 44 years old, bowling against a guy in his twenties – especially if it's your third or fourth match of the day – the younger guy starts to get the edge. You got to rely on your skill and command of the game, saving up your energy, using experience instead of strength, and your ability to psych the other guy out. Luckily, I'm in a state of continuous prayer to my Higher Power, and it seems like I'm running off a battery that never runs out of juice.

So before you know it, I make it into the top 64, out of all them gunslingers from all over the country. Man, I'm on a roll. I know I'm going to do good. I might even be able to grab the brass ring in this thing. This is the furtherest I ever got in the High Roller before – in the past, if I even got to the top 128, I'd collect my $2,000 or $3,000 and then I just wouldn't show up for no more matches. I'd be down at the bar, having this heart-to-heart with the bartender and getting wasted – wasting my promise, wasting my potential, wasting my life. I'd also be hustling the guy for money.

I didn't know it at the time, but by this point in the tournament, I am developing a fan club down at the federal building, back in Manhattan. It's 1996, and some people are using this new-fangled thing called the Internet so they can follow the High Roller. And an amazing number of judges and lawyers like to bowl, so it's gotten around the courthouse through the grapevine that Robert Purzycki, inmate #857435757, the defendant in the Mob extortion case, is doing real good out at the Super Bowl High Roller, in Las Vegas. So all these judges and lawyers and FBI agents are starting to follow the action, and rooting for me. Who knows? Maybe some of them are even betting on me. Now even the guys that arrested me – that FBI agent John Triolo, and his pal, Louie – even they are rooting for me. They want to see me do good. They want to see me make something of myself.

Can you imagine that?

But my most important fan is Maurice.

"Look, Bobby, I got some news," he tells me on the phone one day. "The judge granted you a continuance. You don't have to be back here until Friday morning, ten o'clock. So if you win Thursday, you'll have to get on the redeye back to New York for the hearing the next morning. But you still got time to make the finals."

"Wow! How'd you get the judge to do that?"

"Didn't you know you got a fan club at One Federal Plaza?"

So now, if I do succeed at getting into the finals, I won't have to drop everything just when I got to the top. The fact that a federal judge would allow a continuance on an extortion case because the defendant is bowling in a tournament in Las Vegas – I mean, how amazing is that?

By Wednesday, I've made it into the final 32. There is nobody left but the world-class bowlers. But the only one I'm worried about is Pat Healey, who is considered the top amateur in the country.

In the years leading up to the High Roller this year, Healey has racked up an amazing string of victories. In 1991, he was Gold Medalist in both doubles and trios at the FIQ World Championships (the international bowling federation, going up against bowlers from around the world). In 1991, 92 and 95, he won World Cup Amateur of the Year. In 1995, he won U.S. National Amateur Champion. And this past year, 1995-96, he won World Amateur Bowler of the Year. Et cetera.

He is also 28 years old, and I'm 44. You'd be surprised how physically taxing competitive bowling can be – all the stress and pressure, especially. Also, I figured this is my last shot at glory, but Healey is in his prime and has a lot more shots to go. Which puts a lot more pressure on me. And, of course, that's not to mention the fact that my body has been dragged through the agonies of hell by all them years on the street. In a tense, close fight, all that damage will count against me.

Whoever wins this match, me or Healey, makes it into the final 16. I know very well that I'll have to use all the power and skill and cunning I've learned in my whole life to beat this guy. Plus a tip of the hat from an old monk.

"Can you beat him?" Jeffrey whispers to me, as I'm getting ready to approach the foul line.

"Forget about it," I says.

"I'm not sure you can beat this guy," he says.

"Shut up," I tell him. I am lost in concentration but having trouble getting into rhyme with my Higher Power.

I don't need Jeffrey asking me to tell him the future.

I decide to start out using the purple ball, Lightning.

And in the first frame, I throw a strike – beautiful, powerful, and very loud. My trademark. Eleven more of those and I'll be fine. Then Healey follows with a strike that's just as powerful and just as loud. Perfect, flying down the lane bed and exploding the tenpins like a bomb.

Healey is a small-step bowler, with a high backswing and a very, very smooth follow-through, with a slight break in his elbow. It's beautiful to watch – very controlled, and much slower than the way I throw the ball.

Among all the different styles of bowling, Healy would be considered a "stroker" – a guy with a high backswing and a smooth-as-silk follow-through. A guy with a lot of accuracy. "Spinners" are bowlers who spin the ball like a top, which can be real effective because of high performance bowling balls. "Heavers" just throw that bitch up the lane as hard as they can. And "crankers" just "grip it and rip it," giving the ball the most power and rotation of any bowling style.

My own style is pretty unique – I'm a stroker with a big breaking ball. I have a very high backswing and then I snap it hard on the back end. My dad had a high backswing, so maybe I copied it from him, but nobody else copied it from me. I have no imitators.

I'm watching Pat Healey's super-smooth approach and delivery, and I don't know what it is, but suddenly I start to lose it. I lose my concentration, lose my nerve. I start thinking to myself: There's no way I can beat the three-time World Cup Amateur of the Year. Who am I trying to kid? Just a few years ago, I was sleeping on the floor of a peep show house on 42nd Street. I was hustling some lonely commuter for a drink in a bar, so I wouldn't have to face up to my miserable life. Why did I ever think I could do this? I can't do this. Back on the street: That's where I belong.

When I had been out here for the High Roller a couple of times when I was homeless, after I got knocked out of the tournament, I took my two grand in winnings (or whatever), hopped the redeye back to LaGuardia, and caught a cab to... where? Where was I going? Where did I live? I'd go to a bar I knew, or a bowling alley, and find somebody to hustle so I could get something to drink, something to eat, someplace to sleep for the night. That's who I was: A grifter. A hustler. A bowling bum.

By the fourth frame, Healey is leading by 42 pins. He's leading because he's better than me. The fact that I'm here at all is a joke. I'm not a championship bowler at all. I'm a junkie and a drunk. Who let me in here?

"You're not winning," Jeffrey whispers, helpfully.

Then a great bowler named James Mack sits down next to me on the semi-circular settee. He can see I'm getting rattled.

"Relax," he says, very soothing, very quiet. "Concentrate. I think you should switch balls and move inside."

So I take his advice, exchanging the purple ball for the black one, Thunder, and focusing on firing it closer to the center of the lane.

I make the sign of the cross.

I ask for help and power.

I beg for mercy from my Higher Power, and from Father Paul.

And then I throw a strike.

And another strike.

And another strike.

Boom, boom, boom!

My rhythm, and my game, is roaring back. Boom! I'm getting better and better. Then Healey throws two more strikes. Then I throw another strike. Then, in the ninth frame, Healey misses a ten-pin. It's an incredible blunder – for Healey to miss something like that is practically a miracle. I get up in the ninth frame and throw a huge, powerful strike – just hook the crap out of it and torch the pins, clattering them all over the place. Now it's come down to the very last frame, against one of the toughest bowlers in the world. Either one of us could win this thing now. But for me, the task is huge: All I need is to throw two strikes in the tenth frame. In other words, I have to bowl perfect.

If I throw the first strike, I'm still in the High Roller. If I don't, I'm out – heading back to New Jersey like all them other times. I get up and address the line. I make the sign of the cross. I ask for Father Paul's blessing. And I throw – and it sails down the lane and just kills those pins. A strike, powerful as a punch in the nose.

The bowling alley explodes in applause.

I don't know what's happening, really, because when the great, near-perfect Pat Healey gets up and throws, he leaves a ten-pin standing – again.

"Concentrate," James whispers to me, as I'm getting ready to walk up to the line.

"You can win," Jeffrey whispers.

"This is why we came out here to the High Roller," I whisper back to them both. "This is what I've been living for."

Then, silently, to my Higher Power and Father Paul, I whisper, "Don't fail me now."

I need this last one to win. If I miss, there will be no hurrah. I'll be going home to face the judge and maybe three to five years in a tiny cell where the lights burn all night and there is no sun, no quiet, and every move outside my cage involves locking or unlocking a steel door.

"It's time to play the game," I whisper to myself. "Win this one, and I'm a champion. Miss this one, and I'm forgotten."

The moment the ball leaves my fingertips and goes sailing down the lane, my whole life flashes in front of me. The whole thing – all my great promise as a kid, getting blinded, getting raped, overcoming it all to become a superstar, all my perfect games, Uncle Raymond and John Gotti and Bobby Cabert, getting hit by a cab and almost crippled, pain and pain pills and alcohol, the dark night of addiction and all those terrible years on the street, the six apparitions of Father Paul, Jack and the steps, the gradual return to the light, then getting arrested and seven months in federal prison and now this, the High Roller, the biggest-money tournament in the country, the pinnacle of my promise.

I throw the ball so hard it goes sailing down the lane like a black missile – a thunderbolt, spinning down those sixty-two feet, ten inches of hard maple. It's arcing sharply to the right, almost to the gutter.

"Hook," I whisper. "Hook!" And just then the ball hooks hard and blasts all ten pins across the pindeck. It makes contact just behind the headpin and – kaboom! – the pins explode, like a collapsing house in a hurricane.

By now the whole bowling center is watching, and they break into wild applause. For a second, I don't even dare to breathe.

Then I hear it, all around me: Wild applause and cheering and wolf-whistles. I've beat Pat Healey, the number one amateur in the world. At least for one frame and one game, I won. I beat him.

Healey doesn't take it well. He throws a temper tantrum, just like a little kid, throwing his bowling ball down the lane.

"Why are you mad?" I says to him. "Are you mad because you lost to me and I'm not any good? Are you mad because I'm more than forty years old and an old man beat you?"

He just glares at me.

"Well, you didn't get beat by no dog," I says. "I'm one of the best bowlers who ever lived."

Finally he cools off and comes over to me.

"Congratulations," he says, holding out his hand. "That was a great match."

And after that, Pat Healey is a total gentleman. In fact, for the rest of the tournament he's right there beside me, rooting for me.

After I beat Pat Healey, I am into the final 16 and now they roll in the big TV cameras and lights (as if I'm not nervous enough already.) Now I have a chance to fuck it up on national TV. Now all the judges and lawyers and FBI agents at the federal building can watch me, and so can Patsy and my other sisters, and everybody else in my life who has completely written me off.

But now I'm on a roll. I beat Robert Smith, who just quit the PBA Tour. Then I'm in the top 8, and up against John Dillard, who just bowled 266 and is the Hudson County Bowler of the Year. I actually know him – he's from my home town of Paterson, and we usually root for each other. But this time, I throw ten spares in a row, like a machine, and he never has a shot. In fact, halfway through the game he chokes. He loses it. I hope it don't sound too egotistical to say this, but I think he chokes partly because the myth of Bob Perry gets to him. He don't think he can possibly beat me, and that destroys his game, just like it almost destroyed me in the match against Pat Healey.

So much of any game, from baseball to pinball, is mainly about what happens between your ears. And this time my mental game beats the crap out of his mental game.

By now, I know that I actually have a shot at winning this thing – not just the happy talk I been telling myself. This is no bullshit, no trash-talking, this is for real. I am on national TV every night, in a bowling alley so quiet you can hear a pin drop, focusing with every ounce of my concentration until the moment my bowling ball shatters those ten-pins and they go clattering down the lane. I know very well that I might never have any more chances to win The Big One. I know I have to dig deep and let my talent come out, just like Father Paul said. I know this might be the last time I will be able to actually reach out and touch my dream.

Sure: I am experienced, I have the chops, and I know how to take advantage of breaks and mistakes other people make. And if they don't make mistakes, I know how to outperform then. But the thing is this: The most important thing I am doing here is spiritual. In my heart, I am imagining myself performing to my greatest ability. I am remembering everything Father Paul told me.

I am manifesting a miracle.

And I am bowling for everybody out there. I am bowling for everybody who never got no chance to bring their dreams to life. I am bowling for everybody whose second chance never came. I am bowling for all those alcoholics and junkies and crackheads down on 42nd Street, guys who could have been something but somehow got sucked down by their disease. I am bowling for C.J. and Annie, who lost everything they had and yet still stuck by me. I am bowling for my sister Jeannie. I am bowling for my kids – Spanky and Jeffrey and Junior and Dustin and Melrock. I am bowling for everybody who ever believed in me, who ever thought I was the greatest in the world. I am bowling because I want to show them that they can reach higher than they ever thought they could. This is the day for me to prove that everyone's dreams, not just my own, can come true.

And, most of all, I am bowling for Patsy who, if anybody deserved to be made a saint, it's her. Patsy never gave up on me, never lost faith in me. Even when Patsy was telling me to get the fuck out of her house, in her heart all she wanted was for me to come back to myself, to overcome the demon that was possessing me and become what I could be – to reach the point in my life that I had reached this day. And when push came to shove, James and Patsy had put up the money to get me out of jail – they laid everything they had on the line.

Now there are only four of us left in the tournament. If I was a gunslinger in the Old West, Main Street would be stacked hip-deep in bodies. If I win the next two matches, I win the whole enchilada – a ten-gallon trophy cup with great big handles on it, a check for $100,000, and the joy of being a role model for everybody in my life.

Next up, I'm bowling a guy from Kansas. I never heard of him, but he's got some incredible chops. Now there are, like, hundreds of people watching in the bowling alley, not to mention these glaring lights and TV cameras, like the set for Let's Make A Deal.

The guy from Kansas starts out with a strike. I don't throw a strike in the second frame, leaving a 3-10 split. It's crucial that I make this, or I could be down 30 pins. I make the split, turning the match around. Then he throws a strike, misses a spare, and from there it is an easy coast to victory. Now there is only one match to go.

Now, if I was a gunslinger, I'd have beat every other gunslinger in town except one. And the last guy standing, besides me, is Chris James, this guy from Springfield, Massachusetts – a phenomenally gifted bowler, like Pat Healey. You go down to your local bowling alley and watch a bunch of guys in the local league, and they all bowl kind of the same. But once you get to the highest levels of the sport, you see guys who just look different. Their whole approach, their swing, their delivery – it's like the difference between Tiger Woods and your local duffer. No comparison.

Well, this guy Chris James is one of them guys. (And so am I.)

To have any chance of beating this guy, I have to put myself into a winning frame of mind, with 100 percent of my focus on the thing at hand, just like Father Paul said. Not thinking about what's for dinner or the other guy throwing two strikes and I'm down 43 pins, or the condition of the lane surface, or whether or not I have the right ball for the lane, or whether the ball is hooking like it oughta, or any other damn thing, even the possibility of federal prison hanging over my head. I know that when I bowl good, I am as good as anybody in the world.

And this particular day, bowling the final match against the Massachusetts guy, I am better than anybody in the world. I am unstoppable. And then I get a break. After the fifth frame, they stop the match for a commercial break. And after the break, Chris James gets up and he throws a bad split, 6,7,10 – almost impossible to throw that for a spare. And he don't do it – the ball goes right over the nose of the head pin, but still leaves two pins standing. So by the fifth frame, he's down 25 pins. All I needed after that was to throw a clean game, and the next four frames I threw a spare, strike, spare, strike. He threw a strike in the ninth frame, but by then it was too late.

When I get down to the last frame, I know it's practically all over. I make a sign of the cross. I say to my Higher Power and Brother Paul, "This strike is for everybody – my mom and dad, Annie, C.J. Jeffrey, everybody. If I'm gonna throw it great, let me throw it now."

I throw. The ball sails down the lane, makes a beautiful hook into the pocket like Michael Jordan sinking a three-pointer, and the ten-pins shatter in every direction. A strike. A beautiful strike. I've won.

For everybody.

The whole place explodes in applause, and 50 or 60 or 70 people come pouring down onto the approach, hugging me, clapping me on the back. I can hardly believe what's happening. All my kids come crowding up, and C.J. and Annie. Even the guy I just beat comes up and shakes my hand (he probably don't feel too bad, because the second-place finisher gets fifty grand).

I can tell you one thing: A lot of people was crying, because everybody knew what I had gone through in my life. They knew what the High Roller meant to me.

A little while later there's an awards ceremony, and Eddie Baur hands me that enormous shiny trophy cup, and a check for a little over $112,000 (which was the prize plus some other things I won).

Not bad for a homeless crack addict with no teeth from 42nd Street.

Talk about floating on air! That was great – terrific, really – but I only had one regret: That Patsy could not be here to share it with me.

It's only a couple of hours later that I get on the redeye back to New York. I arrive at LaGuardia at 6:15 in the morning, and there's a federal probation officer waiting for me. He takes me over to One Federal Plaza, in Manhattan, and a little while later I'm standing in the hall with Mr. Rodriguez, my PTI guy (Pre-Trial Intervention), when a couple of very important-looking federal judges come walking by.

"Are you the guy we let go to Vegas?" one of the judges asks me.

"Yes, sir, Your Honor."

"And you won?"

"Yes, sir."

"Good job!"

When the judge walks away I says to the PTI,

"Who's that guy?"

"One of the top judges in the Southern District of New York."

So, you know, that was good.

Even so, the contrast between today and yesterday is like the difference between yes and no. Yesterday there was screaming and yelling and trophies and TV cameras on the Las Vegas strip, and thrill rides on the 108th floor. Today there is only serious, silence and scary. After all, Judge Cederbaum seems like a nice lady, but she has the power to send me back to federal prison for five years – which, considering my damaged condition, could be the rest of my life.

I really don't know if winning the High Roller had anything to do with it

– going out into the world and showing I could make something of myself. All I know is that when I went in front of Judge Cederbaum later that morning, she decided to cut me a break. She didn't send me back to my high-security shoebox at MCC or Otisville. She gave me supervised release, and I began to honorably serve out my federal parole, which I finished a couple of years later, with no problems.

There's no way to express what a relief that was.

When I came back home to Union City, to the wild applause of everybody at Bowl-Rite lanes, I paid off some debts, gave money to C.J. and Annie, gave all the kids a couple of hundred bucks (which was probably more money than they ever seen), and of course, I bought everybody shrimp. I bought myself a TV and a VHS player. And I gave the kids a few short words of advice (which I give to you, too):

"Never give up, no matter what."

A couple of months later, there was another honor.

It was a vote by some of the big-name sportswriters who covered bowling. Every couple of years they would give out this award for people who had been through some real tough shit, a heart transplant, cancer, beating MS, personal difficulties, and then returned to the sport of bowling, and to life. They hadn't gave it out for the past three years.

But this year, they decided to give the award to me.

It was called "Comeback Bowler of the Year."

Which, I gotta tell you, almost made me choke up when they gave it to me. The last thing in this world I wanted was to go back to them dark, lost years on the street. Even so, I couldn't think of no award I was happier to get. And, for better or worse, I couldn't think of no award I actually deserved less. Because my "comeback" from the gates of hell wasn't anything I done myself.

It was a miracle made manifest.

ALBUM

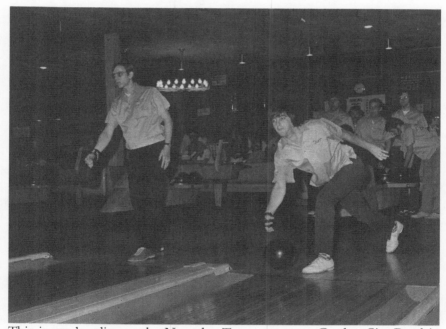

This is me bowling at the Newsday Tournament, at Garden City Bowl in Garden City, Long Island in the early 1970s. I was 20 or so, arrogant as hell, and still wore my hair disco-style.

Another tournament, another trophy – this one in a local east coast scratch tournament, when I was 18. I look exhausted in this picture not because I was high but because I'd been bowling around the clock for three days – tournament bowling in the day, bowling for the action at night.

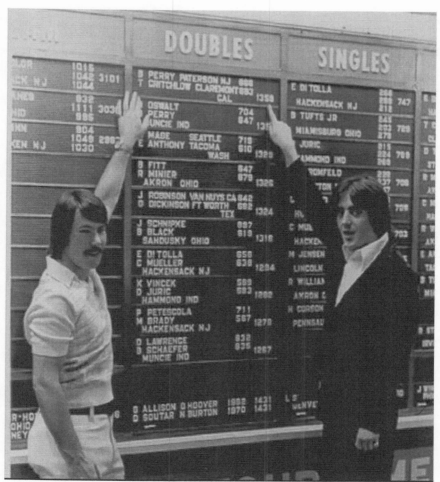

In 1973, my partner Gary Page and I won the ABC National Doubles Championship, beating 1,500 other bowlers. Here I'm pointing to my name at the top of the leaderboard, with Earl Anthony, maybe the greatest bowler ever, two places behind.

The beginning of the end. Somebody snapped this sad picture when I showed up uninvited at my sister's house for Thanksgiving sometime in the 1980s. By then I'd been homeless a couple of years, and my mouth was swelling from rotten, infected teeth (which later fell out). My sister gave me a few bucks and then kicked me out of the house. I used the money to go get high.

When I was homeless I always wore a hoodie sweatshirt pulled up over my head, like in this photo recreation made for the documentary "High Roller."

I was 12 when I won the New Jersey State Youth Championship. After that, I entered the National Youth Championships at the 1964 World's fair – but I never made it, because I got blinded in one eye a couple of days before the tournament. I wasn't sure I'd ever bowl again

This picture was taken for my mom and dad's 25th anniversary. I'm the cute one in the middle at age 12, with my sisters (from left) Jeannie, Joan, Pat and Ann.

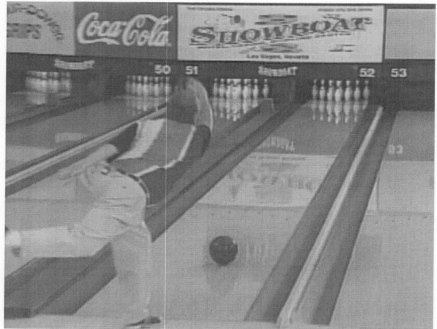

This still picture is from TV footage taken during the Super Bowl High Roller, in 1997, in Las Vegas. The High Roller was the biggest-money tournament in the country – the big enchilada.

This is me at the High Roller tournament in Vegas. I was dead focused on beating the more than 2,000 great bowlers I was competing against, and also trying to forget the federal extortion charges – and years in prison – that loomed over me when I got back to New Jersey.

EPILOGUE

"We have been called to heal wounds, to unite what has fallen apart, and to bring home those who have lost their way." -St Francis of Assisi

Well, here it is fifteen years after that incredible night at the High Roller in Las Vegas. I'm 61 now, and my life has been a roller-coaster of good fortune and bad, but the main thing is that I have maintained my sobriety no matter what for 21 years. Man, it's a miracle! Believe me, if I can do it, anybody can.

You know what's one of the main keys to my spiritual transformation? Helping other people. Not too long after the High Roller was when my sister Patsy and I set up the little nonprofit business in an old train station in Pompton Plains, New Jersey we called "Last Stop". Our business was to sell (at no profit) a whole line of spiritual books from Alcoholics Anonymous and Hazelden. We also carried literature for other Twelve Step programs, too, helping people break addictions to overeating, smoking, sex, whatever. People would come into our store in such pain and suffering – nobody knew how to help a family member or friend, nobody knew what to do. And since I'd pretty much gone as low as you can go without actually dying, I was able to help them by using my own experience. I probably helped over 300 people get into treatment programs. I was paid in the spiritual satisfaction of seeing somebody else get help. Patsy knew about the sorrow of addiction from the point a view of a scared and angry family member, so she could talk to people whose kids or spouses or friends were in trouble too. That was her service work.

Me and Patsy would have kept doing that work but we got shut down (the city of Pompton Plains took the train station by eminent domain, because it was supposedly of historical significance). Afterwards we tried to set up shop in a church around the corner, but we lost 80 percent of our "business" so we quit.

After that, I went down to Texas and opened a bowling center with some partners, but we got hammered by a hurricane and driven out of business. Then I decided to go back to Las Vegas and see if I could win the High Roller another time. I spent a long time getting my chops back and then, in 2008, I returned to Vegas and fought my way to the finals in front of a standing-room-only house. In the ninth frame my finger slipped and I left an almost-impossible split – the two pin and the ten, at opposite ends of the pin deck. My opponent jumped up and started yelling "yes! yes!" because the odds of hitting a two-ten split are astronomical. So I got up in the tenth, threw the ball like a friggin' heat-seeking missile, and wasted both pins. The place went wild.

I actually made it pretty far in the High Roller in 2009, too, but by then my health was coming to pieces and I didn't have no stamina left. I had developed cancer of the prostate at the same time I was struggling with diabetes, brought on partly by all those years on the street, and all those years of alcohol and drug abuse.

In 2012 I decided to leave Las Vegas and move to Charlottesville, Virginia, where I live now, for a couple of reasons. First, I could get great cancer treatment here at the University of Virginia hospital. But, second, I wanted to write a book about my life and my friend Howard Barnett, who'd grown up in Paterson, thought he could help me. It was Howard who put me in touch with the great writer Stefan Bechtel, who helped shape and craft the book you're reading, and asked me a million questions to bring out the details.

All them movie stars get to thank people when they get their Academy Awards, so I'd like to thank people too. I'd like to thank my sisters Patsy and Jeannie, for never giving up on me, and my brother-in-law James Spadafora. I want to thank the men who helped me stay sober, Jack, Billy and George, and also my current sponsor Doc. I'd like to thank Howard and his wife Beth, who are the greatest friends a guy could ask for. I'd like to thank C.J. and Annie and all the kids at the bowling alley – Jeffrey Butler, Jimmy and Timmy Mack, Chris Hayden, Melrock Castillo, Spanky Penafiel, Dustin, Ed Baur, Steve Chiarella and Rocky Salemmo. And I'd like to thank all the people who live one day at a time.

At the end of the day, after all I been through, what would I say to anybody who is reading this? I'd say dreams do come true, no matter how old you may be and no matter what has happened to you in life. Keep moving forward no matter what happens. Never give up. Like Father Paul told me, "God helps those who help themselves." I believe that, because it's true.

If you'd like to contact me directly, you can do it by sending a note to bob.purzycki@facebook.com. You can watch the documentary film that was made about my life at highrollerthemovie.com. Or you can also find it on Netflix under "The Bob Perry Story."

God bless!

Bob

SAINTHOOD AND FATHER PAUL

I went back up to Graymoor in the summer of 2013, because I wanted to revisit the place where my miracles happened, and because I wanted a couple of days of peace and quiet. There's such a spiritual feeling in that place, up in the mountains, where you're all alone with yourself.

I think I was the only visitor the morning I got there. I told the lady at the front desk that I wanted to stay one night, and as she was signing me in I started telling her the story of what happened to me there, 21 years earlier, about Father Paul and everything. Funny thing was, she didn't act like I was crazy. In fact, her eyes were kind of bugging out. Then she called in an elderly man wearing a brown robe, like all them guys, who said his name was Father Kelly. He explained that he was the head of the archive division, and that he was interested in my story because Father Paul had been nominated for canonization as a saint.

He said he was in the process of gathering documentation about miraculous occurrences involving Father Paul because they needed, I think, three miracles for him to qualify for the gold medal of sainthood. He told me to write down my story with as much detail as I could remember, so when I got back home I just sent him Chapters 8 through 11 from this book. If that helps the Franciscans give Father Paul his due, I'll jump over the moon. He deserves it. Thank you, Father Paul.

TOP TIPS ON GETTING BACK TO BOWLING:
YOU CAN HAVE YOUR DREAMS BACK

Sometimes people come so close to touching their own inner greatness when they are young, like I did, that it almost hurts. They discover they have enough natural talent – maybe even fabulous talent – to reach their highest dreams. It might even be possible to reach the stars.

For me, the dream was the sport of bowling. But it really doesn't matter what your dream is. Living out a dream is a magical, powerful way to live. There is nothing greater, or more inspiring to other people, than to live your dream.

But, like me, a lot of people lose sight of their childhood dreams as they get older. Stuff happens. You get sick or injured, you make terrible mistakes, you fail to recover from setbacks. Or sometimes you lose sight of the dream because of good things: A satisfying long-term job, or getting married and having children. And, for a long while, it seems like the dream is dead and buried, or simply forgotten.

But later in life – say, when you're 40 or 50 or 60 or even older – sometimes a whole new world opens up, and you have a second chance at achieving your inner greatness. It looked like I had absolutely ruined my life and should have been dead, and then I won the High Roller at the age of 44. And I won it again when I was 55. I didn't want to sit next to Chris Barnes, one of the greatest bowlers on the pro tour; I wanted to beat him. I wanted to jump into the game of life and participate again. And I'm not the only one who had the greatest triumph of his life, late in life. Jack Nicklaus won the Masters and beat the world when he was 46. Nolan Ryan pitched in Major League baseball games over four decades. He just kept tapping into his inner greatness, year after year after year. And you can do it, too. OK, so you're not Nolan Ryan or Jack Nicklaus. But if you'd like to get your glory back as a bowler, late in life, here's a couple of things to remember.

1. **Who cares if you're a little bit older?** Bowling is unique among sports (except for perhaps golf) in that you can hit your career best when you're older than 50. It requires strength, stamina, skill and strategy, but nothing like, say, baseball. In fact, when it comes to bowling, age is your hidden advantage. You're smarter, more experienced, calmer and – let's face it – sexier than ever. You know how to conserve energy for the long haul, how to "psych out" opponents, how to last. In many ways you're just a better athlete than you ever were. So instead of just sitting there counting the days going by, get your gear together, go down to the bowling alley and step up onto that approach. Then try to be the best that you can be. Don't just bore people by saying, "I used to be a great bowler." Become a greater bowler.

2. **Don't forget exercise.** It's easy to forget that you can't be a great bowler unless you're physically fit. So take the time do some cardiovascular conditioning, stretching, and work the muscles you may not have used in years. It will really pay off. Be sure to talk to your doctor to find the training program that is right for you. Patience is required. The dumb things we did at the gym that we bounced right back from when we were twenty can be dangerous in our golden years.

3. **Catch up with the technology.** When I was starting out – and, hey, it wasn't that long ago! – bowling balls were made of solid rubber and the lanes were made of solid maple, coated first with shellac and then later with lacquer. But the technology has changed dramatically since then, and keeps changing. First they started making balls out of plastic, and now they're made of urethane. The lanes are made of various synthetic substances. What that means is it's easier to throw strikes now, so bowling scores are much higher than they were back in the day. But if you're coming back to bowling after a long siesta, you need to get comfortable with the new high-performance bowling balls and the rest of the new technology. These balls were designed by engineers to knock down anything, so they behave differently in the lane than rubber balls. Don't fight the technology, accept it. Because, in a way, all these improvements to balls and lanes are just extending your longevity as a bowler.

4. **Play the lane, not the other guy.** An old bowler once told me that you're not bowling against the other guy, you're bowling against the lane. That may sound simple, but it's profound. Instead of worrying about what the other bowler is doing or not doing, you're focusing on the lane conditions, the behavior of the ball, and – what's probably the centerpiece of bowling – all the angles involved in the spinning ball, the trajectory of the hook, and the explosion of the pins as they fall. That's where the game takes place, and that should be the focus of your attention.

5. **Find a good instructor.** Bowling is actually a surprisingly complex game, and getting really good at it takes skill, practice and some expert help. It's worth finding a good instructor to work with you on your game, to teach you how to play all the patterns, how to match the ball to the pattern, how to adapt to all different lane conditions. You can go online to the United States Bowling Congress (www.bowl.com), and you may be able to locate a reputable instructor that way. Instructors advertise in the bowling magazines, or online. I don't really believe in videos. I think you need to find somebody to work with you personally.

6. **It's also worth finding a good ball-driller** – somebody who knows how to drill a bowling ball to fit your hand. This is important, because unless the ball leaves your hand clean, it's difficult to throw the ball the exact same way, every time. That's the key to success. Try going to the pro shop at your bowling alley to find a ball-driller.

7. **Practice.** Maybe it goes without saying, but there's no substitute for practice. You have to bowl often enough that your moves get to be second nature again. Sign up for tournaments, no matter how small. Learn to compete again. Learn to stay calm under stress. And, with good instruction, focus, a good ball-driller and pure motives, you can become great again.

8. **Consider your motives and live your dream.** It doesn't matter what you do in life, or what you aspire to do, your actions are driven by your motives. Sometimes people are driven by shallow or shameful or even illegal motives, like trying to make a lot of money or belittle other people or get revenge. But those motives show through in your actions. They don't lead you to greatness, only to some short-term advantage. They might even lead you to disaster. But if your motive is to reach the stars, to harness your dreams to become the best that you can be, that's obvious in your behavior. It inspires other people. And it can jack up your game to a whole new level. If you're 62 years old and you ask yourself, "Why do I want to go back to bowling after all these years?" and the answer is, "I'm doing this to fulfill a childhood dream that was never fulfilled. I'm willing to go to any lengths to achieve my inner greatness," that motive will be quickly reflected in your game. Living out a dream is a magical, powerful way to live. There is nothing greater, or more inspiring to other people, than to live your dream.

ABOUT THE AUTHORS

Robert "Bob Perry" Purzycki was born in the gritty industrial town of Paterson New Jersey, achieving fame in bowling and infamy for his Mob ties before committing to a life of serving others.

Stefan Bechtel is the author of "Mr. Hornaday's War" and ten other books that have sold more than two million copies and been translated into ten languages.   *Headshot, back cover, Peggy Harrison*

Made in the USA
San Bernardino, CA
07 January 2014